D1526415

# Global Issues in Family Law

By

## Ann Laquer Estin
*Professor of Law*
*University of Iowa*

## Barbara Stark
*Professor of Law*
*Hofstra University*

**AMERICAN CASEBOOK SERIES®**

Mat #40569881

© 2007 Thomson/West
   610 Opperman Drive
   P.O. Box 64526
   St. Paul, MN 55164–0526
   1–800–328–9352

Printed in the United States of America

**ISBN:** 978–0–314–17954–8

*TEXT IS PRINTED ON 10% POST CONSUMER RECYCLED PAPER*

# Preface

This book introduces students to a range of global issues in family law, including comparative perspectives on marriage and divorce, international adoption, international child abduction, and domestic violence as grounds for asylum. As the practice of family law becomes increasingly globalized, lawyers across the country confront these and other complex transnational legal problems.

While it is impossible to cover all these subjects comprehensively in a short volume, these materials raise a broad range of questions within each area and suggest useful sources for further study. This book can serve as a supplement to the basic family law course or as the text for a stand-alone class or seminar. The chapters can be used in any combination and in any order. They are intended to be accessible to students with no background in family law or international law.

Please note that the cases and materials included here have been edited, sometimes extensively. Where material has been eliminated, this is noted with an ellipsis (\* \* \*) or with a bracketed summary of the omitted portion of the text. Footnotes and citations have been omitted without indicating this omission in the text. When footnotes are included, the original numbering has been retained.

Our thanks to the *Global Issues* series editor, Franklin A. Gevurtz, and to Louis Higgins at Thomson-West for providing us with the opportunity to take part in this project. We have benefited from the help of many others as well. Thanks are due to Melanie Stutzman at the University of Iowa who managed the manuscript preparation and production with her customary cheerfulness and efficiency. Thanks also to Professor Arthur Bonfield, for his years of stewardship in building the world-class international and comparative law collection in the University of Iowa Law Library, which proved once again to be a terrific resource. At Hofstra Law School, international research librarian Patricia Kasting provided invaluable research assistance and Maureen E. Quinn prepared the manuscript with good humor, patience, and unfailing attention to detail. Professor Andrew Schepard and the students in the Hofstra Child and Family Advocacy Fellowship program provided an endless stream of real-world examples of global issues in family law.

ANN LAQUER ESTIN
BARBARA STARK

April 2007

\*

iii

# Acknowledgements

Deborah E. Anker, Membership in a Particular Social Group: Recent Developments in U.S. Law, 1514 PLI/Corp 119, 131.

D. Marianne Blair & Merle H. Weiner, Family Law and the World Community, 434–35, 986–87 (2003).

Margaret F. Brinig, Choose the Lesser Evil: Comments on Besharov's "Child Abust Realities", 8 Va. J. Soc. Pol'y & L. 205 (2000).

Carol S. Bruch, The Unmet Needs of Domestic Violence Victims and Their Children in Hague Child Abduction Convention Cases, 38 Fam. L.Q. 529 (2004).

June Carbone, Law, Politics, Religion, and the Creation of Norms for Market Transactions: A Review of the Birth of Surrogacy in Israel by D. Kelly Weisberg, 39 Fam. L.Q. 793, 800–81 (2005).

Ann Laquer Estin, Families and Children in International Law: An Introduction, 12 Transnat'l L. & Contemp. Probs. 271 (2002); Toward a Multicultural Family Law, 38 Fam. L.Q. 501 (2004).

Hugues Fulchiron, Egalité, Vérité, Stabilité: The New French Filiation Law After the Ordonnance of 4 July 2005, International Survey of Family Law 203 (Andrew Bainham, ed. 2006).

Hague Conference on Private International Law, Hague Conference Info Sheet.

Berta Esperanza Hernández-Troyol, Asking the Family Question, 38 Fam. L.Q. 481 (2004).

Theresa Hughes, The Neglect of Children and Culture: Responding to Child Maltreatment With Cultural Competence and a Review of Child Abuse and Culture: Working with Diverse Families, 44 Fam. Ct. Rev. 501 (July 2006).

Ursula Kilkelly, Annual Review of International Family Law, International Survey of Family Law 1, 5–6 (Andrew Bainham, ed. 2006).

Suzana Kraljic´, Legal Regulation of Adoption in Slovenia—De We Need Change?, International Survey of Family Law 1, 403–406 (Andrew Bainham, ed. 2006).

Emmanuel Quansak, Progress and Retrogression on Domestic Violence Legislation in Ghana, International Survey of Family Law 1, 241–242 (Andrew Bainham, ed. 2006).

Restatement (3d) Foreign Relations Law of the United States, copyright 1987 by the American Law Institute. Reprinted with permission. All rights reserved.

Barbara Stark, Baby Girls from China in New York: A Thrice Told Tale, Utah L. Rev. 1231, 1293-95 (2003);

A Career In International Family Law, ASIL, Careers in International Law: A Guide to Careers and Internships in International Law (2006–2007 Edition) Reproduced with permission from (c) The American Society of International Law;

Crazy Jane Talks with the Bishop: Abortion in Germany, South Africa and International Human Rights, 12 Tex. J. Women & L. 287 (Spring 2003);

Domestic Violence and International Law: Good Bye Earl, 47 Loy. L. Rev. 255 (2001);

International Family Law: An Introduction, 1–3, 5–9, 53–56, 57–59, 138–39, 148, 227–228, 251 (2005);

Introduction: Practical Applications and Critical Perspectives in International Family Law, Symposium on International Family Law, 38 Fam. L.Q. 475 (Fall, 2004);

Lost Boys and Forgotten Girls: Intercountry Adoption, Human Rights, and African Children, 22 St. Louis U. Pub. L. Rev. 275 (2003).

Violence Against Children in the Home and Family, United Nations 2006 Report.

# Global Issues Series

Series Editor, Franklin A. Gevurtz

## Titles Available Now

**Global Issues in Civil Procedure** by Thomas Main, University of the Pacific, McGeorge School of Law
ISBN 978–0–314–15978–6

**Global Issues in Constitutional Law** by Brian K. Landsberg, University of the Pacific, McGeorge School of Law and Leslie Gielow Jacobs, University of the Pacific, McGeorge School of Law
ISBN 978–0–314–17608–0

**Global Issues in Contract Law** by John A. Spanogle, Jr., George Washington University, Michael P. Malloy, University of the Pacific, McGeorge School of Law, Louis F. Del Duca, Pennsylvania State University, Keith A. Rowley, University of Nevada, Las Vegas, and Andrea K. Bjorklund, University of California, Davis
ISBN 978–0–314–16755–2

**Global Issues in Corporate Law** by Franklin A. Gevurtz, University of the Pacific, McGeorge School of Law
ISBN 978–0–314–15977–9

**Global Issues in Criminal Law** by Linda Carter, University of the Pacific, McGeorge School of Law, Christopher L. Blakesley, University of Nevada, Las Vegas and Peter Henning, Wayne State University
ISBN 978–0–314–15997–7

**Global Issues in Family Law** by Ann Laquer Estin, University of Iowa and Barbara Stark, Hofstra University
ISBN 978–0–314–17954–8

**Global Issues in Labor Law** by Samuel Estreicher, New York University School of Law
ISBN 978–0–314–17163–4

**Global Issues in Legal Ethics** by James E. Moliterno, College of William & Mary, Marshall-Wythe School of Law and George Harris, University of the Pacific, McGeorge School of Law
ISBN 978–0–314–16935–8

**Global Issues in Property Law** by John G. Sprankling, University of the Pacific, McGeorge School of Law, Raymond R. Coletta, University of the Pacific, McGeorge School of Law, and M.C. Mirow, Florida International University College of Law
ISBN 978–0–314–16729–3

*

# Summary of Contents

\*

# Table of Contents

# Table of Cases

The principal cases are in bold type. Cases cited or discussed in the text are roman type. References are to pages. Cases cited in principal cases and within other quoted materials are not included.

# Global Issues in Family Law

*

# Chapter 1

# INTRODUCTION

This chapter first explains why international family law matters. Global issues have become increasingly important in family law practice, from mail-order brides seeking divorce to inter-country adoption, and American lawyers need new skills to respond to these new demands. Second, this chapter defines international family law, including its sources. Third, it explains how international family law functions, how international standards are incorporated and enforced in domestic law. Finally, it considers the options when it does not function, when legal resolution is needed but there is no readily applicable law. The objective here is simply to introduce the subject and provide a basic framework for analysing and addressing the growing numbers of global issues facing family lawyers. The chapters that follow address a range of topics, reflecting those found in most American family law texts.

## A. WHY IT MATTERS

The excerpts below explain how the globalization of the family is transforming family law and why it matters to lawyers as well as to their clients.

### ANN LAQUER ESTIN, FAMILIES AND CHILDREN IN INTERNATIONAL LAW: AN INTRODUCTION

12 Transnat'l L. & Contemp. Probs. 271 (2002).

Although marriage, divorce, child custody, and adoption are rarely considered as international law subjects, the field of international family law is growing in importance and complexity. In

1

contemporary understanding, "international law" extends both to nations and to individuals, and international family law includes both a private law dimension and an increasingly substantial public law component. On the private international law side, also referred to as conflict of laws, there are treaties with a history stretching back more than a century governing such matters as international recognition of marriages and divorces, or enforcement of judgments for family support. In recent years, "private law" questions have taken on a substantial public law character, as international agreements have established new systems of intergovernmental cooperation on matters such as support enforcement, child abduction, and intercountry adoption. Moreover, these systems now fit within a larger framework of international human rights agreements, which articulate a broad set of normative standards applicable to both international and domestic family law.

* * *

Family life and domestic family law around the world have been subject to sweeping transformations during the past half-century, changes that have had a significant impact on international law. With the process of globalization has come an increase in the migration of individuals and families. This has in turn increased the incidence of transnational families, bringing into sharper focus the need for workable rules of international family law. With the development of international human rights has come a greater understanding of the need to protect both families and individual family members. The articulation of human rights norms concerning the family is based on a remarkable international consensus that has served to anchor the development of international and domestic family law principles. In addition, these norms provide a framework for addressing some of the difficult questions of citizenship and asylum that have followed the transformation and globalization of the family.

## BARBARA STARK, A CAREER IN INTERNATIONAL FAMILY LAW

ASIL, Careers in International Law: A Guide to Careers and Internships in International Law (2006–2007 Edition)

There are at least three compelling reasons to pursue an international law career in international family law. The first two derive from the simple fact that international family law is an absolute necessity, something that people cannot live without. In an increasingly globalized world, families are torn apart, forming new families, terminating old relationships, and trying to sustain long distance parent-child relationships. They seek international custody awards, property distribution, and the return of their abducted children. International family law enables increasingly attenuated families to define and maintain their most fundamental human relationships. It is the legal equivalent of the cell phone. Thus, the first compelling reason to practice international family law is that it is the bread-and-butter for an international law practice. When support for human rights litigation is hard to come by, international divorce, maintenance, and child custody cases can pay the rent.

The second reason is similarly grounded in the idea of international family law as absolutely necessary: nothing is more important to your clients. The oil field concessions you may be able to negotiate are important, but visitation with a beloved child is infinitely more so. The third reason is related to the first two: you will never be bored. International family law is about love, sex, money, betrayal and heartache. It is also intellectually rigorous, demanding, and rapidly changing.

## BARBARA STARK, INTRODUCTION: WHY STUDY INTERNATIONAL FAMILY LAW?

International Family Law: An Introduction, 1–3 (2005).

The practice of family law has in fact become globalized. Lawyers inevitably encounter clients whose family law problems extend beyond national boundaries, including problems in which the laws of more than one state must be taken into account. Lawyers everywhere are increasingly confronted with issues regarding international adoption, child abduction, divorce, custody and domestic violence, where the parties reside in, or are citizens of, different states.

This is not surprising. As the United Nations notes, families are the primary unit of social organization, and families are changing, trying to adapt to new demands and taking advantage of new mobility. Globalization is transforming family law. Women are seeking asylum as refugees, fleeing domestic violence. Workers are following jobs, leaving their families behind and sometimes starting new families in their new countries. Child abduction has become an increasing threat as parents of different nationalities divorce, and both want their children to be raised in their own national traditions.

Even as ties to such traditions become increasingly attenuated, their appeal may become stronger for some. Local religious leaders, similarly, may insist on even stricter adherence to local customs, especially those related to marriage, divorce, and the care and custody of children, as their authority is challenged by competing customs and international norms. In many States, such as Saudi Arabia, family law is basically left to religious authorities. This reflects both its relatively low importance to national governments (compared to matters of trade and finance, for example) and its paradoxically high importance to those who seek to shape the national identity. As Article 9 of the Basic Law of Saudi Arabia states, "the family is the kernel of Saudi society, and its members shall be brought up on the basis of Islamic faith." There are powerful trends and countertrends everywhere, and competing norms of family law are at the core of each.

These play out in a range of contexts, such as the recognition of marriage, child custody jurisdiction, enforcement of foreign support awards, and adoptions, which already claim a significant amount of class time in family law courses and account for a similarly significant number of hours in family law practice. The extraterritorial expansion of family law poses new challenges, but the basic analytic framework remains the same. First, we identify procedures that do not mesh, distinguishing those that are better characterized as procedural from those that reflect more substantive differences in underlying policy. Second, we find or create mechanisms for reconciliation, where possible, or for the orderly resolution of disputes where reconciliation is not possible.

While major issues in international family law [IFL], such as those addressed in the Hague Convention on Child Abduction, can be at least touched upon in a general course, growing numbers of students go on to specialize in family law. For these future lawyers, IFL is increasingly a necessity. In fact, the failure to anticipate international family law issues, such as the removal of children to another country during visitation, may well expose a lawyer to a malpractice claim.

\* \* \*

[W]hy study 'international' family law as opposed to 'comparative' family law? 'International' here refers to shared or agreed upon rules and norms among a group of States, while 'comparative' refers to the respective rules and norms applicable in two or more particular States. Comparative family law is an essential component of IFL. The ways in which different domestic legal systems address custody disputes or invalidate marriages must be understood in the practice of IFL. The study of comparative law is also invaluable for gaining insight into other cultures and expanding horizons. Lawmakers increasingly look abroad for new approaches to intractable domestic problems.

They must keep in mind, however, that legal norms do not operate in the abstract, but in specific cultural contexts. A particular reform, such as retroactive laws opening adoption records, might be functional because it is compatible with the underlying social norms in one context but not in another. Comparative family law requires lawyers to focus on the ways in which culture supports or undermines law. The comparative perspective not only provides a window into another culture, but exposes the often unquestioned assumptions of one's own. Studying custodial presumptions in Islamic states, for example, exposes ways in which culture shapes such presumptions, which may not be as visible when dealing with the culture in which we are immersed . . .

\* \* \*

'International Family Law' vs. *'Private* International Family Law'

'Private' international law historically referred to the rules regarding conflicts of law in disputes between private legal persons, including individuals or corporations. Public international law, in contrast, historically referred to the rules and norms governing disputes among nation States. As many commentators have observed, the distinction between public and private international law has steadily eroded. States increasingly engage in the same kinds of commercial activities as private entities. In addition, because of the growing influence of international human rights, the individual has increasingly become the subject of public international law.

Historically, IFL has been regarded primarily as the province of private international law, requiring familiarity with conflicts of law principles in general and the conventions promulgated by the Hague Conference on Private Law in particular. Public international law plays an increasingly important role, however. Even as the Hague Conference studies the problem of transnational child support, for example, States enter into growing numbers of bilateral treaties addressing the issue.

\* \* \*

Such treaties are governed by public international law. International human rights law, moreover, has become an increasingly pervasive factor in international family law, from the refusal to recognize institutions such as polygamy (as a violation of human rights) to the recognition of reproductive rights. International human rights law also recognizes affirmative economic, social, and cultural rights, such as the right to maternal protection before and after the birth of a child, which are explicitly identified as rights owed to the family as such. Finally, rights of individuals within the family, such as the child's rights to freedom of religion, raise issues of State interference with family privacy. The State has an obligation to protect the child's rights without violating the rights of the family unit.

In sum, the erosion between public and private international law has been so thorough in the context of IFL that the subject can no longer be understood merely as a part of private international law. Rather, it requires a grasp of the applicable public international laws, especially human rights law, as well.

## B. WHAT IT IS

This section first describes some of the recurring tensions in globalized family law, including domestic resistance to international norms. This section next sets out the international law, including treaty law and customary international law, which attempts to reconcile, or harmonize, these divergent domestic systems.

### ANN LAQUER ESTIN, TOWARD A MULTICULTURAL FAMILY LAW

38 Fam. L.Q. 501 (2004).

As the United States becomes a more diverse and multicultural society, law and legal institutions face new challenges ... For family law, there are issues posed for courts when disputes involve unfamiliar ethnic, religious, and legal traditions. Over the past two decades, courts around the country have encountered Islamic and Hindu wedding celebrations, Muslim and Jewish premarital agreements, and divorce arbitration in rabbinic tribunals. In these cases, courts have struggled to understand and accommodate the tremendous cultural and religious diversity of America today within a legal framework established long ago.

The project of building a multicultural family law is complicated by the fact that American family law is based on specifically Christian norms. In England, before the colonization of North America, family law was ecclesiastical law, and it remained within the jurisdiction of the church until the mid-nineteenth century. Although jurisdiction over family matters in the American colonies was in secular courts, the content of our early family law was firmly rooted in English ecclesiastical law. Beyond the specific legal rules governing marriage, annulment, and divorce, American marriage policies grew from a set of religious and political ideas that were directly enforced through governmental policies over more than a century. Family law rules appear to be secular and neutral to the contemporary observer, but they still reflect this religious heritage. As a result, our rules do not always fit well with practices drawn from different traditions, and it can be difficult to determine to what extent accommodation is appropriate.

## BARBARA STARK, INTRODUCTION: WHY STUDY INTERNATIONAL FAMILY LAW?

International Family Law: An Introduction 5–9 (2005).

### Private International Law Conventions

Family law in many States is a matter of national or subnational, i.e., state or provincial, law. A major exception is those States in which family law is basically delegated to religious authorities ... [T]hese various systems are harmonized, [to some extent] on the international level.

This has been accomplished through private international law conventions, such as the Hague Convention on Child Abduction, the Hague Convention on Intercountry Adoption, and the Convention on the Law Applicable to Maintenance Obligations Toward Children. A list of the Hague Conventions on Private International Law can be found at www.hcch.net/e/conventions/index.html (Lists of States Parties are also available at this site.) These treaties are binding on States parties. In many States, such treaties become enforceable in national courts through implementing legislation. Under international law, a State is legally obligated under a convention it has ratified even if it has not yet enacted domestic law to implement that treaty.

\* \* \*

### Public International Law

State family law is also subject to public international law, including international human rights law. As set out in the Statute of the International Court of Justice, there are three sources of international law. First, international law may be made by treaty; that is, a binding agreement entered into by two or more States. Examples include the U.N. Charter and the human rights conventions discussed below, all of which are multilateral treaties, and the bilateral treaties regarding child support * * * and spousal maintenance * * *

Second, international law may be found in customary international law, which has two elements: (1) State practice, and (2) *opinio juris*; that is, the belief that such State practice is legally mandated. Torture, for example, is a violation of customary international law. No State claims that it may legally engage in torture. On the contrary, all States have official policies against torture, reflecting their common understanding that it is prohibited in the international community. This does not mean, of course, that no State actually engages in torture. It simple means that it does so secretly, or contends that a particular practice is not in fact "torture." * * * [F]or example, domestic violence may amount to torture although this is not recognized by most States.

Customary international law may be shown through State practice over time, in the form of State adherence to international treaties, declarations, or General Assembly resolutions, through the enactment of domestic legislation, through executive action, and through a State's own judicial decisions. The accretion of such practice, accompanied by evidence that the State believed that such practice was legally mandated, constitutes customary international law. Where consensus among States is clear and no State objects, less practice may be needed.

Third, and finally, international law may be found in the 'general principles' of law recognized by States. These include principles such as *res judicata* or the commonly accepted understanding that statements made to one's lawyer are privileged. In the context of ILF, however, general principles may not be applicable. *Res judicata*, for example, may not apply to the custody determination of one State because another considers that determination subject to its modification, or contrary to the best interest of the child.

The major international human rights treaties affecting family law are the International Covenant on Civil and Political Rights ('ICCPR' or the 'Civil Covenant,') the International Covenant on Economic, Social, and Cultural Rights ('ICESCR' or the 'Economic Covenant'), the Convention on the Elimination of All Forms of Discrimination Against Women ('CEDAW' or the 'Women's Convention'), and the Convention on the Rights of the Child ('CRC' or the 'Child's Convention'). The pertinent sections of each of these instruments are set forth in the chapters in which they apply most directly. There is some cross-referencing in order to avoid repetition, but there is also some repetition for the reader's convenience. Complete texts of the instruments can be found in the treaty series cited in the chapters or at http://www1.umn.edu/humanrts/instree (Lists of States Parties are also available at this site.)

Some States ratify human rights conventions subject to reservations regarding specific provisions. This means that the State accepts its obligations under the treaty with the exception of the particular article to which it has taken a reservation. Many Islamic States, for example, have taken reservations to Article 16 of the Women's Convention, addressing family rights. The usual reservation provides that the State accepts the cited article to the extent that it is consistent with Shari'ah, Islamic personal law.

### Regional Conventions

[Other sources of IFL] include the European Convention on Human Rights, the Inter–American Convention on Human Rights, and the African Charter on the Rights and Welfare of Children. The European Convention has been useful in protecting the rights of sexual minorities, particularly gays, lesbians and transgendered persons. The Inter–American Convention has been used to establish State responsibility in connection with domestic violence. The African Charter restricts intercountry adoption in Africa, explicitly preferring institutionalization in the child's country of origin to intercountry adoption. Where there are no feasible alternatives, intercountry adoption may be considered, but even then, it is limited to those countries which are also parties to the Charter or to the CRC. This has recently been challenged under the South African Constitution.

### Notes

1. What specific global issues in family law would you expect to encounter in your local family court? Why?

2. The Vienna Convention on the Law of Treaties, which the U.S. accepts as legally-binding law, provides that: "A signatory shall not defeat the object and purpose of the treaty." (Art. 18). The United States is not a party to the Children's Convention, the Women's Convention, or the Economic Covenant, although it has signed (but not ratified) all three. Can you nevertheless raise violations of these instruments in family courts? How? How would you counter such arguments if raised by opposing counsel?

## C. HOW IT FUNCTIONS

This section explains how international family law develops on the national as well as the international levels. It includes with a call for strengthening international norms, which suggests how the domestic and international levels interact. The section concludes by noting the gaps in international family law, and suggests ways in which lawyers can protect their clients.

International family law may be triggered in cases involving parties from different countries, or with ties to different countries, or in wholly domestic matters subject to international law, such as human rights law. The mechanisms for raising these issues in U.S. family courts are addressed in a burgeoning practitioner-orientated literature. An excerpt from an Introduction to one such Symposium follows.

## BARBARA STARK, INTRODUCTION: PRACTICAL APPLICATIONS AND CRITICAL PERSPECTIVES IN INTERNATIONAL FAMILY LAW

Symposium on International Law, 38 Fam. L. Q. 475 (Fall, 2004).

\* \* \*

\* \* \* This is not the first time the Family Law Quarterly has focused on international family law. In 1995, a Special Symposium on International Marriage and Divorce Regulation and Recognition discussed laws in sixteen countries. In 1998, an issue, Selected Topics in International Family Law, featured four articles, focusing primarily on international child support and abduction.

There are two major differences between the 1998 symposium and this one, reflecting two emerging trends over the past six years. First, human rights questions have come to the fore in international family law, as noted in virtually all of the articles that follow. Second, growing efforts to coordinate and harmonize divergent, often competing, systems have exposed the increasing complexity of international family law, and the growing need for practical guidance like that offered by the contributors to this Symposium.

In this issue, a stellar group of experts begins with two perspectives on the shifting terrain of international family law, and proceeds with four in-depth, practitioner-oriented analyses of three different contexts, all of which involve children. It concludes with a hands-on account of the actual law-making process through which such dilemmas may be addressed, and the difficulties in reaching closure on the international level.

\* \* \*

\* \* \* Professor Duncan's cogent piece provides a rare glimpse into the necessarily time-consuming process of achieving international consensus. More provocatively, it suggests why such consensus might sometimes be impossible. Jurisdiction, for example, may be predicted on fundamentally incompatible notions of the role of the state. The extent to which states are willing to compromise on such issues remains an open question. Professor Duncan sets out the alternatives, as well as the costs, where consensus cannot be achieved.

As this Symposium suggests, there are many such areas, and much international family law remains unsettled. Those who pick up this Symposium for guidance on a particular narrow question may at first be disappointed that their question is not directly addressed. Even if the authors do not answer a particular question, however, they may well cite a text, or a Web site, or suggest an analytical framework that will bring a workable resolution closer. Equally important, they demonstrate the crucial role of the family law practitioner in shaping international family law.

Hague Conference on Private International Law

## HAGUE CONFERENCE INFO SHEET
## HAGUE CONFERENCE ON PRIVATE
## INTERNATIONAL LAW

MACROBUTTON HtmlResAnchor http://www.hcch.
net/index_en.php?act=text.display & tid=26.

## A WORLD ORGANISATION . . .

With over 60 Member States representing all continents, the Hague Conference on private international law is a global inter-governmental organisation. A melting pot of different legal traditions, it develops and services multilateral legal instruments, which respond to global needs.

An increasing number of non-Member States are also becoming parties to the Hague Conventions. As a result, the work of the Conference encompasses more than 120 countries around the world.

## . . . BUILDING BRIDGES BETWEEN LEGAL SYSTEMS . . .

Personal and family or commercial situations which are connected with more than one country are commonplace in the modern world. These may be affected by differences between the legal systems in those countries. With a view to resolving these differences, States have adopted special rules known as "private international law" rules.

The statutory mission of the Conference is to work for the "progressive unification" of these rules. This involves finding internationally-agreed approaches to issues such as jurisdiction of the courts, applicable law, and the recognition and enforcement of judgments in a wide range of areas, from . . . child protection to matters of marriage and personal status.

Over the years, the Conference has, in carrying out its mission, increasingly become a centre for international judicial and administrative co-operation in the area of private law, especially in the fields of protection of the family and children, of civil procedure and commercial law.

### ... AND REINFORCING LEGAL CERTAINTY AND SECURITY

The ultimate goal of the Organisation is to work for a world in which, despite the differences between legal systems, persons—individuals as well as companies—can enjoy a high degree of legal security.

### A LONG–STANDING ORGANISATION ...

The Conference held its first meeting in 1893, on the initiative of T.M.C. Asser (Nobel Peace Prize 1911). It became a permanent inter-governmental organisation in 1955, upon entry into force of its Statute.

### ... GOVERNED AND FUNDED BY ITS MEMBER STATES ...

The Organisation meets in principle every four years in Plenary Session ... to negotiate and adopt Conventions and to decide upon future work. The Conventions are prepared by Special Commissions or working groups held several times a year, generally at the Peace Palace in The Hague, increasingly in various member countries. ... The Organisation is funded principally by its Member States ...

### ... BASED IN THE HAGUE, CENTRE OF INTERNATIONAL JUSTICE

Activities of the Conference are co-ordinated by a multinational Secretariat–the Permanent Bureau–located in The Hague. The Conference's working languages are English and French.

The Secretariat prepares the Plenary Sessions and Special Commissions, and carries out the basic research required for any subject taken up by the Conference.

\* \* \*

### THE HAGUE CONVENTIONS

\* \* \*

Between 1951 and 2005, the Conference adopted 36 international Conventions, the practical operation of many of which is regularly reviewed by Special Commissions. Even when they are not ratified, the Conventions have an influence upon legal systems, in both Member and non-Member States. They also form a source of inspiration for efforts to unify private international law at the regional level, for example within the Organisation of American States or the European Union.

The most widely ratified Conventions deal with:

\* \* \*

International child abduction
Intercountry adoption
Maintenance obligations
Recognition of divorces

The most recent Conventions are the Convention on Jurisdiction, Applicable Law, Recognition, Enforcement and Co-operation in respect of Parental Responsibility and Measures for the Protection of Children (1996), the Convention on the International Protection of Adults (2000).

\* \* \*

Negotiations on a new global instrument on the international recovery of child support and other forms of family maintenance are currently in progress.

\* \* \*

## EDUCATION AND EXCHANGE

With the aim of harmonising the implementation of the Conventions, the Secretariat organises, assists in organising and participates in conferences and seminars held at both international and national levels to educate the various persons involved in the implementation of the Conventions, including judges, Central Authority personnel and members of the legal profession. A judicial newsletter on international child protection is also published...

## A SOURCE OF INFORMATION CONSTANTLY UPDATED

\* \* \*

The Conference website, MACROBUTTON HtmlResAnchor www.hcch.net, presents general information concerning the Hague Conference as well as detailed and updated information on the Hague Conventions: text of the Conventions, full status reports, bibliographies, information regarding the authorities designated under the Conventions on judicial and administrative co-operation, explanatory reports, etc.

INCADAT, the International Child Abduction Database, MACROBUTTON HtmlResAnchor www.incadat.com, is a special initiative which provides easy access to many of the leading judicial decisions taken by national courts around the world in respect of the 1980 Hague Convention on international child abduction.

## BERTA ESPERANZA HERNÁNDEZ-TRUYOL, ASKING THE FAMILY QUESTION

38 Fam. L.Q. 481 (2004).

\* \* \*

\* \* \* I urge that a key component to all international norm-making and relations be the asking of the family question. This approach requires, as a central inquiry in any process of international norm creation, that the norm-makers ask what impact, if any, a particular international law or policy will have on children and families. It emphasizes the need for a holistic approach to all matters of international norm-making that includes the consideration of the impact of a norm on the "natural and fundamental unit of society" in any and all of its culturally diverse forms. \* \* \*

### II. THE FAMILY IN INTERNATIONAL LAW

Although family units in myriad forms and expressions have been the central unit of social cohesion since time immemorial, international norms addressing the family are a relatively new phenomena. Because of the strong cultural underpinnings of family formations and expression, family-centered norms have been viewed as a matter of local, not global, concern. Thus, it is not surprising that family norms at the international level have been heavily influenced by the concepts of nationality and domicile. These ideas were influenced by the Italian politician, Pasquale Mancini, who, embracing the idea of family as local, posited that matters relating to a person's status should be governed by that individual's domicile. Inspired by Mancini's nationality principle, Latin American countries joined together to create international treaties that accorded superiority to and expressed a preference for the local as family regulator and protector. Indeed, in the attempt to reach an international consensus regarding the treatment of the family, a number of European and Latin American countries created multilateral treaties that codified the domicile principle. Despite these treaties, families, mainly children, did not receive adequate protection under international law.

Largely as a result of the World Wars, family separation, family support and, particularly, child protection became a great concern for most countries. Emphasizing the need to protect the interests of the child, the League of Nations, in 1924, passed the Declaration on the Rights of the Child, which was followed in 1959 by the United Nations Declaration on the Rights of the Child. As declarations, however, these instruments were not binding on states. The first binding document specifically protecting rights of the child was created in 1961, namely the Convention Concerning the Powers of Authorities and the Law Applicable in Respect of the Protection of Infants, a convention that dealt largely with choice-of-law issues in guardianship cases. This convention and subsequent ones, such as the 1989 Convention on the Rights of the Child (CRC), which codifies the "best interests of the child" standard first articulated in the 1959 Declaration, have guided states in protecting children all over the world.

Through international proclamations, the world has acknowledged the special and precarious status of families and children and has taken measures to protect them. One of the principal ways of protecting children is by protecting families through human rights instruments recognizing the family as the "natural and fundamental group unit of society entitled to protection by society and the State." Significantly, one finds the same conceptualization of the family—in terms of its key role in society and its technical definition—across the spectrum of human rights documents: those that protect civil and political rights, such as the right to vote, free speech, and fair trials, as well as those that protect social, economic, and cultural rights, such as the right to health, work, education, shelter, and cultural expression. Other instruments, such as the Declaration on Race and Racial Prejudice, acknowledge the sensitive and often precarious location of families and provide for their protection.

The right to family life is protected by a number of international conventions. In many instruments, the right to family is protected in tandem with privacy protections, with the underlying theme of these instruments being the prevention of arbitrary interference with the family. For example, Article 12 of the Universal Declaration of Human Rights (Universal Declaration) provides: "No one shall be subjected to arbitrary interference with his[/her] privacy, family, home or correspondence, nor attacks upon his[/her] honour and reputation. Everyone has the right to the protection of the law against such interference or attacks." Article 17 of the International Covenant on Civil and Political Rights (ICCPR) provides similarly-worded protection of privacy rights for the family and prohibits arbitrary interference with the right to family.

Article 10 of the International Covenant on Economic, Social and Cultural Rights (Economic Covenant) also acknowledges the need to protect the family, specifically providing that "the widest possible protection and assistance should be accorded to the family, which is the natural and fundamental group unit of society, particularly for its establishment and while it is responsible for the care and education of dependent children." This is significant in light of this author's proposal to make the family question a central consideration in international norm-making because Article 10 creates a positive obligation on states not only for the protection of the family in general, but also, in particular, with respect to the well-being of children. Thus, state policies that consciously or inadvertently erode family establishment and protection run afoul of this positive state duty . . .

* * *

There are many lacunae in international family law. If a state is not a party to the particular private international law convention addressing an issue, for example, the parties are left to the vagaries of domestic law. This often produces precisely the uncertainty—the races to the courthouse, the conflicting orders, the refusal of one tribunal to recognize or enforce the order of the other—that the conventions were drafted to avoid. In the absence of law binding on all parties—and their respective states—all is not lost, however. As in the domestic context, the possibility of private ordering, through negotiation or mediation, remains a constructive alternative. The critical caveat here is that counsel for the parties must assure that the resulting agreement will in fact be recognized and enforced in all of the pertinent jurisdictions.

### *Notes*

1.  There is a vast literature on mediation and negotiation in domestic family law. See, e.g., Jay Folberg et al., Divorce and Family Mediation: Models, Techniques, and Applications (2004); Robert H. Mnookin & Lewis A. Kornhauser, "Bargaining in the Shadow of the Law: The Case for Divorce," 88 Yale L.J. 950 (1979). Many of the concerns are similar in the international context, including the importance of taking the public policies of the interested states into account, see e.g., Jehan Aslam, Note, "Judicial Oversight of Islamic Family Law Arbitration in Ontario: Ensuring Meaningful Consent and Promoting Multicultural Citizenship," 38 N.Y.U. Int'l L. & Pol. 841–876 (2006).

2.  There is also a vast literature on dispute resolution in the international context. See, e.g., Mary Ellen O'Connell, International Dispute Resolution (2006); Christine Chinkin, Alternative Dispute Resolution Under International Law in Remedies in International Law (Malcolm D. Evans, ed. 1998); Cohen, Negotiating Across Cultures (1991); Christine Gray & Benedict Kingsbury, "Developments in Dispute Settlement: Inter State Arbitration Since 1945", 63 Brit. Ybk. Int'l L. (1992). It should be noted, however, that some of the legal instruments developed to implement and enforce private ordering in the international context exempt family law matters, often implicitly (as 'contrary to public policy').

3.  Your client, an American citizen, plans on adopting a baby from Guatemala. Before turning to the materials on adoption, how would you proceed in general? What law would you research first? What would be your next step?

4.  For an excellent overview of international family law from a practitioner's perspective, see Jeremy D. Morley, International Family Law, New York Law Journal, Nov. 24, 2004.

# Chapter 2

# MARRIAGE

## A. COMPARATIVE PERSPECTIVES

Marriage is a nearly universal human phenomenon, but there is enormous variety to the forms in which it is constructed and celebrated in different corners of the globe. As a social and legal institution, marriage offers a unique window into different cultures and systems of thought. This section introduces several different legal approaches to marriage, including the civil law in France, religious law in Pakistan, customary law in South Africa, and the recent establishment of same-sex marriage in Canada.

### 1. *Marriage in Civil Law: France*

Before the French Revolution, marriage in France was primarily a matter of religious law. With the Revolution, the French overthrew the rule of both the monarchy and the Roman Catholic Church. In 1789, the Declaration of the Rights of Man declared that all sovereignty came from the nation, from the will of the people, and emphasized the equality of all citizens. The equality principle suggested that the law should be uniform, clear, and accessible. One expression of this ideal was the French Civil Code, the first rational, systematic, modern legal code, promulgated under Napoleon in 1804.

The Civil Code addresses private law matters, including the law of persons, the law of property, and modes of acquiring property including inheritance, contracts, sales, and agency law. Provisions of the Code are short statements of general principles that define the rights and obligations of all French citizens. Under the Code, judges are forbidden from pronouncing or making law when they decide particular cases; as a result, judicial decisions are not treated as a binding source of law.

Since 1804, marriage in France has been defined in Book One of the Civil Code as a purely secular institution. Marriage is a civil contract, which requires the consent of the parties. It is preceded by a period of public notice, and celebrated before a public official in a ceremony held at the town hall in a place where one of the spouses resides or is domiciled. Although the civil ceremony may be followed by a religious one, the religious ceremony has no legal significance. In conducting a marriage, the designated official, traditionally the mayor, reads to the couple the sections of the Civil Code printed below, receives from each party the declaration that they wish to take each other for husband and wife, pronounces them to be married, and prepares a marriage certificate.

## FRENCH CIVIL CODE
### Book One: Persons
### Title V: Marriage
### Chapter VI: Duties and Rights of the Spouses Respectively

**Art. 212** Spouses mutually owe each other fidelity, assistance, presence.

**Art. 213** The spouses together assure the material and moral guidance of the family. They provide for the education of the children and prepare for their future.

**Art. 214** If the matrimonial agreements do not regulate the contributions of the spouses to the charges of the marriage, they contribute thereto in proportion to their respective abilities.

**Art. 215** Spouses are mutually bound to a community of life.

### *Notes*

1. The original Civil Code was strongly patriarchal, according a husband broad authority over his wife and children. In contrast to the contemporary language quoted above, Article 213 provided that the husband owed protection to his wife, and the wife obedience to her husband. Article 214 provided that the wife was obligated to live with her husband and to allow him to determine their residence, while the husband was required to receive her in his home and furnish her with all the necessities of life, according to his means and station. In addition, the community property regime of the Civil Code extended to the husband power to administer community property and to manage his wife's separate estate. Under the Code, sons younger than 25 and daughters younger than 21 could not marry without their parents' consent, and even adult children who wished to marry were required to make a formal request for the advice of their parents and wait for a response.

A series of amendments to the Code beginning in 1938 gradually extended to wives full legal capacity along with equal rights to make decisions concerning the couple's property, finances, and children. In addition, the age of capacity for marriage was reduced to 18 for men and 15 for women, with the requirement of parental consent for women younger than 18. See generally John Bell, et al., Principles of French Law 249–276 (1998); Mary Ann Glendon, The Transformation of Family Law 41–43, 61–63, 71–73, 89–91, 1112–114, 118–123 (1989).

2.   French matrimonial property is addressed in Book Three of the Civil Code. Before their marriage, a couple may choose to meet with a lawyer known as a notary (*le notaire*) who specializes in preparing and authenticating legal instruments such as wills, marriage contracts, and mortgages. The notary advises the couple of their legal options and then drafts a marital agreement (*le contrat de marriage*), which must be signed several days before their marriage. There are four standard matrimonial property regimes (*les régimes matrimoniaux*) enumerated in the Civil Code. The spouses may also come up with their own terms, and they may modify their agreement or change regimes with the approval of a court after the old regime has been in place for at least two years. If the couple does not sign an agreement, their matrimonial property rights are defined by a system of community property, which treats any property acquired by either spouse after the marriage as the joint property of the couple. Alternatively, the couple may agree to a broader community property regime, under which property owned by the spouses before the marriage also becomes community property. Couples may choose a separate property system, under which all of their assets remain separate, or a hybrid system which operates as a separate property system during the marriage but which entitles each member of the couple to half of the increase in value during the marriage of the other party's assets when the marriage ends in death or divorce.

3.   The French Civil Code was based on a framework drawn from Roman law, and has been widely influential in the development of civil law system in many different countries, including Europe and Latin America as well as Asia and the Middle East. See generally John Henry Merryman, David S. Clark, and John O. Haley, The Civil Law Tradition: Europe, Latin America, and East Asia (1994).

## 2.   *Marriage in Religious Law: Pakistan*

When Pakistan gained independence in 1947, its legal system was based on a mixture of British and Islamic law. The majority of the population are Sunni Muslims from the Hanafi school, with significant minorities of other Muslim traditions and small groups of individuals of other religious faiths. Pakistan's Muslim Family Laws Ordinance 1961 (MFLO) codified and enacted a series of reforms of traditional marriage and divorce law. Under Islamic law or *Shariah*, marriage (*nikah*) is a contractual matter, negotiated by representatives of the parties (*vakil*), and concluded before two witnesses with a marital agreement (*nikahnama*). The marital agreement specifies a marriage gift or dower payment that the husband is obligated to pay to his wife (*mahr*). Although marriages are typically arranged by the parents or guardians of the parties to be married, both individuals must have reached the age of puberty and both must consent to the marriage.

Section 5 of the MFLO mandated registration of marriages with a *nikah* register and provided for standardization of the forms for marital agreements. The law now requires that the *nikahnama* be put in writing and signed by the bride and groom, their *vakil*, if any, and by the witnesses. The standard form includes clauses that address the details of the dower payments and various legal rights under Islamic law that wives may negotiate at the time of the marriage. The MFLO provisions are not always followed, however, and the courts in Pakistan uphold the validity of marriages even when the statutory formalities are not observed.

Since 1973, Pakistan's Constitution has declared the nation to be an Islamic Republic, and for decades there have been vigorous debates over the Islamization of Pakistani law. At one end of the spectrum are traditionalists, conservative Islamists who emphasize traditional jurisprudence, while at the other are modernists, who stress passages of the Quran and Sunna that support greater scope for protection of women's rights. In this debate, personal status matters including family law and inheritance have been particularly contentious. Constitutional amendments in 1985 provided for the establishment of a Federal Shariat Court with original jurisdiction to determine whether any provision of law is repugnant to the injunctions of Islam. This has set the stage for a series of decisions from the Shariat Court over provisions of the MFLO.

Islam permits polygamy but discourages it, limiting men to a maximum of four wives and requiring a husband to treat each of his wives equally. This is a controversial issue, and many Muslim countries have restricted the practice of polygamy. Under MFLO § 6, a married man must obtain the advance written permission of an Arbitration Council before marrying again, and may be subject to penalties if he does not follow this procedure. In applying for permission, the husband must state his grounds for wishing to marry again and indicate whether he has obtained the consent of his existing wife or wives. The applicant and each wife nominate a representative to the Arbitration Council, which determines whether to grant permission for the marriage.

## ALLAHRAKHA v. FEDERATION OF PAKISTAN

Federal Shariat Court, Pakistan, 2000.
PLD 2000 Federal Shariat Court 1.

MIAN MEHBOOB AHMED, C.J. 37 petitions detailed hereunder have been filed under Article 203–D of the Constitution of the Islamic

Republic of Pakistan questioning the validity of various provisions viz. sections 4, 5, 6 and 7 of the Muslim Family Laws Ordinance 1961 (hereinafter called the Ordinance) on the touchstone of Injunctions of Islam. * * *

* * *

## SECTION 6 OF MUSLIM FAMILY LAWS ORDINANCE, 1961

* * *

82.  [I]n the pre-Islamic era there was no restriction on the number of wives and in addition the morality of society was so degenerative as to have concubines and also resort to prostitution, the Qur'anic Injunctions in this regard appear to be blessings in the society as a whole and for the women a matter of respectability. The Qur'an has allowed ploygamy [sic] but not without restrictions and we quote from Qur'an:—

"If you fear that you shall not be able to deal justly with orphans, marry women of your choice two or three or four but if you fear that you shall not be able to deal justly with them, then only one." (4:3)

* * *

88.  There is no doubt that a Muslim male is permitted to have more than one woman as wife, with a ceiling of 4 at a point of time as the ultimate, but the very *Ayat* which gives this permission also prescribes a condition of *Adal* and the Holy Qur'an has laid emphasis in the same Verse on the gravity and hardship of the condition which Allah Himself says is very difficult to be fulfilled.

89.  Now section 6 of the Ordinance as framed, in no manner places any prohibition in having more than one wife. It only requires that the condition of *Adal* prescribed by the Holy Qur'an itself should be satisfied by the male who wants to have more than one wife. The provision for constituting an Arbitration Council, therefore, cannot in itself be said to be violative of the Injunctions of the Qur'an as only a procedure has been described as to how the Qura'nic verse will be observed in its totality with reference to the condition of *Adal* placed in the Verse itself.

90.  Here we may also refer to Sura Nisa, Ayat 35 which provides for the resolution of dispute between husband and wife and the Qur'anic Injunction as ordained in the said Ayat also is to refer the matter in dispute to representatives of each of the parties to the dispute. The provisions contained in section 6 are, therefore, derivable on a conjunctive reading of Ayat 3 and 35 of Sura Nisa.

* * *

92. * * * However, it may be reiterated that the status of polygamy in Islam is no command more or less than that of a permissible act and has never been considered a command, and therefore, like any other matter made lawful in principle may become forbidden or restricted if it involved unlawful things or leads to unlawful consequences such as injustice. Misuse of the permission granted by Almighty Allah could be checked by adopting suitable measures to put an end to or at least minimize the instances of injustice being found abundantly in the prevalent society. The Arbitration Council in such circumstances would be needed to look into the disputes arising between the husband and existing wife/wives with respect to another marriage and after taking into consideration the age, physical health, financial position and other attending factors, come to a conclusion to settle their disputes. However, we are of the view and accordingly recommend that the Arbitration Council should figure in when a complaint is made by the existing wife or her parents/guardians. The intention is to protect the rights of the existing wife/wives and the interests of her/their children. The wife, who is the best judge of her cause, or her parents may initiate the proceedings if her husband intends to contract another marriage. Moreover, we feel that since a Nikah validly performed with a wife, whether a first or fourth, necessarily entails various consequences including those related to dower, maintenance, inheritance, legitimacy of children, etc., non-registration of the nikah thus performed could not only be a source of litigation between the parties but would also lead to a lot of injustice to such wife/wives.

93. ... Since this section has not expressly declared the subsequent marriage as illegal and has merely prescribed a procedure to be followed for the subsequent marriages and punishment for its non-observance, we find that the spirit of this section is reformative only as in fact it has prescribed a corrective measure for the prevention of injustice to the existing wife/wives.

94. In light of the above discussion we would hold that subject to our observations and recommendation * * * the said provisions are not violative of the Injunctions of Islam.

* * *

### Notes

1. The decision in *Allahrakha* is discussed in Rashida Mohammad Hussain Patel, Woman Versus Man: Socio–Legal Inequality in Pakistan 41–42 (2003). Patel argues that the Shariat Court's recommendation that the Arbitration Council be brought in when a complaint is made by an existing wife or her parents serves to weaken the current

requirement that any man who wishes to marry another wife seek advance permission to do so.

2.   Another recent debate in Pakistan concerned the competence of an unmarried adult Muslim woman to contract a marriage without the consent of her guardian, or *wali*. In a 1977 judgment from the Lahore High Court, two of the three judges on the panel concluded that such a marriage was not invalid, but the decision was appealed. See Abdul Waheed v. Asma Jehangir, PLD 1997 Lahore 331. Despite this ruling, women who marry without their families' consent face such risks as allegations of or prosecutions for illicit sexual relations (*zina*) or even "honor killing" (*karo kari*). The judges in the *Abdul Waheed* case noted that the woman had been living in a shelter for her own protection as the litigation progressed. Patel discusses family pressure concerning marital choice in her book, supra, at 46–71, and discusses domestic violence and murder for male honor at 110–181.

3.   Useful general sources on Islamic family law include Abdullahi An–Na'im, ed., Islamic Family Law in a Changing World: A Global Resource Book (2002); David Pearl and Werner Menski, Muslim Family Law (3d ed. 1998). The country profiles included in the An–Nai'im book are also available online at the website of the Islamic Family Law Project at Emory University. See http://www.law.emory.edu/IFL/.

## 3.   *Marriage in Customary Law: South Africa*

The pluralist legal system that emerged during the colonial period in South Africa included both formal law based on European principles—a hybrid of English common law and Roman–Dutch civil law—and customary law applicable within indigenous communities to family, succession, and property matters. In some instances, official versions of "customary law" were codified and enforced in colonial courts. T.W. Bennett has summarized the features that distinguished customary marriage in South Africa from the European model as follows:

> [P]olygyny was not only tolerated but even approved; the validity of the union depended on payment of lobolo; the relationship was between two families rather than two individuals; the union was achieved gradually over time, not immediately with the performance of a particular ceremony; and marriage was a private affair not requiring any intervention by civil or religious authorities to give it the stamp of validity.

T.W. Bennett, Customary Law in South Africa 188 (2004).

Since the end of the apartheid regime in 1993, South Africa has retained its pluralist system within a new framework of constitutional human rights principles. Section 30 of the 1996 Constitution provides: "Everyone has the right to use the language and to participate in the cultural life of their choice, but no one exercising these rights may do so in a manner inconsistent with any provision of the Bill of Rights." This provision protects customary law, while subjecting it to broader constitutional norms including prohibitions of discrimination on grounds such as age, gender and sex. Section 9(3) of the Constitution states: "The state may not unfairly discriminate directly or indirectly against anyone on one or more grounds, including race, gender, sex, pregnancy, marital status, ethnic or social origin, colour, sexual orientation, age, disability, religion, conscience, belief, culture, language and birth."

The Recognition of Customary Marriages Act, enacted in 1998, defined customary law as "the customs and usages traditionally observed by the indigenous African peoples of South Africa and which form part of the cultures of those peoples." In addition to validating all existing customary marriages, the act provided that future customary marriages would be valid if the spouses were over the age of 18 and consented to be married under customary law, and if the marriage was negotiated and entered into or celebrated in accordance with customary law. The Act provided for registration of customary marriages, but also provided that failure to register a marriage does not affect its legal validity.

## MABENA v. LETSOALO

Supreme Court, Transvaal Provincial Div, South Africa, 1998.
(1998) 2 SA 1068.

Du PLESSIS J.: The late Mr. Joseph Mabena passed away on 23 April 1994. His estate was administered by the magistrate, Pretoria–North in accordance with the provisions of § 23 of the Black Administration Act 38 of 1927 and of the regulations promulgated thereunder. The respondent in this appeal avers that she and the late Mr. Mabena had been parties to a customary marriage. Regulation 2(d) of the regulations referred to above provides that the Minister of justice may in certain circumstances, where a deceased person had been a party to a customary marriage, determine that property of the deceased person shall devolve as if he had been married out of community of property. * * * [T]he Director–General wrote to the magistrate instructing her to obtain from the late Mr. Mabena's parents confirmation of the respondent's averment that she and the deceased had been parties to a customary marriage. Should such confirmation not be obtained, the Director–General wrote, the magistrate was to hold an inquiry in order for her to ascertain whether the marriage existed or not. Mr. Mabena's parents denied the existence of such a marriage, and a formal inquiry was held. The learned magistrate found that a customary marriage between the respondent and the deceased had existed. The father of the deceased lodged an appeal to this Court against

the finding of the learned magistrate. That appeal is now before us.
\* \* \*

Before the magistrate the respondent testified that she became pregnant in 1988. The late Mr. Mabena was the father. Apparently in accordance with customary law the parents of the deceased paid R200 'damages' in respect of the pregnancy to the family of the respondent. (The evidence later was that the respondent's father had deserted the family long ago. However, the respondent did say that her father was involved in the negotiations regarding these damages. In view of the unequivocal evidence that he had abandoned the family, this probably is an error.) A child was born to the couple. In 1988 the deceased purchased a house in Mamelodi, a township in the urban area of Pretoria. Since about March or May 1989 until Mr. Mabena died, the respondent and the child lived with him in the house. The couple decided to regularise their relationship because, to quote the respondent 'we could not proceed staying together whereas no lobolo was paid for me'. However, relations between the respondent and the parents of the deceased were poor, and the latter were not prepared to agree to a customary marriage between the respondent and the deceased. The deceased then 'entered into negotiations' with the respondent and her mother, and an amount of R600 in respect of lobolo was agreed upon. The deceased arranged with two of his friends to go and pay the lobolo to the respondent's mother. As the respondent's father had abandoned his family an uncle of the respondent was by arrangement present to receive the lobolo. Those present then had a 'small party'. The respondent and the child thereafter returned to the common home in Mamelodi.

The respondent is a Pedi while the deceased was a Ndebele. The respondent said that their marriage was performed according to Pedi custom. However, she also said:

> 'My people and I, we do not engage in these customary traditions. We did it as it pleased my mother. It is how we do it at home, it is how we do it according to our custom.'

When it was put to her in cross-examination that they did in several respects not properly follow the Pedi custom, she replied:

> 'Well, customs differ, it depends on an individual, how does he or she want to do it.'

Mr. M.R. Madisa, a friend of the deceased testified that the deceased sent him together with Mr. Skosana and Mr. Mkobane to go and pay the lobolo to the family of the bride. He realized that it was the deceased and not his family who was sending them. When asked whether that is customary, he said that it did happen in the case of a groom who 'has his own house'.

Mr. Michael Mkhwebane is an uncle of the respondent. He was requested by the Letsoalos to be present to receive the lobolo. He did that. Although he had known the deceased for a long time, he said that he did not know that the men bringing the lobolo were not of the Mabena-family.

The respondent's mother testified that the respondent and the deceased lived together after the birth of their child. The deceased told her that they wished to marry. The witness knew that the parents of the deceased were opposed to the marriage. In the circumstances she and the deceased did the best they could; the deceased arranged with her that he would come and pay lobolo. The respondent returned to the home of the witness. A date for payment of lobolo was arranged. The witness arranged for her brother and other family members to be present. The lobolo was paid as testified to by the other witnesses. After the ceremony, the respondent resumed living with the deceased. The witness confirmed that Mr. and Mrs. Mabena were unaware of the payment of the lobolo.

\* \* \*

The essential issue is whether the learned magistrate was correct in holding that a customary marriage existed between the respondent and the deceased.

Mr. Bekker for the appellant submitted that 'the essence of a customary marriage is unification of the two family groups', ie those of the bride and the bridegroom. In this instance it is common cause that the parents of the bridegroom did not consent to the marriage nor participated in the negotiations regarding the marriage and the lobolo. Mr. Bekker argued that the absence of a relationship between the two family groups is fatal to the existence of a customary marriage.

It is true that a customary marriage is not purely a matter between the bride and the bridegroom. It also is 'a group concern, legalising a relationship between two groups of relatives'. However, it does not follow that the father of the bridegroom's consent or his participation in the negotiations regarding the lobolo is essential to the existence of a customary marriage. *Olivier* says that, traditionally, a young man would not have possessed sufficient means to deliver the lobolo for his first wife. From that it followed, writes the author, that the father ordinarily ('gewoonlik') provided the lobolo for his son's first wife and thus consented to the marriage and participated in the negotiations. \* \* \*

*Seymour* puts it even stronger:

'When he disapproves of his son's choice for a first wife, the bridegroom's guardian may refuse to pay lobolo; although he may thus dissociate himself from the customary marriage, he cannot prevent it, if the bridegroom is able to find lobolo himself. The consent of the bridegroom's guardian, therefore, affects only his liability or otherwise ... in the matter of lobolo, but seems to have no bearing on the validity of the customary marriage completed without his help or approval.'

Neither of the latter two authors, when enumerating the essentials of a customary marriage, mentions the consent of the bridegroom's father or guardian as an essential. See also the South African Law Commission's *Report on Marriages and Customary Unions of Black Persons* (Project 51, dated October 1986 at 26 and 27). * * * At present many unmarried men live on their own and fend for themselves. There is no reason to hold that an independent, adult man is not entitled to negotiate for the payment of lobolo in respect of his chosen bride, nor is there any reason to hold that such a man needs the consent of his parents to marry. That that is how the customary law has developed is evident from what *Seymour* and *Olivier* write. It is in addition borne out by the evidence of Mr. Madisa that a man could negotiate for lobolo if he 'has his own house'. It is accordingly held that the fact that the appellant did not consent to the marriage under discussion has no effect on the validity of the marriage. By the same token his lack of involvement in the lobolo negotiations is of no consequence.

* * *

Mr. Bekker's final argument was that because the respondent's father did not consent to the marriage and was not involved in the negotiations regarding the lobolo, the marriage is void. The customary marriage comprises two distinct legal actions: there is on the one hand the marriage itself. On the other hand there is the lobolo agreement with the handing over of the bride. For the first the consent of the bride, the bridegroom and the 'guardian' of the bride is required. For the second, where the father of the bridegroom is not involved, the consent and agreement of the bridegroom and the guardian of the bride is required; the bride is not involved in the lobolo agreement. The thrust of Mr. Bekker's argument is this: in terms of customary law a female person cannot be the guardian of the bride, it has to be a male person, in the ordinary course her father. As the lobolo agreement *in casu* was contracted by the respondent's mother, no valid customary marriage ensued.

It is manifest that all the authorities on customary law accept that only the father of the bride or another male guardian could validly contract for and receive lobolo. (See all the authorities quoted above.) According to traditional customary law the mother of the bride could not be the guardian of her daughter; she was herself under the guardianship of her husband or of her own father or of their successors.

The evidence in this case is that the respondent's father had abandoned the family. The evidence further is that the respondent's mother as a matter of fact functioned as head of the family (consisting as far as one can ascertain from the evidence, only of the two women). No authority was quoted to us as to what the rule of customary law is in such circumstances. Mr. Bekker's argument proceeded on the assumption that such a state of affairs cannot exist where people apply customary law. However, those are the facts in this case, and that is what we have to deal with. The respondent said that they performed the marriage according to their custom. Her evidence in this respect is somewhat ambiguous: she might have been referring to a custom practised by her and her mother and not to a general custom she knows about. However, there are authorities which indicate that the circumstances of this case are not unique. * * *

The South African Law Commission Project 90 'The Harmonisation of the Common Law and the Indigenous Law' *Discussion Paper* 74 at 64 discusses the need for the consent of the bride's father and submits that the consent of the mother (in the case of minors) should also be required. They then state:

'If a mother is entitled to supply the consent to her ward's marriage, then she would also be entitled to arrange the bride wealth. Under the KwaZulu/Natal Codes (§ 59) de jure emancipated women already have this power.'

It must therefore be accepted that there are instances in practice where mothers negotiate for and receive lobolo, and consent to the marriage of their daughters. The present case is clearly not an isolated one. Seen against that backdrop, the respondent was probably referring to the custom followed by people in similar circumstances to their own. A rule that a woman who is the head of her family may negotiate for and receive lobolo is not repugnant to the customary law of marriage. This is clear from the views expressed by the Law Commission. Customary law does recognise that a woman may act as head of a family in certain circumstances.

From what has been said regarding the bridegroom's entitlement to negotiate for and pay lobolo, it is evident that customary law is, as any system of law should be, in a state of continuous development. It has been able to develop the rule that a bridegroom can negotiate for and pay lobolo and thus has met the actual demands of society. Moreover, customary law exists not only in the 'official version' as documented by writers; there also is the 'living law', denoting 'law actually observed by African communities'. (Law Commission Project 90 at 12 para 2.3.2; see also T R Nhlapo 'The African Family and Women's Rights: Friends or Foes' 1991 *Acta Juridica* 135.) The quoted passages by *Labuschagne* and the

Law Commission seem to be the first notations (there might of course be more) of a rule of the 'living law' actually observed by the community and testified to by the respondent. It might be argued that because of the dearth of authority on this point, the rule cannot be 'ascertained readily and with sufficient certainty' as is provided for in § 1(1) of the Law of Evidence Amendment Act 45 of 1988, and that the Court cannot take judicial notice thereof. The evidence of the respondent, admissible in terms of § 1(2) of the said Act, lends support to what the authorities say. This Court should readily recognise the rule. Such recognition would constitute a development in accordance with the 'spirit, purpose and objects' of chap 3 of the Constitution of the Republic of South Africa Act 200 of 1993. * * *

It is held that on the facts of this case the respondent's mother was in law entitled to negotiate for and receive lobolo in respect of the respondent. She was also in law entitled to act as guardian and consent to the marriage of the respondent.

The appeal is accordingly dismissed with costs.

### Notes

1. *Mabena* is discussed in Lisa Fishbayn, "Litigating the Right to Culture: Family Law in the New South Africa," 13 Int'l J.L. Pol'y & Fam. 147 (1999). Fishbayn argues that the case illustrates a post-modern understanding of culture, in which the judge "was able to integrate a commitment to preserving continuity with traditional cultural norms and respect for gender equality by using a notion of culture as a fluid narrative rather than a closed system." Id. at 167.

2. Traditional societies in southern Africa were strongly patriarchal, with clear gender roles in marriage and limited property rights for women. Section 6 of the Recognition of Customary Marriages Act provides that a wife has full legal status and capacity, "on the basis of equality with her husband and subject to the matrimonial property scheme governing the marriage," and section 7(2) provides for a community property regime unless the spouses agree to a different matrimonial property regime in an antenuptial agreement. The Act does not prohibit polygynous marriages, but section 7(6) requires a husband to apply to the court for approval of a written contract defining the property rights of existing and future wives. How can polygyny be consistent with women's equality rights under section 9(3) of South Africa's Constitution, quoted above?

## 4. Same-sex Marriage: Canada

Canada shares in the Anglo–American legal tradition, which has historically defined marriage in Christian religious terms as "the voluntary union for life of one man and one woman, to the exclusion of all others." Hyde v. Hyde and Woodmansee (1866) L.R. 1 P. & D. 130 at 133. At the same time, Canada has built a strong human rights tradition under section 15(1) of its Charter of Rights and Freedoms, which provides that "[e]very individual is equal before and under the law and has the right to the equal protection and equal benefit of the law without discrimination and, in particular, without discrimination based on race, national or ethnic origin, colour, religion, sex, age or mental or physical disability." Applying section 15(1), the highest courts of several Canadian provinces concluded that limiting marriage to opposite-sex couples was a violation of the Charter. See, e.g., Halpern v. Canada (Attorney General) [2003] 65 O.R. (3d) 161 (Ontario Ct. App.). The Canadian government decided not to appeal these decisions to the Supreme Court of Canada, and introduced this legislation which became law in 2005.

# AN ACT RESPECTING CERTAIN ASPECTS OF LEGAL CAPACITY FOR MARRIAGE FOR CIVIL PURPOSES (BILL C–38)

Statutes of Canada 2005, Chapter 33, 53–54 Elizabeth II.
[Assented to 20th July, 2005].

### PREAMBLE

WHEREAS the Parliament of Canada is committed to upholding the Constitution of Canada, and section 15 of the Canadian Charter of Rights and Freedoms guarantees that every individual is equal before and under the law and has the right to equal protection and equal benefit of the law without discrimination;

WHEREAS the courts in a majority of the provinces and in one territory have recognized that the right to equality without discrimination requires that couples of the same sex and couples of the opposite sex have equal access to marriage for civil purposes;

WHEREAS the Supreme Court of Canada has recognized that many Canadian couples of the same sex have married in reliance on those court decisions;

WHEREAS only equal access to marriage for civil purposes would respect the right of couples of the same sex to equality without discrimination, and civil union, as an institution other than marriage, would not offer them that equal access and would violate their human dignity, in breach of the Canadian Charter of Rights and Freedoms;

WHEREAS the Supreme Court of Canada has determined that the Parliament of Canada has legislative jurisdiction over marriage but does not have the jurisdiction to establish an institution other than marriage for couples of the same sex;

WHEREAS everyone has the freedom of conscience and religion under section 2 of the Canadian Charter of Rights and Freedoms;

WHEREAS nothing in this Act affects the guarantee of freedom of conscience and religion and, in particular, the freedom of members of religious groups to hold and declare their religious beliefs and the freedom of officials of religious groups to refuse to perform marriages that are not in accordance with their religious beliefs;

WHEREAS it is not against the public interest to hold and publicly express diverse views on marriage;

WHEREAS, in light of those considerations, the Parliament of Canada's commitment to uphold the right to equality without discrimination precludes the use of section 33 of the Canadian Charter of Rights and Freedoms to deny the right of couples of the same sex to equal access to marriage for civil purposes;

WHEREAS marriage is a fundamental institution in Canadian society and the Parliament of Canada has a responsibility to support that institution because it strengthens commitment in relationships and represents the foundation of family life for many Canadians;

AND WHEREAS, in order to reflect values of tolerance, respect and equality consistent with the Canadian Charter of Rights and Freedoms, access to marriage for civil purposes should be extended by legislation to couples of the same sex;

NOW, THEREFORE, Her Majesty, by and with the advice and consent of the Senate and House of Commons of Canada, enacts as follows:

Short title

1.   This Act may be cited as the Civil Marriage Act.

Marriage—certain aspects of capacity

2.   Marriage, for civil purposes, is the lawful union of two persons to the exclusion of all others.

Religious officials

3.   It is recognized that officials of religious groups are free to refuse to perform marriages that are not in accordance with their religious beliefs.

Freedom of conscience and religion and expression of beliefs

3.1   For greater certainty, no person or organization shall be deprived of any benefit, or be subject to any obligation or sanction, under any law of the Parliament of Canada solely by reason of their exercise, in respect of marriage between persons of the same sex, of the freedom of conscience and religion guaranteed under the Canadian Charter of Rights and Freedoms or the expression of their beliefs in respect of marriage as the union of a man and woman to the exclusion of all others based on that guaranteed freedom.

Marriage not void or voidable

4.  For greater certainty, a marriage is not void or voidable by reason only that the spouses are of the same sex.

### Notes

1.  After the Canadian legislation was introduced, it was referred to the Supreme Court of Canada to determine whether the legislation fell within Parliament's legislative authority, and whether the legislation would be consistent with the Canadian Charter of Rights and Freedoms. The Supreme Court answered these questions affirmatively in 2004. See Re Same–Sex Marriage: In the Matter or Section 53 of the Supreme Court Act, R.S.C. 1985, c. S–26 [2004].

2.  Contemporary laws granting legal recognition to same-sex partner relationships began with the Registered Partnership Act in Denmark in1989. Several European nations subsequently extended the right to marry to same-sex couples, beginning with the Netherlands in 2001, Belgium in 2003, and Spain in 2005. After Canada joined this group in 2005, South Africa became the fifth nation in the world to permit same-sex marriage with passage of the Civil Union Act in 2006.

3.  In the United States, only Massachusetts permits same-sex couples to marry, but states including California, Connecticut, Hawaii, New Jersey and Vermont recognize some form of registered domestic partnership or civil union. Many European countries have established different forms of civil union or registered partnership. In the United Kingdom, same-sex couples may register under the Civil Partnership Act, and in France a contract-based regime known as Civil Solidarity Pacts or PACS (*Pacte civil de solildarité*) is available to both same-sex and opposite-sex couples. See Claude Martin and Iréne Théry, "The PACS and Marriage and Cohabitation in France," 15 Int'l J.L. Pol'y & Fam. 135 (2001).

4.  Cohabitation relationships receive varying levels of legal recognition and protection in these countries. New Zealand extended the same property rules governing married couples to partners in "*de facto* relationships" with legislation in 1999 that defines a de facto relationship as one between two persons, both age 18 or older, who live together as a couple and are not married to one another. See generally Bill Atkin, "The Challenge of Unmarried Cohabitation: The New Zealand Response," 37 Fam. L.Q. 303 (2003). Cohabitants may lose the legal recognition their relationship receives under domestic law when

they travel to another country. See, e.g., American Airlines v. Mejia, 766 So.2d 305 (Fla. Ct. App. 2000) (holding that *union marital de hecho* under Columbian law is not equivalent to common law marriage under wrongful death statute); Estate of Huyot, 169 Misc.2d 805, 645 N.Y.S.2d 979 (Surr. Ct 1996) (rejecting claim that French *concubinage* relationship should be treated as a common law marriage for estate purposes).

# B. MARRIAGE AND INTERNATIONAL HUMAN RIGHTS

International human rights instruments protect the right to marry and found a family. Within the normative boundaries established by the Universal Declaration of Human Rights in 1948 and the treaties that followed it, there is room for a wide diversity of approaches to marriage and family life. Under these treaties, however, some marriage practices are a violation of human rights.

Human rights groups have focused particular attention on child marriage and forced marriage, which violate the consent principle that is central to these norms. In those regions and cultures where marriages are traditionally arranged by the families of the bride and groom, it is necessary to draw a careful distinction between arranged marriage and forced marriage. In a forced marriage, one party does not or is not able to consent, and some element of duress is usually present.

## SINGH v. SINGH
Supreme Court, Tompkins County, New York, 1971.
67 Misc.2d 878, 325 N.Y.S.2d 590.

FREDERICK B. BRYANT, JUSTICE.

This is an action brought by the plaintiff to have his purported marriage to the defendant declared null and void pursuant to Section 5 of the Hindu Marriage Act (Act. No. 25 of the Laws of India, 1955).

The complaint alleges that the purported marriage took place in Allahabad, India, on January 19, 1964 when both parties were residents of India. The plaintiff asserts that he is now and has been for more than two years prior to the commencement of this action a resident of the State of New York. The complaint and the evidence submitted show that the marriage was arranged by the respective parents of the plaintiff and the defendant without the consent of either of the parties and that certain ceremonies and rites customary and essential in marriages performed according to the Hindu Marriage Act were not observed. The plaintiff asserts that because of this the purported marriage was a nullity. These ceremonies include the invocation before the sacred fire and the 'saptapadi'— this is, the taking of seven steps by the bride and bridegroom before the sacred fire. The plaintiff alleges that the defendant refused to participate in these two rites and that the purported marriage was never consummated. The parties have never lived together as husband and wife.

Service of the summons in the action by personal service upon the defendant in India is shown by affidavit in accordance with Section 232 of the Domestic Relations Law. The plaintiff appeared and testified before the Court together with a cooperating witness and the proof required by Section 144 of the Domestic Relations Law has been completed. The defendant has not appeared in the action nor answered the complaint. The Court finds that it has jurisdiction of the subject matter of the action by reason of the plaintiff's uncontested allegation of residence in the State required by Section 230(5) of the Domestic Relations Law.

Section 7 of the Hindu Marriage Act of 1955 reads as follows:

*'Ceremonies for a Hindu marriage*: (1) A Hindu marriage may be solemnized in accordance with the customary rites and ceremonies of either party thereto.

(2) Where such rites and ceremonies include the Saptapaid (that is, the taking of seven steps by the bridegroom and the bride jointly before the sacred fire), the marriage becomes complete and binding when the seventh step is taken.'

The meaning and effect of the quoted section is the principal question before this Court. Plainly, where the customary ceremonies of either party to the marriage include the saptapadi the marriage is complete when the saptapadi is performed. But when the saptapadi is not performed the question arises as to whether the marriage is thereby invalid. Numerous Indian authorities on this point have been studied, including 'The Hindu Marriage Act of 1955' by D. H. Chandhari; 'Hindu Law of Marriage' by S. V. Gupte; 'Indian Law of Marriage and Divorce' by Kumaid Desai; 'The Hindu Marriage Act' by P. V. Deolalkar; 'The Hindu Marriage Act' by Kashi Prasad; 'The Hindu Marriage Act' by P. S. Bendra; 'The Hindu Code' by Shiva Gopal; 'The Hindu Law and Usage' by Nirmal Kumar Roy; and 'The 'Hindu Marriage Act, 1955' by S. K. Shanglo. While these writers are not completely unanimous in their view as to the absolute necessity for performance of the saptapadi in order that a valid marriage be contracted, it seems to be the consensus that if the saptapadi is included among the customary rites and ceremonies of the parties to a marriage a marriage without the saptapadi is invalid and no marriage at all. Apparently, the customary beliefs and practices of the parties are determinative on this issue.

In the present case the plaintiff established that his purported marriage to the defendant was to be a Hindu marriage, solemnized by a Hindu priest. In such circumstances the saptapadi was an essential part of the rite. The refusal of the defendant to take the seven steps, although urged by the priest and her father several times to do so, amounted in effect to a refusal of her consent to the marriage. The plaintiff later learned that the reason for this refusal was that the defendant was in love with someone else and did not want to marry the plaintiff. She told the plaintiff she was not his wife and did not consider him to be her husband and another witness testified to the defendant's failure to perform the saptapadi and to her present refusal to acknowledge herself the plaintiff's wife.

Under all of these circumstances it is this Court's opinion that the defendant's failure to perform the saptapadi—an essential element in the marriage rites—makes the marriage invalid under New York law and likewise invalid under the The Hindu Marriage Act of 1955. This is not a situation of a voidable marriage. The marriage in the present case was void *ab initio* in accordance with the Hindu Marriage Act and this annulment action merely declares that to be the fact.

The plaintiff is therefore entitled to a decree declaring his purported marriage to the defendant on January 19, 1964 to be null and void.

## HIRANI V. HIRANI

Court of Appeal (Civil Division), England 1982.
4 FLR 232.

ORMROD L.J.: This is an appeal by a wife petitioner from a judgment of Judge Roger Willis on 11 February 1982 sitting in the Family Division. He had before him an undefended petition by the wife for a decree of nullity on the ground that she had entered into the marriage under duress, the duress being exerted by her parents. Although it was an undefended suit the judge rejected the petition and dismissed it. The wife now appeals.

The brief facts are these. At the time the wife was 19 years of age, living with her parents in England. They are Indian Hindus. She made the acquaintance of a young Indian, Mr Hussain, who is a Muslim. Her parents were very upset when they discovered this and naturally objected to her association with this man. According to Mrs Hirani's evidence, which the judge accepted, her parents immediately made arrangements for her to marry Mr Hirani. That was in early January 1981. Her evidence went on to say that she had never seen Mr Hirani, nor indeed had her parents ever seen Mr

Hirani, but, within a fortnight of that first conversation, they had arranged for her to marry Mr Hirani at a registry office on 17 January. They put great pressure on her to go through with this ceremony, the threat being:

'You want to marry somebody who is strictly against our religion; he is a Muslim, you are a Hindu; you had better marry somebody we want you to, otherwise pack up your belongings and go. If you do not want to marry Mr Hirani and you want to marry Mr Hussain, go.'

Of course she had no place to go and no means of supporting herself at that age if she did leave the family home, and so, in those circumstances, in spite of her opposition, she was forced to go through with the civil ceremony and after that she returned to her parents. She did not go to live with her husband until after the subsequent religious ceremony which took place on 27 February. She said that she was crying all the way through it and was utterly miserable, but after that ceremony she did live with Mr Hirani for 6 weeks. After that she left and went to Mr Hussain. She has never been back and there was no sexual intercourse between her and Mr Hirani during that 6 weeks.

On that evidence Mr Fox invited the judge to pronounce a decree on the ground of duress, but the judge asked in the course of argument whether that evidence '. . . was anything like enough to say that her mind was overborne by this threat?' Mr Fox referred the judge to two cases: *Parojcic v Parojcic* [1959] 1 All ER 1 and *Scott v Sebright* (1886) 12 PD 31 and the well-known passage in the judgment of Butt J, but the judge had *Rayden on Divorce* before him and it is clear from his judgment that he was greatly influenced by an extract from a judgment of Sir Jocelyn Simon P which appears in the current edition of *Rayden* at p. 179 at the end of note (b). It is an extract which comes right at the end of the judge's judgment in a case called *Szechter v Szechter* [1971] P 286. The passage cited in *Rayden* reads thus:

'. . . while it "is insufficient to invalidate an otherwise good marriage that a party has entered into it in order to escape from a disagreeable situation, such as penury or degradation", this was a case where "the will of one of the parties hereto has been overborne by genuine and reasonably held fear by the threat of immediate danger, for which the party is not responsible to life, limb or liberty, so that the constraint destroys the reality of consent to ordinary wedlock". . . .'

Reading that passage—and one can understand what the judge had in mind—he felt that he had to find threat to life, limb or liberty in order to find duress. With respect I do not for one moment think that the President intended that result. He was merely contrasting a disagreeable situation with one which constituted a real threat. But the matter can be dealt with quite shortly by referring to a recent case in the Privy Council dealing with duress and its effect on a contract. It is a case called *Pao On v Lau Yiu Long* [1980] AC 614. Lord Scarman, giving the opinion of the Privy Council and dealing with the duress question, at p. 635 said this:

> 'Duress, whatever form it takes, is a coercion of the will so as to vitiate consent.'

He then quoted a dictum of Kerr J in another case [*The Siboen and The Sibotre* [1976] 1 Lloyd's Rep. 293 at p. 336]:

> 'There must be present some factor "which could in law be regarded as a coercion of his will so as to vitiate his consent".'

The crucial question in these cases, particularly where a marriage is involved, is whether the threats, pressure, or whatever it is, is such as to destroy the reality of consent and overbears the will of the individual. It seems to me that this case, on the facts, is a classic case of a young girl, wholly dependent on her parents, being forced into a marriage with a man she has never seen and whom her parents have never seen in order to prevent her (reasonably, from her parents' point of view) continuing in an association with a Muslim which they would regard with abhorrence. But it is as clear a case as one could want of the overbearing of the will of the petitioner and thus invalidating or vitiating her consent.

In those circumstances I would allow the appeal and pronounce the decree nisi.

### Notes

1. See also Kaur v. Singh, 2005 SCLR 1000 (Ct. of Session Scotland 2005). A number of English cases involving duress and marriage are discussed in Sebastian Poulter, English Law and Ethnic Minority Customs 27–33 (1986). Some forcible marriage cases involve conduct by parents that amounts to abduction of their children; see, e.g., Re KR (Abduction: Forcible Removal by Parents) [1999] 2 FLR 542 (England), in which English authorities intervened after parents removed their daughter from London to India against her will, apparently for the purpose of arranging a marriage. American consular officials in foreign countries may similarly become involved when U.S. citizens are subjected to coercive marriage practices during trips to other countries. See 7 U.S. Department of State Foreign Affairs Manual (Consular Affairs) 1459 and 1740. See also Alison Symington, "Dual Citizenship and Forced Marriages," 10 Dalhousie J.Leg.Stud. 1 (2001); Sara Hossain and Suzanne Turner, "Abduction for Forced Marriage: Rights and Remedies in Bangladesh and Pakistan," 2001 Int'l Fam. L. 1–64 at 15 (April 2001).

2. UNICEF and a number of international NGOs have campaigned against child marriage as a fundamental violation of human rights. Among other issues, girls married at a young age are likely to be denied access to education, and face higher risks of HIV infections and complications from childbirth. See generally Jaya Sagade, Child Marriage in India (2005); Annie Bunting, "Child Marriage" in 2 Women and International Human Rights Law (Kelly D. Askin & Doreen M. Koenig eds. 2000). While child marriage practices have drawn particular attention in African and Asian countries, it should also be noted that several states in the United States still permit the marriage of girls in their early teenage years with parental consent.

## UNIVERSAL DECLARATION OF HUMAN RIGHTS
United Nations, 1948.
G.A. Res. 217A, U.N. G.A.O.R., 3d Sess. Pt.
1, Resolutions, at 71, U.N. Doc. A/810.

### Article 16

1. Men and women of full age, without any limitation due to race, nationality or religion, have the right to marry and found a family. They are entitled to equal rights as to marriage, during marriage, and at its dissolution.

2. Marriage shall be entered into only with the free and full consent of the intending spouses.

3. The family is the natural and fundamental group unit of society and is entitled to protection by society and the State.

## CONVENTION ON CONSENT TO MARRIAGE, MINIMUM AGE FOR MARRIAGE, AND REGISTRATION OF MARRIAGES
United Nations, 1962.
521 U.N.T.S. 231.

### Article 1

1. No marriage shall be legally entered into without the full and free consent of both parties, such consent to be expressed by them in person after due publicity and in the presence of the authority competent to solemnize the marriage and of witnesses, as prescribed by law.

2. Notwithstanding anything in paragraph 1 above, it shall not be necessary for one of the parties to be present when the competent authority is satisfied that the circumstances are exceptional and that the party has, before a competent authority and in such manner as may be prescribed by law, expressed and not withdrawn consent.

### Article 2

States parties to the present Convention shall specify a minimum age for marriage. No marriage shall be legally entered into by any person under this age, except where a competent authority has granted a dispensation as to age, for serious reasons, in the interest of the intending spouses.

### Article 3

All marriages shall be registered in an appropriate official register by the competent authority.

## CONVENTION ON THE ELIMINATION OF ALL FORMS OF DISCRIMINATION AGAINST WOMEN (CEDAW)

United Nations, 1979.
1249 U.N.T.S. 13, 1989 U.K.T.S. 2, 1982 Misc. 1, Cm. 643, Cmnd. 8444.

### Article 1

For the purposes of the present Convention, the term "discrimination against women" shall mean any distinction, exclusion or restriction made on the basis of sex which has the effect or purpose of impairing or nullifying the recognition, enjoyment or exercise by women, irrespective of their marital status, on a basis of equality of men and women, of human rights and fundamental freedoms in the political, economic, social, cultural, civil or any other field.

### Article 5

States Parties shall take all appropriate measures:

(a) To modify the social and cultural patterns of conduct of men and women, with a view to achieving the elimination of prejudices and customary and all other practices which are based on the idea of the inferiority or the superiority of either of the sexes or on stereotyped roles for men and women;

(b) To ensure that family education includes a proper understanding of maternity as a social function and the recognition of the common responsibility of men and women in the upbringing and development of their children, it being understood that the interest of the children is the primordial consideration in all cases.

### Article 9

1. States Parties shall grant women equal rights with men to acquire, change or retain their nationality. They shall insure in particular that neither marriage to an alien nor change of nationality by the husband during marriage shall automatically change the

nationality of the wife, render her stateless or force upon her the nationality of the husband.

2.  States parties shall grant women equal rights with men with respect to the nationality of their children.

## *Article 16*

1.  States Parties shall take all appropriate measures to eliminate discrimination against women in all matters relating to marriage and family relations and in particular shall ensure, on a basis of equality of men and women:

(a) The same right to enter into marriage;

(b) The same right freely to choose a spouse and to enter into marriage only with their free and full consent;

(c) The same rights and responsibilities during marriage and at its dissolution;

(d) The same rights and responsibilities as parents, irrespective of their marital status, in matters relating to their children; in all cases the interests of the children shall be paramount;

(e) The same rights to decide freely and responsibly on the number and spacing of their children and to have access to the information, education and means to enable them to exercise these rights;

(f) The same rights and responsibilities with regard to guardianship, wardship, trusteeship and adoption of children, or similar institutions where these concepts exist in national legislation; in all cases the interests of the children shall be paramount;

(g) The same personal rights as husband and wife, including the right to choose a family name, a profession and an occupation;

(h) The same rights for both spouses in respect of the ownership, acquisition, management, administration, enjoyment and disposition of property, whether free of charge or for a valuable consideration.

2.  The betrothal and the marriage of a child shall have no legal effect, and all necessary action, including legislation, shall be taken to specify a minimum age for marriage and to make the registration of marriages in an official registry compulsory.

*Notes*

1.   What restrictions do these treaties place on child marriage? See also United Nations Recommendation on Consent to Marriage, Minimum Age for Marriage, and Registration of Marriages, G.A. Res. 2018, U.N. GAOR 20th Sess., Supp. No. 14, at 36, U.N. Doc. A16014 (1965) (recommending minimum marriage age of 15). What marriage laws or practices in the United States or around the world might pose problems under these human rights principles?

2.   Many of the 185 nations that are parties to the Convention on the Elimination of All Forms of Discrimination Against Women (CE-DAW) have made reservations to various provisions of the treaty. Article 16 has drawn particular opposition in those countries in which family matters are governed by Islamic law. See generally Michele Brandt & Jeffrey Kaplan, "The Tension Between Women's Rights and Religious Rights: Reservations to CEDAW by Egypt, Bangladesh and Tunisia," 12 J.L. & Religion 105 (1995–96). Detailed information on ratification and reservations is available on the United Nations web site; see http://www.un.org/womenwatch/daw/cedaw/. The United States has signed but has not ratified CEDAW; see generally Ann Elizabeth Mayer, "Reflections on the Proposed United States Reservations to CEDAW: Should the Constitution be an Obstacle to Human Rights?" 23 Hastings Const. L.Q. 727 (1996).

3.   In 1992, the United States ratified the International Covenant on Civil and Political Rights (ICCPR), Dec. 19, 1966, 993 U.N.T.S. 171, 1966 U.N.J.Y.B. 193, 1977 U.K.T.S. 6, Cmnd. 6702 (1967). Article 23 of the ICCPR includes language that parallels the provisions of Article 16 of the 1948 Universal Declaration of Human Rights, reprinted above.

4.   In Gao v. Gonzales, 440 F.3d 62 (2d Cir. 2006) the court allowed a Chinese woman to pursue a claim for asylum based on a well-founded fear that if she remained in China she would be subjected to a forced marriage, a practice "sanctioned by society and by the local authorities." Forced marriage is one important aspect of the global human trafficking problem; see Sigma Huda, Report of the Special Rapporteur on the Human Rights Aspects of the Victims of Trafficking in Persons, especially Women and Children, U.N. Doc. A/HRC/4/23, Jan. 24, 2007.

## C.   MARRIAGE RECOGNITION

Given the frequency of marriage between citizens of different countries, and the increasing mobility of individuals and families across continents and around the globe, principles governing the recognition of foreign marriages have taken on increasing importance. As suggested by the materials above, there are large differences between nations on the law of marriage. How should a nation that prohibits child marriage, or same-sex marriage, or polygamous marriage, respond to an immigrant who has contracted a valid marriage of this type at home?

In the United States, the rule generally applied to marriages is that a marriage is valid everywhere if it is valid under the law of the place where it is celebrated (*lex loci celebrationis* or *lex loci contractus*). E.g. Marriage of Ma, 483 N.W.2d 732 (Minn. Ct. App. 1992). See Eugene F. Scoles, et al, Conflict of Laws § 13.5 (3d ed. 2000); see also Restatement (Second) of Conflict of Laws § 283 (1971). Conflict of laws principles may operate differently depending upon whether an issue arises as to the substantive or formal validity of the marriage. When the foreign marriage is one that contravenes a strong public policy of the forum state, recognition of the marriage may be denied. The determination whether to extend or deny recognition may also depend on the context of the claims being made. Compare, e.g., In re Dalip Singh Bir's Estate, 83 Cal.App.2d 256, 188 P.2d 499, 502 (1948) (recognizing polygamous foreign marriage for purpose of determining child's inheritance rights) with People v. Ezeonu, 155 Misc.2d 344, 588 N.Y.S.2d 116 (Sup. Ct. 1992) (denying recognition of alleged polygamous marriage under Nigerian law raised as defense to statutory rape charge) and In re Mujahid, 15 I. & N. Dec. 546 (BIA 1976) (holding that polygamous foreign marriage was not valid to confer preferential immigration status). In civil law systems, issues concerning the substantive or "essential" validity of a marriage are governed by the law of the parties' domicile (*lex domicilliae*) or nationality (*lex patriae*).

The 1977 Hague Convention on Celebration and Recognition of the Validity of Marriages ("Marriage Convention") provides that a marriage valid under the law of the place of celebration is valid in all contracting states, without regard to the nationality or domicile of the parties. The Marriage Convention allows contracting states to deny recognition to a marriage based on the prior marriage of one of the spouses, a direct lineal or sibling relationship between the spouses, because either party did not consent freely to the marriage or if either party was not of age. A contracting state may also refuse to extend recognition to a marriage that is incompatible with its public policy. See generally Willis L.M. Reese, "The Hague Convention on Celebration and Recognition of the Validity of Marriages," 20 Va. J. Int'l L. 25 (1979). Only a handful of countries have ratified the Hague Marriage Convention, and as a result these issues are typically addressed at a national level through the application of more general principles of private international law. See "Special Symposium: International Marriage and Divorce Regulation and Recognition," 29 Fam. L.Q. 497 (1995).

When the formal validity of a marriage is challenged, usually on the basis of a defect in the process of licensing or solemnization,

American courts apply a variety of rules and presumptions designed to uphold the marriage. Thus, in Xiong v. Xiong, 255 Wis.2d 693, 648 N.W.2d 900 (Ct. App. 2002), the court allowed a Hmong husband to sue for the wrongful death of the wife he had married according to "traditional Hmong ceremonial rites" in Laos in 1975, at a time when husband was a member of a guerilla army working with the United States Central Intelligence Agency and could not procure formal documentation required by Laotian law. The court concluded that the couple had a putative marriage, based on their good faith belief that they had properly solemnized their marriage. See generally Homer H. Clark, Jr., The Law of Domestic Relations in the United States § 2.7 (Student 2d ed. 1988) for a discussion of various presumptions in support of marriage.

Some of the most complex marriage recognition cases arise when individuals contract a series of marriages. One presumption holds that a marriage once contracted continues in existence until its termination is proved; another presumption holds that the latest of a series of marriages is valid. Traditionally, the doctrine held that the presumption in favor of the later marriage is stronger. In the international context, the challenge of litigating these cases is increased by the need to establish the validity of foreign marriages and divorces.

## GOMEZ v. WINDOWS ON THE WORLD

Supreme Court, Appellate Division, New York, 2005.
23 A.D.3d 967, 804 N.Y.S.2d 849.

CARDONA, P.J.

Appeal from a decision of the Workers' Compensation Board, filed July 6, 2004, which ruled that claimant is the legal widow of decedent and awarded her workers' compensation death benefits.

Wilder Gomez (hereinafter decedent) died on September 11, 2001 in the terrorist attacks upon the World Trade Center in New York City. When claimant applied for a workers' compensation death benefit as decedent's surviving spouse, Elisa Gomez Escalante objected and likewise sought a death benefit as decedent's surviving spouse. It appears that decedent married Escalante in his native Colombia in 1984 and, following his solitary emigration to the United States in 1991, decedent married claimant in New York in 1992.

After decedent's work-related death was established, a Workers' Compensation Law Judge (hereinafter WCLJ) concluded that claimant was decedent's surviving spouse and awarded benefits. Upon Escalante's application for further review, the Workers' Compensation Board affirmed, prompting this appeal.

Initially, we agree with Escalante that the Board should have formally considered certain evidence which had not been presented to the WCLJ but which was submitted as part of her application for Board review. Escalante indicated to the WCLJ that she had been married to one Guillermo Rojas in 1981 but divorced him before her marriage to decedent. In support of this claim, Escalante submitted her Colombian "civil registry record of birth" which noted, among other facts, that she had obtained a "separación de cuerpos" from Rojas and thereafter "contracted civil matrimony" with decedent. Based upon the Spanish-to-English translation provided and representations made by Escalante's counsel, the WCLJ apparently concluded that Escalante and Rojas had merely been legally separated (see generally Domestic Relations Law art. 11) and that, as a result, her subsequent marriage to decedent was "questionable." Therefore, according to the WCLJ, that proof failed to overcome the presumptive validity of decedent's marriage to claimant (see Matter of Seidel v. Crown Indus., 132 A.D.2d 729, 730, 517 N.Y.S.2d 310 [1987]).

In her application for Board review, however, Escalante submitted a copy of the actual order of separación de cuerpos and an affidavit of an experienced Colombian attorney, Sulamita Kaim Torres. Kaim Torres attested that the "birth registry" submitted by Escalante is a statutorily-derived, "unique and definitive" catalogue of facts relating to a person's legal capacity and status. Moreover, Kaim Torres indicated that, under then-existing Colombian law, a separacion de cuerpos was used to civilly dissolve a canonic or religious marriage—such as purportedly existed between Escalante and Rojas—and that the device served as the functional equivalent to a divorce in that context.

Assuming the Board's unfamiliarity with the laws of Colombia, which are pertinent to the resolution of the instant dispute, and inasmuch as Escalante proffered a credible excuse for failing to present the evidence in question to the WCLJ, we conclude that the Board should have formally considered this additional proof. However, in light of the fact that the Board stated that the new evidence, even if considered, would not change its determination, we decline to remit the matter for additional factfinding and will instead review the record before us to ascertain whether the Board's determination in favor of claimant is supported by substantial evidence (see generally 111 NY Jur.2d, Workers Compensation §§ 772, 773).

It has long been the rule that, where a marriage has been proven by the facts adduced, there exists a presumption that such marriage is valid. However, where, as here, two competing putative spouses have come forth with adequate proof establishing the existence of their respective matrimonies, the law further presumes that it is the second marriage which is valid and that the first marriage was dissolved by death, divorce or annulment. Thus, it was Escalante's burden to prove that the more recent marriage of decedent to claimant was invalid due to the continued existence of her own marriage to decedent. Regardless of whether Escalante's burden of persuasion is set at a clear and convincing standard or something less stringent, it is our view that Escalante has sufficiently established the vitality of her marriage to decedent and thus rebutted the presumptive validity of claimant's marriage to decedent.

As discussed above, Escalante produced documentary proof that a Columbian court issued a judgment of separación de cuerpos dissolving her marriage to Rojas, a fact further evidenced by a consistent notation on her Colombian civil registry form. This evidence, in conjunction with Colombian documentation of her subsequent marriage to decedent, sufficiently resolves any question concerning Escalante's capacity to marry decedent. Moreover, Escalante affirmatively testified that she and decedent never divorced and that decedent continued to provide for her and their three children following his emigration. Escalante's assertion is further buttressed by the fact that decedent disavowed any prior marriages on the marriage certificate associated with his marriage to claimant. Significantly, the notarized Colombian marriage registration documenting the union between Escalante and decedent, as well as Escalante's civil registry, both of which were generated by Colombian authorities after decedent's death, make no mention of any dissolution of the marriage. Again, Kaim Torres explained the significance of the absence of such notation on Escalante's registry form and, further, there is record evidence indicating that no divorce action involving decedent or Escalante has been commenced anywhere within New York City. Accordingly, inasmuch as we find the presumptive validity of decedent's marriage to claimant to be sufficiently rebutted by Escalante's proof, and insofar as claimant has failed to adduce affirmative proof of the invalidity of Escalante's marriage to decedent, we find the decision unsupported by substantial evidence.

ORDERED that the decision is reversed, without costs, and matter remitted to the Workers' Compensation Board for further proceedings not inconsistent with this Court's decision.

### Notes

1. *Gomez* suggests some of the complexity of cases involving foreign marriages and divorces. Issues of foreign law are generally treated as questions of fact which must be pleaded and proved under the rules of evidence. See generally McCormick on Evidence 942 (3d ed.

1984). As illustrated by *Gomez*, foreign lawyers are often utilized as expert witnesses for this purpose.

　2.　Marriage validity questions frequently arise in the context of immigration disputes, because immigration and citizenship rights are often determined by family relationships. See generally Nora V. Demleitner, "How Much Do Western Democracies Value Family and Marriage? Immigration Law's Conflicted Answers," 32 Hofstra L. Rev. 273 (2003).

　3.　Historically, married women's citizenship depended on their husbands: it could be acquired by marriage to a citizen, and lost by marriage to a foreign national. See Mackenzie v. Hare, 239 U.S. 299, 36 S.Ct. 106, 60 L.Ed. 297 (1915). Article 9(1) of CEDAW, reprinted above, mandates that men and women have equal rights to acquire, change, and retain nationality, but a significant of nations have made reservations to this article and continue to differentiate the citizenship status of married women and men. See Karen Knop & Christine Chinkin, "Remembering Chrystal Macmillan: Women's Equality and Nationality in International Law," 22 Mich. J. Int'l L. 523 (2001).

# Chapter 3

# DIVORCE

The past fifty years have seen dramatic changes in divorce practices around the globe, with notable increases in divorce rates and a shift in many societies toward laws allowing greater freedom to divorce. Two important scholarly accounts of this transition are William J. Goode, World Changes in Divorce Patterns (1993) and Mary Ann Glendon, The Transformation of Family Law: State, Law and Family in the United States and Western Europe (1989). With the passage of a new law permitting divorce in Chile in 2004, Malta and the Philippines are now the only countries in the world that prohibit divorce.

Despite the world-wide trend toward easier divorce, there remains a great diversity of approaches to the grounds, procedures, and financial incidents of divorce. International divorce disputes raise complex conflict of laws questions concerning jurisdiction over divorce proceedings and recognition of foreign divorce decrees.

## A. COMPARATIVE PERSPECTIVES

### MATTER OF NWANGWU
Board of Immigration Appeals, 1976.
16 I. & N. Dec. 61, Interim Decision (BIA) 2542.

The lawful permanent resident petitioner applied for preference status for the beneficiary as her spouse under section 203(a)(2) of the Immigration and Nationality Act. In a decision dated April 9, 1976, the District Director denied the petition on the ground that proof of the termination of the beneficiary's prior marriage was lacking. The petitioner appeals from that decision. The appeal will be dismissed.

The petitioner was born on December 7, 1937, in Nigeria and was admitted as a lawful permanent resident to the United States on October 22, 1969. The beneficiary was born on April 4, 1937, in Nigeria and entered the United States as a visitor on December 18, 1972. He and the petitioner were married in Detroit, Michigan on April 16, 1973.

It appears that the beneficiary was previously married in Nigeria in 1960 according to the native laws and custom of that country. It is the petitioner's contention that this customary marriage has been dissolved since the beneficiary's Nigerian wife remarried another in 1966, while the beneficiary was living in England. The assertion is that this "automatically" dissolved the customary marriage and, as evidence, the petitioner submits a sworn affidavit by the beneficiary's brother attesting to the same. In addition, the beneficiary submitted a letter to the District Director in March 1974, in which, among other things, he stated that Nigeria is essentially a polygamous country; that a man could marry one, two or three women, and that not infrequently a woman might refuse to live with her husband, and marry another man without going through the courts to obtain a divorce. In the letter he also stated that "desertion and remarriage of one party effectively dissolves the marriage."

In a visa petition proceeding the burden of proof is on the petitioner. Under 8 C.F.R. 204.2(c)(2) the petitioner must submit proof of the legal termination of the parties' previous marriages. Any pre-existing valid marriage is a bar to our recognition of the marriage on which the visa petition is based. The petitioner has failed to prove the legal termination of his previous customary marriage.

In Matter of Akinsete, Interim Decision 2369 (BIA 1975), we recognized that in the Mid–Western State of Nigeria a divorce must be obtained from a competent customary court in order to dissolve a tribal marriage. The law of the East–Central State of Nigeria, in which the beneficiary's prior marriage took place, is different. We have the benefit of a Library of Congress report dated October 6, 1975, entitled "Divorce in the East–Central State of Nigeria Between Persons Married Under Customary Law," which we are attaching hereto as Appendix A. It appears that, in the East–Central State of Nigeria, a customary law marriage may be dissolved not only judicially but also extra-judicially. An extra-judicial divorce requires the observance of certain ceremonial formalities in accordance with the current customary divorce law of the particular ethnic group or tribe of the parties. A mere voluntary separation of the parties or desertion does not effectively dissolve the existing marital relationship.

The only evidence submitted in support of the petitioner's claim that the beneficiary's first marriage was dissolved in 1966 is an affidavit of the petitioner's brother, which states that the first wife deserted the beneficiary, and married another man. The contents of that affidavit are at variance with statements previously submitted by the petitioner, and do not show the legal termination of the beneficiary's marriage under the laws of East–Central Nigeria.

In view of the fact that there has been no showing of the minimum formalities required to dissolve a marital relationship in Nigeria, we must agree with the District Director's decision that the beneficiary's first marriage was not legally terminated prior to his present marriage to the petitioner. We find, accordingly, that the beneficiary's prior marriage is a valid pre-existing marriage preventing recognition for immigration purposes of the marriage between the petitioner and the beneficiary. The appeal will, therefore, be dismissed.

ORDER: The appeal is dismissed.

## APPENDIX A

### DIVORCE IN THE EAST–CENTRAL STATE OF NIGERIA BETWEEN PERSONS MARRIED UNDER CUSTOMARY LAW

Some formality is required to bring a Nigerian customary law marriage to an end.[1] These formalities may take place in or out of court:

> Unlike in English law dissolution of marriage under native law and custom could be either judicial or extra-judicial.[2]

Non-judicial divorce, however, is on the decline in Nigeria, even among people living in traditional societies:

> In the areas where non-judicial dissolution of marriage is permitted, divorce may also be obtained in ... court. Indeed, it appears that more and more people are using these courts, rather than the more informal non-judicial means, in order to make their divorces "official" so as to be protected against any future claim that the marriage was never dissolved ...[3]

The court system of the East–Central State of Nigeria was altered in 1971 to place jurisdiction in cases of divorce "between persons married under customary law" in the Magistrates' Courts.[4]

---

**1.** S.N. Chinwuba Obi, Modern Family Law in Southern Nigeria (1966) 368.

**2.** Okpanum v. Okpanum, 2 ECSLR 561, at p. 564.

**3.** Alfred B. Kasunmu and Jeswald W. Salacuse, Nigerian Family Law (1966) 175.

**4.** E.C.S.N. Edict No. 23 of 1971, Section 17(1)(h).

It is not always an easy task for a court having jurisdiction in the locality in question to determine issues of customary law. In Inyang v. Ita the court made the following observation:

> A good deal of evidence was given by both sides on this question of native law and custom. This kind of so-called expert evidence must always be treated with very great caution. The evidence of these experts is invariably coloured each by his own personal interests. The only way in which such testimony can be safely treated is to refrain from attempting to estimate individual credibility and to concentrate on drawing conclusions from the general trend of the evidence.[5]

In Okpanum v. Okpanum, a case contesting the validity of an alleged customary divorce, the court based its decision upon evidence of a formal meeting attended by representatives of both families of the parties to the marriage.[6] There, the husband formally renounced or terminated the marriage before both families which had been called together for that purpose.[7]

S.N. Chinwuba Obi, whose book on Nigerian family law is cited by the court in the Okpanum case, provides information on the details of the formalities required to bring an Ibo customary marriage to an end.[8] In rejecting the idea that a woman is free to abandon her husband and marry another man without divorce formalities, Obi comments as follows:

> Contrary to popular opinion in certain quarters, customary marriage is not dissolved by the mere fact that one spouse has left, or been sent away by the other with the express intention of never again living together with him or her as husband and wife. Where this happens, there is no more than desertion or voluntary separation as the case may be: the parties remain husband and wife in the eyes of the law nonetheless.[9]

Commentators have expressed the difficulties surrounding proof of a non-judicial divorce as follows:

> It is necessary to determine the acts necessary under the applicable customary law which will sever the marital bonds and the point at which the marriage is terminated. Then, too, it may be difficult to decide whether these acts were actually performed and what the intentions of the parties were at the time.[10]

---

**5.** 9 Nigeria Law Reports 84.

**6.** Okpanum v. Okpanum, supra, at p. 564.

**7.** Okapnum v. Okapnum, supra, at p. 565.

**8.** Obi, supra, p. 368.

**9.** Obi, supra, at p. 368.

**10.** Kasunmu and Salacuse, supra, 172.

For a foreign agency or tribunal to decide the issue of the validity of a divorce in these circumstances it would have to determine (1) the ethnic group or tribe of the parties, (2) the current customary divorce law of that group, and (3) proof of the facts alleged. These are the issues which the local Nigerian courts, on the other hand, are uniquely equipped to determine. For purposes of its use abroad, a judgment of a Nigerian court should be certified as a true copy by the court and, in turn, by the United States embassy or consulate as being the judgment of the court.

Prepared by Neil R. McDonald
Senior Legal Specialist
Near Eastern and African Law Division
Law Library, Library of Congress
October 1975

### Notes

1. Immigration and citizenship rights in the United States depend heavily on family relationships. For an overview of these issues, with extensive references to case law and regulations, see Daniel Levy, "The Family in Immigration and Nationality Law: Part 1," 92–09 Immigr. Briefings 1 (1992). See also Nicole Lawrence Ezer, "The Intersection of Immigration Law and Family Law," 40 Fam. L.Q. 339 (2006).

2. Research and proof of foreign law is a complex process, often accomplished by use of expert witnesses. See generally Susan Van Syckel, "Strategies for Identifying Sources of Foreign Law: An Integrated Approach," 13 Transnat'l Law. 289 (2000).

## ALLAH DITTA v. JUDGE, FAMILY COURT
Pakistan, 1995.
1995 M L D 1852 [Lahore].

Before MUHAMMAD NASEEM, J.

Writ Petition No. 1654/F of 1995/BWP, decided on 19th July, 1995.

West Pakistan Family Courts Act (XXXV of 1964)—

Akhtar Munir Pirzada for Petitioner.

Date of hearing: 19th July, 1995.

### JUDGMENT

Allah Ditta petitioner was married to Mst. Mumtaz Bibi respondent No. 2. Unfortunately the relations between the spouses became strained and Mst. Mumtaz Bibi respondent No. 2 instituted a suit to obtain a decree for the dissolution of marriage against the petitioner on the grounds of cruel treatment of Allah Ditta towards her, his bad character, his second marriage without the consent of the plaintiff, misappropriation of belongings of the plaintiff and false charge of adultery against her. She also pleaded for dissolution of marriage on the basis of Khula'. The suit was resisted by Allah Ditta petitioner who in the written statement refuted the allegations made by Mst. Mumtaz Bibi. He showed his desire to accommodate her.

2. According to the pleadings of the parties following issues were framed for determination:—

(1) Whether behaviour of the defendant has been cruel towards the plaintiff on the grounds of bad character of the defendant, association of the defendant with women of ill-repute, habitual beatings by the defendant, second marriage of the defendant without consent of the plaintiff, false charges of adultery against the plaintiff and misappropriation of belongings of the plaintiff?

(2) Whether the plaintiff is entitled for decree of dissolution of marriage on the basis of Khula'? If so, on what terms and conditions.

(3) Relief.

The parties produced their evidence. Holding that Mst. Mumtaz Bibi was not willing to live with Allah Ditta who had contracted his second marriage without her permission, the trial court held that Mst. Mumtaz Bibi was entitled to a Khula' divorce. In the absence of any evidence she was allowed the unconditional Khula' divorce. Thus issue No. 2 was decided in her favour. However, issue No. 1 was disposed of against her in view of the non-production of cogent evidence. The suit of Mst. Mumtaz Bibi has been decreed and feeling aggrieved Allah Ditta petitioner has filed this writ petition.

3. I have heard the preliminary arguments addressed by the learned counsel for the petitioner. He has not been able to convince me that Mst. Mumtaz Bibi is not entitled to unconditional Khula' divorce. It is the admitted position that Alluh Ditta petitioner contracted the second marriage without the permission of Mst. Mumtaz Bibi respondent No. 2. In such a state of affairs her aversion towards him can well be imagined. Obviously the first wife feels an insult if the husband contracts his second marriage. Thus the inception of hatred by Mst. Mumtaz Bibi respondent No. 2 towards Alluh Ditta petitioner is a natural conduct which has correctly been given the legal weight by the trial Court. Such conduct of the husband towards the wife certainly breaks her heart if not the bones and when heart is broken it is simply immaterial if the bones are intact. In this view of the matter the trial Court has correctly granted Khula' divorce to Mst. Mumtaz Bibi. There being no cogent evidence about the passing of the consideration, respon-

dent No. 2 has rightly been granted the unconditional Khula' divorce. I therefore affirm the findings of the trial Court.

4. Finding no force in this writ petition I dismiss the same in limine.

C.M. No. 1–95;

5. This application for dispensation of certified copies of the documents has become infructuous in view of the dismissal of the writ petition in limine.

Petition dismissed.

### *Note*

Nadya Haider, in "Islamic Legal Reform: The Case of Pakistan and Family Law," 12 Yale J. L. & Feminism 287 (2000), discusses the *Allah Ditta* case as an example of the "on-going liberalization of Pakistan's divorce law through the creative construction of judge-made common law." As she notes, Islamic law gives a husband the right to terminate his marriage by a unilateral repudiation (*talaq*). A wife's rights to divorce are more limited, although there are variations in these rules between different schools and in different countries with Islamic legal systems. In Pakistan, in addition to divorce by *talaq*, a husband and wife may divorce by mutual agreement (*mubara'a*), or a wife may offer a divorce to her husband (*khula*) in exchange for some compensation, such as giving up her rights to dower (*mahr*). There are also fault-based divorce grounds available to wives under the 1939 Dissolution of Muslim Marriages Act and the 1961 Muslim Family Law Ordinance. Since 1959, the Pakistani courts have recognized a judicial *khula,* available without the consent of the husband on proof that she cannot live with her husband "within the limits prescribed by Allah." Haider reports that although a husband can claim compensation from his wife for a judicial *khula*, judges in cases like *Allah Ditta* have granted divorces even without payment of financial consideration. See also Rubya Mehdi, The Islamization of the Law in Pakistan 173–84 (1994).

## TAL v. TAL

Supreme Court, Nassau County, New York, 1993.
158 Misc.2d 703, 601 N.Y.S.2d 530.

Marvin E. Segal, Justice.

### Findings of Fact

The parties were married in Iran on February 19, 1977 in an orthodox religious ceremony. After the marriage, the parties moved to Israel. The parties have four children, to wit: Ronit, born December 16, 1977; Yair, born December 6, 1981; Raphael, born

January 17, 1986 and Ariel, born October 30, 1987. The wife and Ronit and Yair moved to the United States in or about October, 1985; the husband moved here on or about December 20, 1985. The two younger children were born in this country. * * *

The wife is 38 years old. She is not fluent in the English language and has never been employed. The husband is 42 years old. He owns and operates clothing stores in Manhattan. He also earns rental income from leases he holds on various commercial properties in Manhattan. The husband alleges that the parties began to experience marital difficulties in December 1990. He accuses the wife of "having an affair" with his best friend and remaining away from home. On or about March 7, 1991 the parties executed and acknowledged a document entitled "Separation Agreement". The agreement provides that the husband shall have custody of the children, subject to the wife's right of visitation. It requires that the husband support the children without contribution from the wife, and that he pay the wife maintenance of $1000.00 per month for a period of six years. The agreement further contains a waiver of inheritance rights and sets forth that all assets have been divided to the parties' mutual satisfaction. On or about April 24, 1991, the husband obtained a religious divorce, "a Get", from the Rabbinical Court of the Rabbinical Alliance of America. The husband alleges that during the religious divorce proceedings, the parties executed a second matrimonial agreement. This agreement requires that the husband pay the wife a lump sum of $125,000.00 in lieu of maintenance. It also provides that in the event custody of the children is transferred to the wife, the husband would pay the sum of $6000.00 per month for the support of the children. The husband retained counsel in Israel and contends that he obtained a formal decree of divorce from the Tel Aviv Jaffa Rabbinical Court in Israel on or about February 11, 1992.

* * *

In or about July, 1992, the wife commenced an action for divorce in this State. Thereafter, she moved for omnibus pendente lite relief. She acknowledges that the husband paid her the sum of $126,000.00 and further states that he has paid expenses of $9500.00 per month for the support of herself and the children. She alleges, however, that the husband earns $850,000.00 per year and that based upon his income, the voluntary support paid to the wife is insufficient to meet her needs and those of the children. The husband contends that as Israeli citizens, the parties were validly divorced by the State of Israel on February 11, 1992. Based upon the Israeli Decree of Divorce he seeks an order dismissing the wife's complaint for divorce. In the alternative, the husband argues that the parties executed two valid and binding separation agreements;

that he has fully complied with his obligations under said agreements and that the wife is therefore precluded from seeking pendente lite relief unless and until said separation agreements are set aside.

The wife denies the husband's allegations that she committed adultery. She responds that she left the marital home and sought refuge with relatives because the husband threatened her life. The wife alleges that the separation agreements and the "Get" were achieved through "fraud, diversion of assets, brutalization, duress and threats". She asserts that the separation agreement dated March 7, 1991 was executed by her as a "blank" piece of paper; that she had no counsel to represent her and no disclosure of the husband's assets or income. The wife further asserts that the agreement is unconscionable on its face; that the husband's affidavit of net worth sets forth assets of over $500,000.00 and the distribution to her of one-fifth of the disclosed marital assets is inequitable. She has amended her complaint so as to set forth a cause of action seeking judgment rescinding the separation agreements and declaring the Israeli Decree of Divorce to be a nullity.

CONCLUSIONS OF LAW

The courts of this state will generally accord recognition to bilateral foreign judgments of divorce, including the terms and provisions of any agreements incorporated therein, under the doctrine of comity. Absent some showing of fraud in the procurement of the foreign country judgment or that recognition of the judgment would do violence to some strong public policy of this state, a party who properly appeared in the action is precluded from attacking the validity of a foreign country judgment in a collateral proceeding brought in the courts of this state. A separation agreement incorporated in a valid foreign divorce judgment is also immune from challenge under the doctrine of comity, because such a challenge would essentially constitute an impermissible collateral attack on the foreign judgment.

In the instant action, the husband contends that the Tel Aviv Jaffa Rabbinical Court of the State of Israel had subject matter and personal jurisdiction over the parties herein such that this court should recognize the decree under the principle of comity. He contends that the divorce proceeding in the State of Israel was a bilateral proceeding based upon the wife's participation in and submission to the Rabbinical Court in the State of New York. He concedes, however, that the wife was never afforded notice of the commencement of any divorce action in Israel.

The decree issued by the Rabbinical Court of the Rabbinical Alliance of America on April 24, 1991, states that the husband herein "divorced his wife in accordance with Jewish Religious Law.

In accordance with Jewish Religious Law he is free to remarry provided he is also civilly divorced. This certificate applies only to the above-mentioned and is not to be taken as evidence regarding the status of the wife." The Decree issued by the Tel Aviv Jaffa Rabbinical Court merely recites that the husband "who is abroad, has appeared before us, presenting us with the divorce certificate stating that (he) has divorced his wife Shahin. The divorce was arranged abroad, in America. We hereby confirm that (he) has divorced his above named wife . . . .". The Decree issued by the Tel Aviv Jaffa Rabbinical Court of the State of Israel does not set forth that the wife appeared before said court, nor does the Decree incorporate by reference the terms of any separation agreement. While the parties herein did execute a purported separation agreement in the context of the proceeding conducted by the Rabbinical Court in this State, the decree resulting from that proceeding does not incorporate the agreement by reference and further specifically provides that the decree is not to be taken as evidence regarding the status of the wife.

The law is clear that judicial involvement in matters touching upon religious concerns has been constitutionally limited, and courts should not resolve controversies touching upon religious concerns in a manner requiring consideration of religious doctrine. *Avitzur v. Avitzur*, 58 N.Y.2d 108, 114, 459 N.Y.S.2d 572, 446 N.E.2d 136 * * *. Thus, the issue as to whether or not the proceedings conducted herein, in the Rabbinical Courts in this country and in the State of Israel, resulted in the religious divorce of the parties according to Jewish Law is beyond the purview of this court. This court is not, however, without jurisdiction to adjudicate the enforceability of a separation agreement executed within the context of a religious proceeding (*Avitzur v. Avitzur*, supra, 58 N.Y.2d at 114, 459 N.Y.S.2d 572, 446 N.E.2d 136; *Hirsch v. Hirsch*, 37 N.Y.2d 312, 372 N.Y.S.2d 71, 333 N.E.2d 371), or to deny comity to a foreign country judgment of divorce procured by extrinsic fraud or which violates strong public policy.

Under the facts and circumstances of this case, wherein the wife has not resided in Israel since 1985, was not given notice of the commencement of any civil divorce action in the State of Israel; and did not appear in said civil action; and where the foreign country judgment does not incorporate the subject separation agreement by reference, the court declines to afford comity to the Decree of Divorce issued by the State of Israel. The portion of the husband's motion which seeks an order dismissing the complaint based upon the Israeli Divorce Decree is therefore denied.

* * *

## *Notes*

1. Within the state of Israel, jurisdiction over personal status matters is determined based on the religious affiliation of the parties involved, and rabbinical courts have jurisdiction over Jewish divorces. If these parties had been domiciled in Israel at the time of the rabbinic divorce proceeding, would the religious divorce have been entitled to respect in an American court? Cf. Shapiro v. Shapiro, 110 Misc.2d 726, 442 N.Y.S.2d 928 (Sup. Ct. 1981). The problem of comity for foreign divorce decrees is considered in more detail below.

2. The *Avitzur* case, cited in *Tal*, involved a Jewish premarital agreement or *ketuba* in which the parties promised to appear before a rabbinic court or *bet din* to resolve any disputes in their marriage. When the couple divorced, the wife sought to compel her husband to appear before the *bet din* to give her a religious divorce, known as a *get.* The New York Court of Appeals held that the promise was analogous to an arbitration clause and was enforceable in a civil court. An observant Jewish woman cannot marry again without a *get,* and there is a substantial literature on the problem of pressuring recalcitrant husbands to cooperate in *get* proceedings. In New York, two statutes have addressed the *get* problem with some success. See generally Lisa Zornberg, "Beyond the Constitution: Is the New York Get Legislation Good Law?" 15 Pace L. Rev. 703 (1995), and Michael J. Broyde, Marriage, Divorce and the Abandoned Wife in Jewish Law (2001).

In Ontario, Canada, Marion Boyd was asked in 2004 to investigate proposals to allow private religious arbitration in family and inheritance disputes. See Marion Boyd, Dispute Resolution in Family Law: Protecting Choice, Promoting Inclusion (2004). Boyd outlined a series of recommendations to allow religious arbitration to go forward with safeguards to protect vulnerable people. In the face of strong political objections against the proposal, however, the recommendations were rejected in 2005.

3. For a comprehensive comparative survey of divorce laws, see Bea Verschraegen, "Divorce" in 4 International Encyclopedia of Comparative Law ch. 5 (Mary Ann Glendon, ed. 2004). Professor Verschraegen points out that despite the broad international trend toward no-fault divorce grounds, many legal systems continue to combine fault and no-fault grounds in their laws. She notes that the grounds asserted in any particular case may not reflect the real cause of the divorce, as parties are influenced by the different procedures, requirements, or time limits connected with different legal grounds. Her survey indicates that most countries now permit divorce by mutual consent, and also allow for agreements between the parties as to the financial and other consequences of divorce. See also William J. Goode, World Changes in Divorce Patterns (1993).

# B. INTERNATIONAL DIVORCE

Historically, one of the principal difficulties in harmonizing family law at the international level is that some legal systems approach jurisdictional and choice of law questions based on the parties' nationality, while others have used an approach based the parties' domicile or residence. See generally Adair Dyer, "The Internationalization of Family Law," 30 U.C. Davis L. Rev. 625, 625–27 (1997). The conventions developed by the Hague Conference on Private International Law have sought to bridge this divide, providing broadly for recognition of marriages and divorces that would be valid under either the nationality or residence principle, unless recognition is incompatible with the public policy or *ordre public* of the state asked to extend recognition. As the following materials demonstrate, however, the United States adheres strongly to the domicile principle in addressing these matters.

At one time, significant differences among the laws of different countries on the permissible grounds for divorce generated substantial conflict of laws problems. With the widespread evolution of mutual consent or no-fault divorce laws, divorce recognition disputes have come to center on either the financial remedies available in different jurisdictions, or on nonjudicial divorces permitted by laws in some countries.

## BOURBON v. BOURBON

Supreme Court, Appellate Division, Second Department, New York, 1999.
259 A.D.2d 720, 687 N.Y.S.2d 426.

* * *

In 1960 the plaintiff wife and the defendant husband, both French citizens, were married in France. Eight children were born of the marriage. However, only one child is currently a minor. The family lived in France until 1984, at which time the parties relocated to New York due to the husband's employment. Starting in 1984, the children attended school in New York. The parties' minor child is currently enrolled in a New York school. In 1985 the husband purchased a home in Larchmont, New York. In 1989, the husband became employed at a French-based bank, and he and the family began traveling between New York, where the wife and the children continued to reside, and France. In 1998 the wife commenced the instant action in New York for a divorce and ancillary relief. Approximately one week later, the husband commenced a similar action in France.

Upon the wife's motion for pendente lite relief, the husband cross-moved to dismiss the action, asserting lack of personal and in rem jurisdiction. The Supreme Court dismissed the New York action on the ground that "another action is pending where similar claims exist and plaintiff has submitted to the jurisdiction of the French Court". Subsequently, the wife moved for renewal and reargument, and the court granted renewal and reargument but adhered to its prior determination. We reverse.

Contrary to the husband's claims, although he is domiciled in France, he is a resident of New York, and is therefore, amenable to the jurisdiction of the New York courts. The husband maintains a home in Larchmont. He files Federal and resident New York income tax returns, and lists the Larchmont home as his residence on those returns. In contrast, he files "non-resident" tax returns in France. He maintains a Citibank account in New York. He also has a New York State driver's license, registers two of the parties' vehicles in New York, and is paid one-half of his salary in New York.

Moreover, the wife established compliance with the durational requirements of Domestic Relations Law § 230(2), which provides that an action for divorce may be maintained when "[t]he parties have resided in this state as husband and wife and either party is a resident thereof when the action is commenced and has been a resident for a continuous period of one year immediately preceding" the commencement of the action.

Assuming, arguendo, that the husband's claim that the wife was in France for portions of the year preceding the commencement of the divorce action is correct, the wife has shown compliance with the statute by proof that she was continuously domiciled in New York for one year immediately preceding the commencement of her action for divorce. The wife has continued to primarily reside in New York since the family moved in 1984. Since 1984 the parties' children have been raised here. The children attended school in New York, and the parties' minor child is currently attending school here. Further, the husband and wife applied for and obtained permanent United States residence status. We note that, by the husband's own admissions in the French petition, the wife has indicated her desire to remain in the United States with the children since 1989.

Moreover, dismissal of the wife's action on the grounds of forum non conveniens is not warranted. The wife's residence in New York provides a substantial nexus to this State. In addition, New York is the forum where the parties' minor daughter has been raised and educated.

We reject the claim that the doctrine of comity serves as a basis for New York to decline jurisdiction. CPLR 5302 makes clear that comity is to be applied in the case of "any foreign country judgment which is final, conclusive and enforceable where rendered". Here, the French court has rendered a temporary support order and not a final judgment of divorce.

## Notes

1. On what basis would the French court have jurisdiction in this case? If the French court had already entered a divorce decree how should the New York court proceed? For later developments in this case, see Bourbon v. Bourbon, 300 A.D.2d 269, 751 N.Y.S.2d 302 (App. Div. 2002) (extending recognition to French divorce decree).

2. How should courts proceed when the married couple live in different places? In the United States, jurisdiction to grant a divorce is based on the petitioner's domicile, but jurisdiction over financial matters such as property and support rights usually requires personal jurisdiction over the respondent spouse. Courts routinely grant divorces to foreign citizens domiciled in the United States, even when their spouses have no contacts with the state. See, e.g., Marriage of Kimura, 471 N.W.2d 869 (Iowa 1991). Conversely, a foreign citizen who is not domiciled in the U.S. will not be granted a divorce here. See, e.g., Adoteye v. Adoteye, 32 Va.App. 221, 527 S.E.2d 453 (2000).

## COLLINS v. COLLINS

Court of Appeals of Ohio, 2006.
165 Ohio App.3d 71, 844 N.E.2d 910.

DOAN, PRESIDING JUDGE.

Plaintiff-appellant, Russell E. Collins, was serving in the United States military in Germany when he married defendant-appellee, Brigitte M.L. Collins, a German citizen, on April 8, 1983. The parties separated in 1999. Russell Collins moved to Ohio and purchased a home. Brigitte Collins remained in Germany.

Russell Collins filed a complaint for divorce on September 16, 2002, in the Domestic Relations Division of the Hamilton County Court of Common Pleas. The complaint included a request for certified mail service upon Brigitte Collins in Germany. The certified mail receipt was returned and filed October 15, 2002. By letter dated November 1, 2002, Brigitte Collins's German counsel notified Russell Collins's counsel that the attempt to serve Brigitte Collins was improper pursuant to the Hague Convention on Service of Process Abroad of Judicial and Extrajudicial Documents in Civil or Commercial Matters ("the Hague Convention").

In her decision of November 15, 2002, the magistrate stated, "Wife was served by certified international mail on September 17, 2002. The parties have not lived in a marital relationship in the state of Ohio and this court has no personal jurisdiction over wife." The magistrate's decision set forth the duration of the marriage, distributed real and personal property, and addressed the issues of spousal support and Russell Collins's military pension. The trial court adopted the magistrate's decision on January 17, 2003. A decree of divorce was entered February 4, 2003. The decree stated that Russell Collins was an Ohio resident and that "service of process [on Brigitte Collins] was made according to law or waived."

On August 8, 2003, Brigitte Collins filed a Civ.R. 60(B) motion for relief from judgment, alleging that she had never been properly served with process pursuant to the Hague Convention and that the trial court had no personal jurisdiction over her. The magistrate granted the Civ.R. 60(B) motion, finding that the motion had been timely filed and that Brigitte Collins had not been properly served with the complaint for divorce in accordance with the Hague Convention. Russell Collins filed objections to the magistrate's decision, which the trial court overruled. He has now appealed, raising four assignments of error for our review.

\* \* \*

For a court to acquire personal jurisdiction, there must be a proper service of summons or an entry of appearance, and a judgment entered without proper service or an entry of appearance is void. *See State ex rel. Ballard v. O'Donnell* (1990), 50 Ohio St.3d 182, 553 N.E.2d 650. "A trial court is without jurisdiction to render judgment or to make findings against a person who was not served summons, did not appear, and was not a party in the court proceedings. A person against whom such judgment and findings are made is entitled to have the judgment vacated." Id. at paragraph one of the syllabus.

The Hague Convention is a multilateral treaty "intended to provide a simpler way to serve process abroad, to assure that defendants sued in foreign jurisdictions w[ill] receive actual and timely notice of suit, and to facilitate proof of service abroad." *Volkswagenwerk Aktiengesellschaft v. Schlunk* (1988), 486 U.S. 694, 698, 108 S.Ct. 2104, 100 L.Ed.2d 722. The Hague Convention "requires each state to establish a central authority to receive requests for service of documents from other countries." Id. The Hague Convention preempts inconsistent methods of service of process prescribed by state law by virtue of the Supremacy Clause of Article VI of the United States Constitution. See id. The Hague Convention, a ratified treaty, is "the supreme law of the land." *Meek v. Nova Steel Processing, Inc.* (1997), 124 Ohio App.3d 367, 370, 706 N.E.2d 374.

Under the terms of the Hague Convention, registered mail service is insufficient service of process on citizens of nations that are signatories. Germany, a signatory to the Hague Convention, has expressed a specific objection to service by international mail and has asserted that the Hague Convention is the exclusive method for international service of process in Germany.

It is clear from the record, and undisputed by Russell Collins, that Brigitte Collins was never properly served with the complaint for divorce pursuant to the terms of the Hague Convention. Therefore, the court had no personal jurisdiction over Brigitte Collins.

A decree of divorce is regarded as a judgment in rem because it determines the marital status of the parties. The marital status, or res, follows the domiciles of the parties to the marriage. In order for the court to have jurisdiction over the res, or marriage, one of the parties must be domiciled within the state granting the divorce. Russell Collins was domiciled in Ohio. Therefore, the trial court had the authority to enter a decree terminating the Collinses' marriage.

In order to determine financial issues, the trial court must have personal jurisdiction based upon notice to and proper service on the defendant. In a divorce proceeding, the trial court must have personal jurisdiction over a nonresident defendant in order to determine issues of spousal support and property division. The trial court had no jurisdiction over Brigitte Collins in this case. Therefore, the court had no authority to distribute property to which she arguably had a claim, to issue orders regarding spousal support, or to issue orders regarding the parties' pensions.

The trial court erred in granting Brigitte Collins's Civ.R. 60(B) motion for relief from judgment as to the granting of the divorce. The trial court did not err in granting the Civ.R. 60(B) motion as to support, property division, and all other financial matters. The first and second assignments of error are sustained solely to the extent that they challenge the trial court's granting of the Civ.R. 60(B) motion in regard to the granting of the divorce, and they are overruled in all other respects.

* * *

The judgment of the trial court is affirmed in part and reversed in part, and this cause is remanded for further proceedings consistent with law and this decision.

Judgment affirmed in part and reversed in part, and cause remanded.

### Note

The Hague Convention on Service Abroad, cited in *Collins*, is one of several that play an important role in coordinating international litigation. For more information on these conventions, see the website of the Hague Conference of Private International Law at www.hcch. net.

# RESTATEMENT (THIRD) OF FOREIGN RELATIONS LAW OF THE UNITED STATES

American Law Institute, 1987.

## § 484. Recognition of Foreign Divorce Decrees

(1) Courts in the United States will recognize a divorce granted in the state in which both parties to the marriage had their domicile or their habitual residence at the time of divorce, and valid and effective under the law of that state.

(2) Courts in the United States may, but need not, recognize a divorce, valid and effective under the law of the state where it was granted,

(a) if that state was, at the time of divorce, the state of domicile or habitual residence of one party to the marriage; or

(b) if the divorce was granted by a court having jurisdiction over both parties, and if at least one party appeared in person and the other party had notice of and opportunity to participate in the proceeding.

(3) A court that would not recognize a divorce that is within Subsection 2(a) or 2(b) may nevertheless recognize such a divorce if it would be recognized by the state where the parties were domiciled or had their habitual residence at the time of the divorce.

# CONVENTION ON THE RECOGNITION OF DIVORCES AND LEGAL SEPARATIONS

Hague Conference on Private International Law, 1970.
978 U.N.T.S. 993, 1975 U.K.T.S. 123, Cmnd. 6248.

The States signatory to the present Convention,

Desiring to facilitate the recognition of divorces and legal separations obtained in their respective territories,

Have resolved to conclude a Convention to this effect, and have agreed on the following provisions:

## *Article 1*

The present Convention shall apply to the recognition in one Contracting State of divorces and legal separations obtained in another Contracting State which follow judicial or other proceedings officially recognized in that State and which are legally effective there.

The Convention does not apply to findings of fault or to ancillary orders pronounced on the making of a decree of divorce or legal separation; in particular, it does not apply to orders relating to pecuniary obligations or to the custody of children.

## Article 2

Such divorces and legal separations shall be recognized in all other Contracting States, subject to the remaining terms of this Convention, if, at the date of the institution of the proceedings in the State of the divorce or legal separation (hereinafter called "the State of origin")—

(1) the respondent had his habitual residence there; or

(2) the petitioner had his habitual residence there and one of the following further conditions was fulfilled—

a) such habitual residence had continued for not less than one year immediately prior to the institution of proceedings;

b) the spouses last habitually resided there together; or

(3) both spouses were nationals of that State; or

(4) the petitioner was a national of that State and one of the following further conditions was fulfilled—

a) the petitioner had his habitual residence there; or

b) he had habitually resided there for a continuous period of one year falling, at least in part, within the two years preceding the institution of the proceedings; or

(5) the petitioner for divorce was a national of that State and both the following further conditions were fulfilled—

a) the petitioner was present in that State at the date of institution of the proceedings and

b) the spouses last habitually resided together in a State whose law, at the date of institution of the proceedings, did not provide for divorce.

## Article 3

Where the State of origin uses the concept of domicile as a test of jurisdiction in matters of divorce or legal separation, the expression "habitual residence" in Article 2 shall be deemed to include domicile as the term is used in that State.

Nevertheless, the preceding paragraph shall not apply to the domicile of dependence of a wife.

* * *

## Article 8

If, in the light of all the circumstances, adequate steps were not taken to give notice of the proceedings for a divorce or legal separation to the respondent, or if he was not afforded a sufficient opportunity to present his case, the divorce or legal separation may be refused recognition.

* * *

### Article 10

Contracting States may refuse to recognize a divorce or legal separation if such recognition is manifestly incompatible with their public policy ("ordre public").

* * *

### Note

How does the Hague Divorce Convention compare with the Restatement approach? Eighteen contracting States have ratified or acceded to the Divorce Convention, including the United Kingdom but not including the United States. Information on ratification is available on the website of the Hague Conference at www.hcch.net. On the American approaches to divorce recognition, see Friedrich Juenger, "Recognition of Foreign Divorces—British and American Perspectives," 20 Am. J. Comp. L. 1 (1972). Within the European Community, recognition and enforcement of divorce judgments is governed by Council Regulation (EC) No 2201/2003 Concerning Jurisdiction and the Recognition and Enforcement of Judgments in Matrimonial Matters and the Matters of Parental Responsibility, known as the "new Brussels II Regulation" or "Brussels II bis."

## IN THE MATTER OF ZAIDA SHERIF v. FAROUK SHERIF*

Family Court, City of New York, New York County, 1974.
76 Misc.2d 905, 352 N.Y.S.2d 781.

DECISION ON MOTION TO DISMISS THE PETITION

HAROLD A. FELIX, JUDGE:

The instant proceeding was instituted upon the Petitioner's filing a petition for support against her alleged husband, the Respondent. There are no children of this marriage. The Respondent claims that he is not the Petitioner's husband, inasmuch as a valid decree was issued on August 25, 1973 in Egypt, and therefore pursuant to Section 412 of the Family Court Act he is not liable for the Petitioner's support:

'§ 412.  Husband's duty to support wife. A husband is chargeable with the support of his wife and, if possessed of sufficient

---

* Names are fictitious for purposes of publication.

means or able to earn such means, may be required to pay for her support a fair and reasonable sum, as the court may determine, having due regard to the circumstances of the respective parties.'

The Petitioner and the Respondent are Egyptian nationals, followers of the Islamic faith. They both were born in Egypt, lived there and were married in that country on July 8, 1971. The marriage contract made provision for the Petitioner's support in the event of divorce seemingly in conformity with the customs of that country. In 1971 they both arrived in the United States and on August 14, 1973 they traveled together back to Egypt where the Respondent on August 25, 1973 obtained a divorce in conformity with Egyptian law, which incorporated the support provisions of the marriage contract.

The Petitioner does not contend that the said divorce is not in compliance with all the laws, and regulations of the Government of Egypt. The Petitioner concedes that the said divorce is recognized within Egypt. The issue thus is whether as a matter of 'comity' this State will recognize the said divorce.

It is a firmly established principle of Anglo–American law that foreign judgments, subject to a few exceptions, are not open to re-examination on the merits before a local forum. If the said divorce decree were of a sister-state the full faith and credit provision of the Constitution would be applicable but inasmuch as this divorce decree is of a foreign country 'the comity of nations' doctrine applies. 'Comity' has been described as 'neither a matter of absolute obligation, on the one hand, nor of mere courtesy and good will, upon the other ... it is ... the legislative, executive, or judicial acts of another nation, having due regard both to international duty and convenience, and to the rights of its own citizens, or of other persons who are under the protection of its laws.' Hilton v. Guyot, 159 U.S. 113, 163—164, 16 S.Ct. 139, 143, 40 L.Ed. 95.

The Egyptian laws with regard to matrimony do not by any means meet with the approval of this Court. However, the Court's approval or benediction of this divorce is not necessary to validate it and the facts of this case do not make it offensive to the public policy of this State to accord it recognition. Although this State, itself, provides for divorces through a judiciary process, it has on prior occasions recognized divorces obtained through other channels.[2]

---

**2.** In Sorenson v. Sorenson, 122 Misc. 196, 202 N.Y.S. 620, aff'd 219 App. Div. 344, 220 N.Y.S. 242, this State recognized a divorce granted by a Danish king.

Even marriages among American Indians according to their laws and customs have been recognized, though both polygamy and termination by mutual consent are permitted. * * *

A basic principle underlying the conflicts of law area is that the foreign forum in rendering a judgment between a native and a foreigner accorded fair and equal treatment to both parties before it. In other words the foreigner should be accorded the same treatment as the native. In the instant case, the Respondent and the Petitioner are both Egyptian nationals and no allegation has ever been raised that they were not accorded the same treatment as other Egyptians wherein the Egyptian–Islamic husband had instituted the divorce proceedings. Thus, this is not a case where there has been less than 'an impartial administration of justice between the citizens of (Egypt) and those of other countries.' Hilton v. Guyot, 159 U.S. at 202, 16 S.Ct. at 158.

The case at bar does not involve a 'mail order' divorce issued by a country having no relationship to the parties' marital status. The divorce was rather granted by a country wherein the parties were domiciled[4] at all crucial points in their marital history. It is not shocking to 'the conscience to conclude that people who marry under a certain set of laws may expect to be bound only so long as that set of laws required it.' Oettgen v. Oettgen, 196 Misc. 937, 941, 94 N.Y.S.2d 168, 172.

Respondent's motion to dismiss is granted the Court concluding that the Respondent is not the Petitioner's husband within the meaning of Section 412. By its action the Court is not passing on the applicability of Section 466(c) of the Family Court Act.

## FARAG v. FARAG

Supreme Court, Appellate Division, New York, 2004.
4 A.D.3d 502, 772 N.Y.S.2d 368.

In an action for divorce and ancillary relief, the plaintiff appeals [from a judgment] which, after a nonjury trial, inter alia, determined that the former marital residence was marital property subject to equitable distribution and awarded the defendant $114,500 representing 50% of the appraised value of the former marital residence, minus $3,000, constituting her share of the marital debt.

* * *

We further reject the plaintiff's contention that the trial court should have recognized the ex parte Egyptian ''Bill of Revocable

---

**4.** Note Gould v. Gould, 235 N.Y. 14, 138 N.E. 490, recognition of French divorce though both parties were domiciled in New York.

Divorce" pursuant to the legal concept of comity. It is axiomatic that comity should be extended to uphold the validity of a foreign divorce decree absent a showing of fraud in its procurement or that recognition of the judgment would do violence to some strong public policy of the state. The general rule is that a "foreign divorce decree obtained on the ex parte petition of a spouse present but not domiciled in the foreign country will not be recognized in New York where the other nonresident spouse does not appear and is not served with process" (Steffens v. Steffens, 238 A.D.2d 404, 405, 657 N.Y.S.2d 339; see Rosenbaum v. Rosenbaum, 309 N.Y. 371, 130 N.E.2d 902). It was undisputed that the plaintiff never informed the defendant that he was traveling to Egypt to obtain the foreign divorce decree. Furthermore, there is no evidence in the record that the plaintiff followed the proper procedures for obtaining the foreign divorce decree. Thus, contrary to the plaintiff's contention, the trial court properly refused to recognize the foreign divorce decree pursuant to the concept of comity. Moreover, the trial court properly rejected the plaintiff's argument that the Egyptian "Marriage Deed" governed the equitable distribution of the parties' marital assets or the maintenance obligations in this case. There was no proof that the Marriage Deed was duly executed pursuant to Domestic Relations Law § 236(B)(3) and nothing in that document speaks to the issues of equitable distribution of assets or maintenance obligations in the event of a divorce. The plain reading of the Marriage Deed merely provides that pursuant to a dowry provision, the plaintiff was obligated to pay the defendant, as consideration for the arranged marriage, the sum of 10,000 Egyptian Pounds at the time of marriage and the "deferred" sum of 10,000 Egyptian Pounds in the event of "divorce or death." While similar marriage documents have been upheld and their secular terms deemed enforceable as a contractual obligation, there is no authority to support the plaintiff's contention that this dowry provision, as written, governed the equitable distribution of the parties' assets or maintenance obligations or waived the defendant's rights thereto in this divorce action.

### Notes

1. Other American cases raising this issue include Shikoh v. Murff, 257 F.2d 306 (2d Cir. 1958); and Chaudry v. Chaudry, 159 N.J.Super. 566, 388 A.2d 1000 (App. Div. 1978). Recognition for foreign, nonjudicial divorces such as the Muslim *talaq* has been problematic in a number of countries. See generally Alan Reed, "Transnational Non–Judicial Divorces: A Comparative Analysis of Recognition Under English and U.S. Jurisprudence," 18 Loyola L.A. Int'l & Comp. L.J. 311 (1996). How would these case be analyzed under the Hague Divorce Convention?

2. *Farag* also considers the enforcement of a Muslim marital agreement including provision for payment of *mahr*. Another decision reaching the conclusion that a *mahr* agreement does not limit the wife's right to property and support remedies in an American court is Marriage of Shaban, 88 Cal.App.4th 398, 105 Cal.Rptr.2d 863 (2001) (including English translation of Egyptian marriage agreement). See generally Ann Laquer Estin, "Embracing Tradition: Pluralism in American Family Law," 63 Md. L. Rev. 540, 569–577 (2004).

## DART v. DART

Michigan Supreme Court, 1999.
460 Mich. 573, 597 N.W.2d 82.

MARILYN J. KELLY, J.

We granted leave to determine whether the parties' English divorce judgment is entitled to full faith and credit under the principle of comity, and whether res judicata bars the action.[1]

We hold that principles of comity and res judicata mandate that the Darts' foreign divorce judgment be enforced. The English court decided the property distribution issue on the merits, and no evidence was presented showing that plaintiff Katina Dart was denied due process. We affirm the decision of the Court of Appeals.

### I. FACTS

Plaintiff and defendant were married in 1980 and were residents of Okemos, Michigan until 1993, when they moved to England. The couple owned a large house in Okemos, situated on thirty-nine acres of land, valued at $1,500,000. The parties had two children. The defendant is the son of the founder of Dart Container Corporation, one of the largest family-controlled businesses in the United States. The defendant's earned income for the years 1992, 1993, and 1994, was $313,009, $563,917, and $281,548, respectively. Between 1990 and 1993, the family's annual expenditures ranged from $300,000 to $600,000. The move to England made possible a September 1993 transfer of several hundred million dollars to the defendant from family trusts.

In 1974, before the marriage, the defendant's father established a trust for the benefit of defendant and his brother. For the transfer to occur, defendant had to renounce his United States citizenship and relocate outside the United States. The plaintiff

1. We note that the lower courts considered whether the Uniform Foreign–Money Judgments Recognition Act (UFMJRA), M.C.L. § 691.1151 *et seq.*; M.S.A. § 27.955(1) *et seq.*, applied to the facts of this case. However, even if the UFMJRA did not apply, we can decide this issue under the general principle of comity. See *Bang v. Park,* 116 Mich.App. 34, 321 N.W.2d 831 (1982). We note, also, that the circuit court's jurisdiction was not raised as an issue in the Court of Appeals.

refused to renounce her United States citizenship, and she also refused to renounce the citizenship of the children. She claims that, despite the relocation to London, England, she has always considered herself a resident and domiciliary of Okemos, Michigan.

[After the parties moved to London in 1993, they jointly purchased a house for £2.75 million, and spent another £3.5 million on renovations. They enrolled the children in the American School of London, but plaintiff and the children made regular trips to Michigan for holidays, medical care, vacations, haircuts and other activities, and plaintiff also maintained her Michigan driver's license and voted regularly in Michigan elections.]

[Defendant received his distribution from the family trust which had a present, net value of £274 million (approximately $500,000,000) and plaintiff announced that she wanted a divorce in the fall of 1994, revealing that she had been involved in a long-standing affair with a man in Greece. Although plaintiff asserted that she and defendant agreed to postpone the divorce action until she and the children returned to Michigan after the 1994–95 school year, defendant filed for divorce in England on February 3, 1995. Plaintiff was served with process at the parties' home the following day. She contacted her American attorneys, and they filed a similar suit on her behalf in Michigan in the Ingham Circuit Court four days later. The parties remained in England until a consent order was entered in the English court on June 9, 1995, allowing plaintiff to return with the children to Michigan.]

[Defendant moved for summary disposition of the Michigan litigation on the bases of lack of jurisdiction and pendency of a prior proceeding, and the plaintiff brought a jurisdictional challenge in England. Both courts concluded that their jurisdiction was proper, and both suits proceeded. The English court entered a "decree absolute" of divorce on October 27, 1995, which was followed by a seven-day trial in March 1996 in which plaintiff filed an answer claiming the "full range of financial ancillary relief available to a wife under the Matrimonial Causes Act [of] 1973." Both sides presented expert witnesses who testified regarding the parties' assets and plaintiff's reasonable needs, and the court made its ruling in "a lengthy opinion" on March 21, 1996.]

[The English court determined defendant's total net worth to be "about £400 million." It awarded plaintiff £300,000 ($450,000) a year for life, a lump sum of £9 million ($13,500,000) to achieve an equitable distribution, the Michigan house with its contents with a value of approximately $1.5 million, and four paintings and her jewelry. The court also set child support in the amount of $95,400 a year for both children. Defendant was awarded four automobiles and the balance of the marital estate. The English court concluded that plaintiff was not entitled to a substantial share of defendant's family wealth, because it was not a product of the marriage and had not been generated by the efforts of either party.]

On March 29, 1996, defendant moved to stay or dismiss the Ingham Circuit Court proceedings, arguing that the English judgment was entitled to enforcement under the principle of comity and under the Uniform Foreign Money–Judgments Recognition Act, M.C.L. § 691.1151 *et seq.*; M.S.A. § 27.955(1) *et seq.* At the hearing on April 8, 1996, he urged, also, that the present action was barred by res judicata.

The circuit court judge denied the motion, finding that the English judgment was not entitled to recognition under the UFMJRA or the principle of comity. He reasoned that the English system of law was repugnant to the public policy of Michigan, and the English decision violated plaintiff's "right to have a fair and equitable distribution of property. . . . "

On appeal, in a per curium opinion, the Court of Appeals reversed, concluding that the "entire judgment, including the property division as well as the child support and lump-sum awards," should be enforced under the UFMJRA. 224 Mich.App. 146, 150, 568 N.W.2d 353 (1997).

\* \* \*

## II. ANALYSIS

The Court of Appeals correctly held that comity dictated that the judgment should be enforced because the plaintiff was accorded due process. Since the English judgment adjudicated the property issue, the plaintiff is barred from relitigating that issue under res judicata.

Comity is defined as the recognition which one nation allows within its territory to the legislative, executive, or judicial acts of another nation, having due regard both to international duty and convenience and to the rights of its own citizens or of other persons who are under the protection of its laws.

Comity mandates that this foreign judgment be given force and effect. The seminal United States Supreme Court case of *Hilton v. Guyot,*[2] set forth the factors that the federal courts use in recognizing and giving full effect to the judgment of foreign countries under comity:

> Where there has been opportunity for a full and fair trial abroad before a court of competent jurisdiction, conducting the

**2.** 159 U.S. 113, 202–203, 16 S.Ct. 139, 40 L.Ed. 95 (1895).

trial upon regular proceedings, after due citation or voluntary appearance of the defendant, and under a system of jurisprudence likely to secure an impartial administration of justice between the citizens of its own country and those of other countries, and there is nothing to show either prejudice in the court or in the system of laws under which it was sitting, or fraud in procuring the judgment, or any other special reason why the comity of this nation should not allow it full effect, the merits of the case should not, in an action brought in this country upon the judgment, be tried afresh, as on a new trial or an appeal, upon the mere assertion of the party that the judgment was erroneous in law or in fact.

* * *

Here, both parties participated and were represented by counsel in the English court proceedings. Plaintiff initially challenged jurisdiction in the English court. She asserted that defendant had not been "habitually" a resident of England for twelve months. Justice Johnson of the Family Division of the High Court of Justice ruled in defendant's favor, concluding that England was his main home and that he intended to stay there.

Plaintiff argues that the English judgment should not be enforced because defendant was not domiciled in England. We find this argument unpersuasive. The present case is distinguishable from the situation presented in *Gray v. Gray,* 320 Mich. 49, 58, 30 N.W.2d 426 (1948). In *Gray,* the wife was not personally served with process and the husband lived in Nevada only for the time necessary to obtain a divorce, then returned to Michigan. Under those facts, we determined that he had not acquired a bona fide domicile in Nevada and refused to recognize the divorce. However, in the present case, the record does not reflect that defendant moved to England for the purpose of obtaining a divorce. Rather, he moved to England to receive a disbursement from his family's trust.

The English court heard evidence pertaining to the value of the Dart Container Corporation, as well as defendant's salary and other real and personal property. It heard evidence regarding plaintiff's nonmonetary contributions to the marriage as well. It considered the home in Michigan, paintings, jewelry, and cars.

The parties agree that the factors that the English courts examine when dividing property are substantially the same as those used in Michigan. In *Sparks v. Sparks, supra,* this Court set forth the appropriate factors to consider in the division of marital property:

(1) duration of the marriage, (2) contributions of the parties to the marital estate, (3) age of the parties, (4) health of the

parties, (5) life status of the parties, (6) necessities and circumstances of the parties, (7) earning abilities of the parties, (8) past relations and conduct of the parties, and (9) general principles of equity. [*Id.* at 159–160, 485 N.W.2d 893.]

Section 25 of the Matrimonial Causes Act[4] requires that an English court consider nearly identical factors in dividing marital property.

Plaintiff argues that English courts apply a different rationale in cases involving large assets. In her brief, she asserts that the English court principally examined her financial needs to determine the appropriate award, not the marital assets.

In *Preston v. Preston,*[5] the English court announced a formula to be applied in cases in which the available resources are large. *Preston* established that there is a maximum sum to be awarded. This so-called "*Preston* ceiling" limits the award to an amount that satisfies the court's estimation of a wife's needs for support. Lord Justice Ormrod wrote in *Preston:*

> I think that on the true construction of § 25 there does come a point, in cases where the available resources are very large, . . . when the amount required to fulfill its terms "levels off," and redistribution of capital as such, in some unspecified ratio begins, which is outside the section. [*Id.* at 339.]

Had the English court actually used this formulation to divide the parties' marital assets, we might agree with plaintiff that she was denied due process. However, the English court did not use the *Preston* ceiling. Instead, it determined that the defendant's holdings and trust income were not marital property. Justice Johnson explained:

> [I]f you had a case where the husband and wife together built up a vast property empire, I see no reason why the wife's contribution should not entitle her to 50%. There is said to be a distinction between the wife whose contribution was child care and the wife who actually worked in the business, doing the books or whatever, it was. If Mr. and Mrs. Dart had started with nothing and in a back street somewhere in Detroit they had started making plastic objects and over the period of 20 or 30 years they had [ended] up with an empire worth £1,000 million, I would see every reason for Mrs. Dart having half of it. Personally, I do not have any difficulty with that. Whether the English law permits it or not is another matter, but that is not this case.

**4.** English Matrimonial Causes Act, 1973, § 25.

**5.** 1981 2 FLR 331.

Normally, property received by a married party as an inheritance, but kept separate from marital property, is deemed to be separate property not subject to distribution. *Lee v. Lee,* 191 Mich. App. 73, 477 N.W.2d 429 (1991). The trust income from the Dart Container Corporation was never marital property. Although the defendant worked for Dart Container Corporation during the marriage, his compensation was the salary and bonuses that he earned. His cumulative salary and bonuses over the course of the marriage were far less than the $14.5 million property award that plaintiff received.

The Dart fortune and defendant's interest in it exist independently of defendant's workplace activities or the marriage partnership.[6]

Thus, the English court's treatment of defendant's interests in the Dart family trusts and assets as separate property, rather than marital assets, did not violate plaintiff's right to due process.

Moreover, plaintiff's assertion that the English court failed to consider marital property is flawed. The English judgment awarded her the $1.5 million house in Okemos, some paintings, and a car. It also awarded child support in the amount of more than $90,000 a year. Certainly, the English court could not have divided these marital assets had there been no discovery. We find that the plaintiff was accorded due process in the English proceeding.

Consequently, res judicata bars the plaintiff from relitigating the property distribution issue. The English court decided this issue on the merits. Res judicata bars a subsequent action between the same parties when the evidence or essential facts are identical. A second action is barred when (1) the first action was decided on the merits, (2) the matter contested in the second action was or could have been resolved in the first, and (3) both actions involve the same parties or their privies.

Michigan courts have broadly applied the doctrine of res judicata. They have barred, not only claims already litigated, but every claim arising from the same transaction that the parties, exercising reasonable diligence, could have raised but did not.

Here, the Michigan divorce action involves the same parties with the same assets and the same children as the English action. We have already determined under our comity analysis that the English judgment is valid. The fact that it does not address custody or visitation is not fatal to its preclusive effect with respect to property distribution. The Ingham Circuit Court has jurisdiction

**6.** We recognize that, in certain situations, a spouse's separate assets, or the appreciation in their value during the marriage, may be included in the marital estate.

over the questions of custody and visitation, pursuant to the Uniform Child Custody Jurisdiction Act, *supra.* Accordingly, res judicata bars relitigation of the present action.

## III. CONCLUSION

We affirm the Court of Appeals decision to give deference to the English divorce judgment under the principle of comity. It was evident from the judgment rendered in England that plaintiff had a fair hearing on the merits, that she was present, represented by counsel, and actively participated. Thus, the present action is barred by res judicata.

### *Notes*

1. Several justices dissented in *Dart*, arguing that "the operation of the English system of marital asset division in cases involving substantial assets reflects considerations very different from our own," and concluding that such considerations "cast a shadow on the decision sufficient to preclude Michigan courts, with our well-established criteria for property distribution in divorce cases, from recognizing a decision that is not only from another land, but truly foreign to the concepts underlying Michigan law." Is this conclusion consistent with the majority's general statement on the law of comity, taken from *Hilton v. Guyot?*

2. When a divorce decree is entered by a court without personal jurisdiction over the respondent spouse, American cases generally allow a separate action to address support and property division matters after the divorce. How should the courts consider this type of claim following an international divorce? When should such relief be made available? Should it matter whether the divorced spouse is domiciled outside the United States? Cf. Chaudry v. Chaudry, 159 N.J.Super. 566, 388 A.2d 1000 (App. Div. 1978).

3. The lower courts in *Dart* also considered whether the English judgment could be enforced under the Uniform Foreign Money–Judgments Recognition Act (UFMJRA). This Act provides a mechanism for enforcing foreign country judgments in state courts as if they were judgments of other states entitled to full faith and credit.

Courts have reached different conclusions on whether the UFMJRA is ever applicable in domestic relations cases. As originally adopted in 1962, the Act extended to "any judgment of a foreign state granting or denying recovery of a sum of money, other than a judgment for taxes, a fine or other penalty, or a judgment for support in matrimonial or family matters." A recent revision of the Act, adopted in 2005 as the Uniform Foreign–Country Money Judgments Recognition Act, provides in § 3(b) that the Act does not apply to any foreign judgment "for divorce, support, or maintenance, or other judgment rendered in connection with domestic relations." The Comments to this provision suggest that this broader exclusion is consistent with the courts' interpretation of the prior statutory language. These Comments, and § 11 of the new Act, emphasize that courts are free to recognize foreign-country judgments not within the scope of the Act under common law principles of comity. What are the arguments for and against using the doctrine of comity to decide these cases, rather than applying the full faith and credit approach taken to other sorts of foreign money judgments?

# Chapter 4

# ESTABLISHING PARENT/CHILD RELATIONSHIPS

This chapter focuses on establishing parent/child relationships. The first section addresses the parent's decision whether or not to enter into such a relationship. The second section considers the changing legal status of non-marital children, for whom questions of legitimacy and paternity may still have important legal consequences. The third section focuses on international adoption, which is often closely related to the first two topics. If contraception is difficult to obtain, or abortion is illegal, or if 'unauthorized' children cannot be registered, for example, foreign adoption becomes an increasingly appealing option.

## A.  ABORTION/CONTRACEPTION

The decision whether or not to have a child, regarded as an important right in the United States, also raises legitimate public health concerns, from population growth to the spread of AIDS. This chapter begins with an asylum case, which highlights the tension between Chinese and American policies. A brief overview is followed by a more in-depth comparison of abortion reform in three countries. The section concludes with a description of recent U.N. initiatives. Each context raises challenging questions about the social construction of reproduction, and the resulting conflicts between individuals and the state.

### XIAO JI CHEN v. GONZALES
Court of Appeals for the Second Circuit, 2006.
434 F.3d 144.

\* \* \*

In the instant case, petitioner argues that she is entitled to withholding of removal under both the INA and the CAT because her alleged subjection to a forced abortion in China would create a rebuttable presumption that it is more likely than not that she will be sterilized, or otherwise persecuted, if she returns to China. She contends that forcible sterilization is particularly likely since, in contravention of China's family-planning policy, she has had more children since arriving in the United States.

The BIA has recognized that "coerced sterilization [should be] viewed as a permanent and continuing act of persecution."

* * *

[The court discusses the treatment of coercive family planning as persecution on the basis of political opinion]. Consequently, if petitioner had demonstrated to the IJ that there was a clear probability that she would be sterilized if she returned to China, she would be entitled to withholding of removal under the INA. Such relief was denied, however, because the IJ found that petitioner had not met her burden of proof, given that her testimony was "inherently improbable, internally inconsistent, [and] inconsistent with her written application as well as some of her supporting documents."

## BARBARA STARK, REPRODUCTIVE RIGHTS AND ABORTION

International Family Law: An Introduction 138–47 (2005).

### Contraception

Access to information and education regarding contraception is the crucial first step. This includes the effects of spacing children on maternal health as well as on infant and child mortality. Second, equally crucial, families must have access to effective, dependable, and safe contraception. This includes sterilization, condoms, spermicides, diaphragms and other barrier methods, as well as intrauterine devices and oral contraceptives. Hormonal emergency contraception (EC), the "morning-after pill," prevents pregnancy by preventing a fertilized egg from becoming attached to the uterine wall. The morning-after pill, accordingly, is also properly considered a form of contraception.

Women's equality is increasingly recognized as a factor in their enjoyment of reproductive rights. If women do not enjoy equal rights within the family, the reproductive rights of the *couple* are apt to be exercised by the husband. If a woman cannot support herself, but is dependant on her husband for her sustenance, her reproductive rights may well be illusory. The Committee on the Elimination of Discrimination against Women has criticized rules requiring women to obtain spousal consent in order to undergo tubal ligation or abortions even when their health was in danger. In its General Comment No. 24 on Article 12 of the Women's Convention, the Committee recognizes that women's health issues are of central importance to the family as a whole but notes that an imbalance of power may effectively deprive women of access to health care. The General Comment concludes that in interpreting Article 12 of the Convention there should be 'no restrictions on the ground that women do not have the authority of husbands, partners, parents or health authorities.'

While the State should recognize the reproductive rights of individuals and couples, the State also has legitimate interests in promoting the use of contraceptives. The UK, for example, launched a national campaign to reduce teen pregnancy in the Spring of 2002. As part of this campaign, the Tesco supermarket chain began distributing free morning-after pills to teenagers. In order to combat the AIDS epidemic, States such as Brazil, in cooperation with international organizations and non-governmental organizations, have initiated widespread condom distribution programs.

Other States, confronted with burgeoning populations, have adopted comprehensive population policies in order to assure basic human rights, including rights to an adequate standard of living, education, and healthcare. The means adopted by the State in connection with such policies cannot be 'compulsory or discriminatory,' according to the Human Rights Committee. Thus, incentives, propaganda, and education are generally considered acceptable, while coerced sterilizations or abortions, criminal sanctions, and onerous fines are not. In China, for example, the infamous one-child policy was adopted in 1980, limiting each family to one or at most two children. This policy was enforced through a broad range of methods, including onerous fines on excess children, forced sterilizations and abortions, the refusal to register 'unauthorized' children, and oppressive campaigns in which committees would monitor women's menstrual cycles and pay unwelcome visits to women who became pregnant, sometimes harassing them for hours until they agreed to abortions.

## Abortion

Abortion refers to the termination of a pregnancy after the fertilized egg has become attached to the uterine wall. Unlike reproductive rights in general, there is no international consensus on abortion in particular. The controversy is grounded in the belief in some States that abortion involves two lives, that of the fetus as well as that of the mother, unlike contraception, which only involves the decision by the mother (or the parents) whether or not to become pregnant. Among those States which recognize a State interest in the preservation of human life, moreover, there is a range of views as to when fetal life comes into being. The Inter–American Convention, for example, refers to "a right to life from the moment of conception." German law, in contrast, accepts as a matter of scientific fact that life begins fourteen days after conception. Under the Hanafi school of Islamic law, 'ensoulment' occurs at four months, before which abortion may be permitted.

Even where abortion is legal, moreover, there is growing condemnation of sex-selective abortions as a 'cleaner' form of female infanticide. In China, for example, almost one million baby girls are missing annually. That is, gender ratios predict that one million more baby girls will be born every year than appear on national registries. Approximately fifteen percent, or 191,089, of these baby girls are missing because of selective female mortality or infanticide, sex-selective abortions, or neglect.

The American Declaration on the Rights and Duties of Man provides, 'Every human being has the right to life, liberty and the security of his person.' The American Convention on Human Rights is more specific: "Article 4.1 Every person has the right to have his life respected. This right shall be protected by law, and, in general, from the moment of conception. No one shall be arbitrarily deprived of his life. In White and Potter v. United States, [Case 2141, Inter–Am. C.H.R. 25, OEA ser. L/V/II.54, doc.9 rev.1 (1981)] petitioners argued that the United States was in violation of the Declaration, which it had signed, and which should be interpreted in light of the American Convention, which the United States had not ratified. The Commission rejected this argument and refused to 'impose upon the United States Government, or that of any member State of the OAS, by means of "interpretation", an international obligation based upon a treaty that such State has not duly accepted or ratified.'

## BARBARA STARK, CRAZY JANE TALKS WITH THE BISHOP: ABORTION IN CHINA, GERMANY, SOUTH AFRICA AND INTERNATIONAL HUMAN RIGHTS

12 Tex. J. Women & L. 287 (Spring 2003).

This paper focuses on the right to abortion and the inability of feminists to generate consensus regarding that right on the international level, despite widespread agreement as to its basic importance. This inability can be traced partly to the different functions abortion serves in different countries and partly to the different strategies that feminists have employed at the national level to safeguard or limit the right to abortion. This paper examines the political and social constructions of abortion in China, Germany, and South Africa—states that have all reformed their abortion laws within the last ten years—to show how subversions of national abortion policies have effectively subverted attempts to produce an intelligible international position.

By way of caveat, this paper does not attempt to provide the rigorous immersion in each culture necessary to understand reproductive rights within a particular cultural context. Such an immersion would necessarily include a full account of reproduction within that culture, including an examination of state population policy, available contraception, access to healthcare, and analysis of women's status. As Vivian Curran has argued, such an immersion necessarily requires an understanding of the language as well as the culture. My purpose here is much more limited; this paper simply explores the kinds of obstacles feminists confront in reaching an international consensus. The international project must take the underlying cultures into account, but it should not be driven by them. Rather, if the international project is realized, it will become the driving force to which the respective cultures must conform. The relationship between the international project and the underlying culture is obviously subject to a shifting dynamic. A key question for international human rights is how to protect the most vulnerable, especially during transition. Yeats's "Crazy Jane" is a crone, a poor woman who somehow gets by, a defiant outsider. She challenges the Bishop to show that his abstract theology addresses her very earthy needs. In the "Crazy Jane" series, written near the end of his life, Yeats assumes a woman's voice to express the range and complexity of women's experience. Just as Crazy Jane challenges the Bishop, the pragmatic strategies adopted by feminists on the national level challenge the abstract, universal constructions of international human rights law.

"Abortion" includes a broad range of procedures, depending in part upon the stage of fetal development at which it is performed. Abortion includes a similarly broad range of social and political meanings. In South Africa, the debate over the new abortion law became a microcosm of national politics as Islamic, tribal, and other factions struggled with the rhetoric of equality and the bitter legacy of apartheid. In China, abortion is both a human rights rally cry against the coerced abortions performed pursuant to the one-child policy (and a ground for asylum claims) and a privilege limited to those who can afford the sex-selective abortions that remain technically illegal. In Germany, unification forced a problematic synthesis between pro-natalists and those eager to exorcise any trace of the Nazi policies in the West and the far more liberal abortion laws of the formerly socialist East.

Part II establishes the backdrop of the abortion debate, briefly describing and contrasting the law in each state before the reforms.

Part III explains what feminists wanted, whether expressed in private interviews with feminists in China or in the very public lobbying and advocacy of women's groups in South Africa and Germany. Part IV describes what they got. Part V explains how the resultant laws, whether incorporating feminist arguments in their respective national debates or silencing them, exemplify the range of discordant approaches that preclude consensus on abortion in international human rights law.

In each state, the abortion law reforms of the 1990s were shaped by the larger domestic political contexts from which they emerged. In China, globalization and the accompanying scrutiny from the international community resulted in a rhetorical nod toward human rights. In South Africa, abortion was reconstructed within the rhetorical frameworks of human rights and liberation, to which the new government was authentically committed. In Germany, the Court (which actually set out the parameters of the new law) crafted an uneasy synthesis between women's rights and the recognition of fetal rights urged by Christian groups and grounded, like the First Abortion Decision, in the recognition of the Basic Law's "human dignity."

## A.  In South Africa

The ANC had promised to decriminalize abortion and to eliminate the onerous procedures that effectively precluded legal abortion for the vast majority of South African women. After the ANC won the election, the old abortion law was discarded along with apartheid. Indeed, reproductive rights were explicitly assured in the new South African Constitution, which establishes the right "to make decisions concerning reproduction" and the right to "security in and control over [the] body."

The Choice on Termination of Pregnancy Act (CTOP) was enacted in South Africa in 1996. It requires the state to provide an abortion on request during the first twelve weeks of pregnancy. Women were deliberately made part of the drafting process. Fifteen women were on the 1995 parliamentary committee which reviewed the restrictive 1975 Act; eleven committee members were men. But polls showed that the majority of South Africans did not want the new, liberalized law. Although most of those who had had illegal abortions, and most of those who died from them, were black, "the black majority was more likely than the white minority to be pro-life."

## B.  In Germany

Under the terms of the German Reunification Treaty, West German law replaced inconsistent East German law. As Florian Miedel notes, however, "The abortion case was different." The Aid for Pregnant Women and Families Act of July 27, 1992 (the "1992 Act") represented a compromise between the very liberal abortion laws of the socialist East and the very restrictive abortion laws of the democratic West. Under the new law, extensive counseling was provided with the express goals of protecting the unborn fetus and preventing future unwanted pregnancies. Like the 1974 Reform law before it, the new law was challenged before the Constitutional Court on the ground that it conflicted with the German Basic Law. The Court found that the law was indeed in conflict with the Basic Law and established a new model.

The core principle of the new law was to prevent abortion through counseling and to simultaneously decriminalize abortion. Some features of the 1992 Act were retained by the Court. Abortions within the first twelve weeks, after counseling, for example, are not criminal. Since criminal sanctions have basically been eliminated in the new law, it is enforced for the most part by denial of state insurance benefits. Women will not be reimbursed for abortions unless they are authorized by certificates of indication. An exception is made, however, for poor women who cannot otherwise afford abortions. The new law is in continuing tension with other provisions of German law, however, because of its characterization of fetuses as legal persons and bearers of rights.

### V.  The New Laws and International Human Rights Law

In general, reproductive rights are not as well-established in international human rights law as equality rights, which have been championed by men for more than 200 years. When women seek "formal" equality, accordingly, they can rely on well-developed equality jurisprudence. Reproductive rights, in contrast, address issues—including conception, pregnancy, and childbirth—historically relegated to the private sphere; that is, such matters have been viewed as better left to the determination of the married couple. This perception both reflects and perpetuates women's subordination within marriage. The idea that women should have control over the number and spacing of their children has been controversial, especially in cultures where large families are viewed as desirable. Nevertheless, reproductive rights are increasingly recognized in international human rights law. These rights, including education about family planning, access to contraception, and freedom from gender discrimination, are widely recognized throughout the world. Almost every state allows access to contraception, and several states provide contraceptives as a free public health benefit.

While reproductive rights are widely recognized as a general principle, the implementation of reproductive rights is more problematic. Major issues include: whose rights they are—that is, are reproductive rights to be exercised by a couple or by each individual within a couple? Second, under what conditions, and through what mechanisms, can these rights be circumscribed by the state? Are state population control policies, for example, inconsistent with these rights?

The controversy is grounded in the belief in some states that abortion involves two lives, that of the fetus as well as that of the mother, unlike contraception, which affects only the mother. Among those states which recognize a state interest in the fetus, moreover, there is a range of views as to when fetal life comes into being. The American Convention on Human Rights, for example, refers to "a right to life from the moment of conception." German law, in contrast, accepts as a matter of scientific fact that life begins fourteen days after conception.

## A.  THE CIVIL COVENANT

The International Covenant on Civil and Political Rights (the "Civil Covenant") addresses civil and political rights, such as freedom of expression and freedom of religion, familiar to Americans from our own Constitution. While Article 3 of the Civil Covenant requires states to "ensure the equal right of men and women to the enjoyment of all civil and political rights," there is no explicit reference to reproductive rights. While Article 17 recognizes a right to "privacy," unlike the right to privacy which the U.S. Supreme Court has found in the U.S. Constitution, the international version has not been construed to include the right to reproductive privacy.

The final South African Constitution explicitly contemplates an expanded conception of equality. As Valorie Vojdik has explained, while section 9(1) assures equal protection, section 9(2) expressly provides for affirmative measures to bring those historically "disadvantaged by unfair discrimination" up to the starting line. Nor does the Constitution require any 'intent' to discriminate.

Article 23 of the Civil Covenant assures the "right of men and women of marriageable age to marry and to found a family" and requires the state to "take appropriate steps to ensure equality of rights and responsibilities of spouses as to marriage, during marriage, and at its dissolution." This applies to state family planning policies, as the Human Rights Committee has pointed out:

> The right to found a family implies, in principle, the possibility to procreate and live together. When States' parties adopt family planning policies, they should be compatible with the provisions of the Covenant and should, in particular, not be discriminatory or compulsory.

China's one-child policy appears to violate even this minimal standard, since it is both "compulsory" and "discriminatory" and the burden of contraception is borne almost exclusively by Chinese women. In times of "public emergency," however, states may derogate from certain rights, including reproductive rights, under the Civil Covenant. As explained above, China certainly viewed the population crisis in the early 1980s as a "public emergency." While forced abortions or sterilizations should be prohibited even under this standard, fines for unauthorized children might be acceptable, if they are not onerous. Even if the population crisis is no longer considered a "public emergency," international human rights laws permit states to limit some rights, if necessary to ensure "the public welfare." Even if incentives are viewed as limits on rights, accordingly, they would arguably be permissible under this standard. Such permissible limits might include incentives for families with only one child, such as preferred housing or bonuses like those currently offered in some regions.

Like the Chinese government, the South African government considers the fertility rate (of 3.3 children per woman) to be too high. Its goal is to reduce the fertility rate to the replacement rate of 2.1 children per woman by 2010. Unlike the Chinese government, the South African government has attempted to do so in a manner compatible with women's rights under the Civil Covenant. Rather than imposing criminal or other sanctions on women, the government supports family planning services and provides free contraceptives at all government medical establishments.

The German government has a different problem. It considers the fertility rate of 1.3 children per woman too low. Reflecting both respect for women's reproductive rights under international human rights and German law, as well as the lack of consensus among the German political parties on this issue, the government has not intervened with respect to fertility levels, although it does provide indirect support for contraceptive use.

### B. THE ECONOMIC COVENANT

The International Covenant on Economic, Social, and Cultural Rights (the Economic Covenant) is the other half of the International Bill of Human Rights. It assures basic economic and social rights, including the right to health and the right to an adequate standard of living. Unlike the Civil Covenant, it has no counterpart in U.S. jurisprudence. Article 2 and Article 3 of the Economic Covenant require states to "ensure the equal right of men and women to the enjoyment of all economic, social, and cultural rights."

Article 10 of the Economic Covenant requires states to ensure "family rights," and Article 12 requires states to ensure the "right to health." Reproductive rights are crucial to any meaningful understanding of either article. Without reproductive rights, parents cannot determine the most fundamental issues of family membership, such as the spacing or number of children. Section 27 of the final South African Constitution "guarantees every person, inter alia, the right to adequate housing, medical care, including reproductive health care, food, water, and education" (emphasis added).

The right to health can also be invoked to argue against state limits on abortion. As the World Health Organization ("WHO") has noted, the absence of safe, dependable contraception and abortion present grave risks to the health of women, whether through unsafe abortions (20 million annually), severe maternal morbidity (20 million cases annually), or perinatal deaths (7.2 million annually). The South African government has expressed particular concern about the complications of child bearing and child birth. The government does not consider morbidity and mortality resulting from induced abortion a serious problem. The German government, in contrast, does not consider complications of child bearing and child birth to be a major problem. Indeed, the maternal mortality rate is 22 (per 100,000 live births in 1990), notably less than the 27 median among developed countries. Morbidity and mortality from induced abortion, similarly, are not a governmental concern.

While it is clear that state-sponsored or state-sanctioned coerced abortions or sterilizations violate the Covenants, it is not clear what kinds of incentives and disincentives, short of brute force, amount to coercion. It has been argued that any incentives or disincentives by the state should be considered impermissible. This assumes a neutral background, a level playing field. Where there is strong social coercion, however, like the pressure on women in rural China to bear sons, it can be argued that some incentives may be necessary as a counter-weight.

Articles 4 and 5 of the Economic Covenant, which address the non-derogation of economic, social, and cultural rights, suggest the parameters for such counterincentives. Article 4 provides that "the State may subject such rights only to such limitations as are determined by law only in so far as this may be compatible with the nature of these rights and solely for the purpose of promoting the general welfare in a democratic society." As Philip Alston notes, this imposes a rigorous standard; "[L]imitations must, in the first place be 'determined by law' in accordance with the appropriate national procedures and must not be arbitrary or unreasonable or retroactive. The limitations must also 'be compatible with the nature' of these rights."

Article 5 extends the prohibition against derogation in three important ways. First, it extends this prohibition to non-State third parties. Thus, while a violation under the Civil Covenant requires a showing of state practice, the "over-zealous" local official defense is expressly anticipated here. Second, it extends the prohibition to activities indirectly aimed at derogation. A monetary inducement for a late-term abortion posing significant risk to the mother's health would arguably violate this standard. Third, it prohibits derogation from any other rights on the "pretext" that the Covenant requires such derogation.

### C.  THE WOMEN'S CONVENTION

The Convention on the Elimination of All Forms of Discrimination Against Women (the Women's Convention) is considerably more expansive. Article 1 begins by defining the term "discrimination against women" to mean "any distinction, exclusion or restriction made on the basis of sex, which has the effect or purpose of impairing or nullifying the recognition, enjoyment or exercise by women . . . of human rights and fundamental freedoms in the political, economic, social, cultural, civil or any other field."

Article 2 of the Women's Convention further requires the state "to take all appropriate measures, including legislation, to modify or abolish existing laws, regulations, customs and practices which constitute discrimination against women." This is an extremely broad formulation, effectively holding the state responsible for all discrimination on the basis of gender, whether through state policy or private prejudice. Thus, the Women's Convention imposes an affirmative obligation on the state to take whatever steps are necessary to counteract discrimination against women.

While women's equality is officially endorsed by all three governments, its meaning is very different in Germany, South Africa, and China. In Germany, formal equality is modified by a system of pro-natalist incentives that reflect and perpetuate women's inequality in the labor force. The view of women in the former West Germany, in short, has prevailed over the view of women in the former East Germany.

South Africa's view of women's equality, in contrast, is among the most progressive in the world. Under the South African Constitution, as under the Women's Convention, de facto inequality is to be addressed by affirmative measures. The new abortion law permits abortion on demand during the first trimester and also allows abortion through the twentieth week of pregnancy on very broad grounds, including socio-economic grounds. The law is firmly based on a notion of individual human rights. The preamble provides that South Africa's Constitution protects the rights of persons to make decisions concerning reproduction and to achieve security in and control over their bodies; that both men and women have the right to have access to safe, effective, and acceptable methods of fertility control of their choice; and that women have a right of access to appropriate health care services to ensure safe pregnancy and childbirth. It also makes the State responsible for providing reproductive health to all, contraception and termination of pregnancy services, as well as safe conditions under which the right of choice can be exercised without fear or harm. South Africa's abortion law has been challenged, however, on the ground that it violates the right to life of the fetus.

While China has arguably gone further than either of the other two states to promote women's equality, the one-child policy remains problematic, raising several issues under the Women's Convention. To the extent that it is enforced through measures which specifically impair women's rights to health, it violates the Convention. Article 11.2 further prohibits the state from penalizing women for pregnancy. Since the purpose of the Women's Convention is to prohibit discrimination against women, however, it is unclear whether penalizing the family for a pregnancy violates the Convention, because women are not being singled out.

Article 12 explicitly requires the state to "ensure access to healthcare services, including those related to family planning" and, more specifically, to "ensure to women appropriate services in connection with pregnancy, confinement in the postnatal period, granting free services when necessary, as well as adequate nutrition during pregnancy and lactation." Article 14 reiterates the right to family planning services for rural women in particular. Article 16, relating generally to women's rights within marriage, again emphasizes that women have "the same rights [as men] to decide freely and responsibly on the number and spacing of their children."

While the Women's Convention provides a clear statement of reproductive rights, and measures to be taken to assure them, enforcement in domestic courts is a separate issue. Although some countries, such as the Netherlands, adopt international human rights treaties as domestic law upon ratification, many, including China and Germany, do not. Although China and Germany have ratified the Women's Convention, it is not enforceable as domestic law in either country. This means that neither Chinese nor German women can claim their rights under the Convention in their national courts.

Nor is there any international tribunal before which they may do so. An Optional Protocol to the Women's Convention enables individual women to file complaints before CEDAW, the Committee responsible for implementation of the Convention. But this is not an option for Chinese women because China is not a party to the Protocol. Although Germany signed the Optional Protocol on December 10, 1999, it has not yet ratified it.

Since the death of Mao Tse-tung in 1976, China has slowly but inexorably been opening its doors. The same forces that led China to develop relations with Western adoption agencies have led to a new era in trade, foreign investment, and educational exchanges. China has become an active participant in U.N. conferences, sending a large delegation to the U.N. World Conference on Population in Cairo in 1994, at which "population" was recast in terms of "women's human rights." China hosted the World Conference on Women in Beijing in 1995, which reaffirmed the importance of reproductive rights. As a result, women in China are increasingly aware of human rights in general and reproductive rights in particular. The extent to which this has curtailed the early abuses of the one-child policy is unclear.

\* \* \*

As this Article has explained, while China, South Africa, and Germany have all undergone significant reforms in their abortion law in the past ten years, and all have been influenced by international human rights, these reforms were grounded in different cultures and subject to different political processes. The three states began with three very different dual systems. Within each of the dual systems, there were multiple, conflicting constituencies and "women" were dispersed among them; they were not a monolithic group. "What feminists wanted" depended upon who was asked and who was considered a feminist. Women who still viewed it as their duty to bear sons in China, like religious women in Germany and South Africa, in general did not view themselves as "feminists." "What they got" reflected the larger domestic political context in which the reforms were crafted. For American feminists, abortion is often viewed as a symbol of women's autonomy. I refer here not to some abstract notion of autonomy, but a profound sense of the social realities in which such a claim is necessarily embedded. In each of these countries, abortion similarly carried great symbolic weight, but the underlying meanings were dramatically different. In South Africa, "abortion" was equated with "liberation," if not by the pro-life black majority who disapproved of it. In Germany, abortion was viewed as a terrible reminder of the Nazis' "lives unworthy of life," and as a desperate measure to which women should have a full range of alternatives. In China, abortion is still perceived, at least by some, as a modern, scientific answer to both the demographic nightmare of overpopulation and the ancient practice of female infanticide.

The inability to reach consensus on this issue is not necessarily a bad thing. Rather, the inability of international law to subvert local subversions highlights both the always questionable claims of "universal" human rights and indicates ongoing feminist ambivalence regarding this very difficult issue. It also reflects the powerful and well-financed coalition opposing abortion on the international level, including the Vatican and, under the Bush administration, the United States. Focusing on other aspects of reproductive rights—such as universal access to the "morning-after pill" or the right to otherwise legal abortions for poor women—may well be a more constructive short-term strategy for internationalists.

## D. MARIANNE BLAIR & MERLE H. WEINER, REPRODUCTIVE FREEDOM, ASSISTED CONCEPTION, AND ABORTION

Family Law in the World Community 986–87 (2003).

Nations have worked together on international population issues for approximately fifty years. Initial cooperation focused on gathering and sharing population statistics, but by the early 1970s participants in international population conferences were concerned about the rapidly increasing world population and its implications for the environment, world hunger, infant and maternal mortality, and a host of other social ills. Nations came together to set policy goals and offer recommendations at the World Populations Conference at Bucharest in 1974, the International Conference on Population at Mexico City in 1984, and again at the International Conference on Population and Development in Cairo in 1994.

Despite differences on particular issues, particularly the need for safe abortion, most countries agreed on most issues at the Cairo Conference, including that rapid unchecked population growth is harmful and the population stabilization is critical. As the Programme of Action for the Cairo Conference said:

> While it had taken 123 years for world population to increase from 1 billion to 2 billion, succeeding increments of 1 billion took 33 years, 14 years and 13 years. The transition from the fifth to the sixth billionth, currently under way, is expected to take only 11 years and to be completed by 1998.

After the Conference reaffirmed the rights and freedoms in the Universal Declaration of Human Rights (principle 1), the right to an adequate standard of living (principle 3), and the right to gender equality (principle 4), among other things, the Conference adopted principle 5: "Population-related goals and policies are integral parts of culture, economic and social development, the principle aim of which is to improve the quality of life of all people."

However, the Programme of Action also recognized limits to population policies. Participants recognize the family-planning programs should not involve any form of coercion, that governmentally-sponsored economic incentives and disincentives were only marginally effective, and that governmental goals "should be defined in terms of unmet needs for information and services" and not quotas or targets imposed on providers. *Id*. § 7.16. Countries were to meet the family-planning needs of their populations as soon as possible, but no later than 2015. *Id*. § 7.16. A number of countries entered reservation, specifically objecting to the word "individuals" in section 7.16.

In addition, the Cairo Programme of Action recognized "reproductive rights," as set out in international human rights documents. The notion of "reproductive rights" includes *both* "the basic right of all couples and individuals to decide freely and responsibly the number, spacing and timing of their children, and to have the information and means to do so" *and* "the right to obtain the highest standard of sexual and reproductive health."

### *Note*

China's discredited one-child policy continues to inspire criticism, as a violation of parents' as well as children's rights. See, e.g., Megan C. Dempsey, Note. "A Misplaced Bright-line Rule: Coercive Population Control in China and Asylum for Unmarried Partners", 92 Iowa L. Rev. 213–243 (2006); Liu Huawen, The Child's Right to Birth Registration in Family Life and Human Rights 441 (Peter Lodrup & Eva Modvar eds. 2004). Under what circumstances, if any, does the state have a legitimate interest in limiting population, or encouraging population growth? What can the state do to promote population policies, without impinging on individual rights?

## B.  LEGITIMACY/PATERNITY

Rules about legitimacy and paternity are grounded in assumptions about identity and citizenship that may be so deeply ingrained that they are unquestioned, accepted as 'natural', in a particular culture. These assumptions are disrupted by contact with other cultures, by new reproductive technologies and by international human rights law that imposes incompatible norms.

### NGUYEN v. IMMIGRATION AND NATURALIZATION SERVICE

United States Supreme Court, 2001.
533 U.S. 53, 121 S.Ct. 2053, 150 L.Ed.2d 115.

* * *

Title 8 U.S.C. 1409 governs the acquisition of United States citizenship by persons born to one United States citizen parent and one noncitizen parent when the parents are unmarried and the child is born outside of the United States or its possessions. The statute imposes different requirements for the child's acquisition of citizenship depending upon whether the citizen parent is the mother or the father. The question before us is whether the statutory distinction is consistent with the equal protection guarantee embedded in the Due Process Clause of the Fifth Amendment.

[I]

Petitioner Tuan Ahn Nguyen was born in Saigon, Vietnam, on September 11, 1969, to copetitioner Joseph Boulais and a Vietnamese citizen. Boulais and Nguyen's mother were not married. Boulais always has been a citizen of the United States, and he was in Vietnam under the employ of a corporation. After he and Nguyen's mother ended their relationship, Nguyen lived for a time with the family of Boulais' new Vietnamese girlfriend. In June 1975, Nguyen, then almost six years of age, came to the United States. He became a lawful permanent resident and was raised in Texas by Boulais.

In 1992, when Nguyen was 22, he pleaded guilty in a Texas state court to two counts of sexual assault on a child. He was sentenced to eight years in prison on each count. Three years later, the United States Immigration and Naturalization Service (INS) initiated deportation proceedings against Nguyen as an alien who had been convicted of two crimes involving moral turpitude, as well as an aggravated felony. Though later he would change his position and argue he was a United States citizen, Nguyen testified at his deportation hearing that he was a citizen of Vietnam. The Immigration Judge found him deportable.

Nguyen appealed to the Board of Immigration of Appeals and, in 1998, while the matter was pending, his father obtained an order of parentage from a state court, based on DNA testing. By this time, Nguyen was 28 years old. The Board dismissed Nguyen's appeal, rejecting his claim to United States citizenship because he had failed to establish compliance with 8 U.S.C. § 1409(a), which sets forth the requirements for one who was born out of wedlock and abroad to a citizen father and a noncitizen mother.

Nguyen and Boulais appealed to the Court of Appeals for the Fifth Circuit, arguing that § 1409 violates equal protection by providing different rules for attainment of citizenship by children born abroad and out of wedlock depending upon whether the one parent with American citizenship is the mother or the father. The court rejected the constitutional challenge to § 1409(a). 208 F.3d 528, 535 (2000).

The constitutionality of the distinction between unwed fathers and mothers was argued in *Miller [Miller v. Albright*, 523 U.S. 420 (1998)], but a majority of the Court did not resolve the issue.

\* \* \*

Since *Miller*, the Courts of Appeal have divided over the constitutionality of § 1409. We granted certiorari to resolve the conflict. We hold that § 1409(a) is consistent with the constitutional guarantee of equal protection.

\* \* \*

Section 1409(a) thus imposes a set of requirements on the children of citizen fathers born abroad and out of wedlock to a noncitizen mother that are not imposed under like circumstances when the citizen parent is the mother. All concede the requirements of [§ 1409(a)(4)], relating to a citizen father's acknowledgment of a child while he is under 18, were not satisfied in this case ... As an individual seeking citizenship under § 1409(a) must meet all of its preconditions, the failure to satisfy § 1409(a)(4) renders Nguyen ineligible for citizenship.

\* \* \*

[III]

For a gender-based classification to withstand equal protection scrutiny, it must be established " 'at least that the [challenged] classification serves "important governmental objectives and that the discriminatory means employed" are "substantially related to the achievement of those objectives." ' " For reasons to follow, we conclude § 1409 satisfies this standard.

\* \* \*

Before considering the important governmental interests advanced by the statute, two observations concerning the operation of the provision are in order. First, a citizen mother expecting a child and living abroad has the right to re-enter the United States so the child can be born here and be a 14th Amendment citizen. From one perspective, then, the statute simply ensures equivalence between two expectant mothers who are citizens abroad if one chooses to reenter for the child's birth and the other chooses not to return, or does not have the means to do so. This equivalence is not a factor if the single citizen parent living abroad is the father. For, unlike the unmarried mother, the unmarried father as a general rule cannot control where the child will be born.

Second, although § 1409(a)(4) requires certain conduct to occur before the child of a citizen father, born out of wedlock and abroad, reaches 18 years of age, it imposes no limitations on when an individual who qualifies under the statute can claim citizenship. The statutory treatment of citizenship is identical in this respect whether the citizen parent is the mother or the father. A person born to a citizen parent of either gender may assert citizenship, assuming compliance with statutory preconditions, regardless of his or her age. And while the conditions necessary for a citizen mother to transmit citizenship under § 1409(c) exist at birth, citizen fathers and/or their children have 18 years to satisfy the requirements of § 1409(a)(4).

The statutory distinction relevant in this case, then, is that § 1409(a)(4) requires one of three affirmative steps to be taken if the citizen parent is the father, but not if the citizen parent is the mother: legitimation; a declaration of paternity under oath by the father; or a court order of paternity. Congress' decision to impose requirements on unmarried fathers that differ from those on unmarried mothers is based on the significant difference between their respective relationships to the potential citizen at the time of birth. Specifically, the imposition of the requirement for a paternal relationship, but not a maternal one, is justified by two important governmental objectives. We discuss each in turn.

The first governmental interest to be served is the importance of assuring that a biological parent-child relationship exists. In the case of the mother, the relation is verifiable from the birth itself. The mother's status is documented in most instances by the birth certificate or hospital records and the witnesses who attest to her having given birth.

In the case of the father, the uncontestable fact is that he need not be present at the birth. If he is present, furthermore, that circumstance is not incontrovertible proof of fatherhood.

\* \* \*

The second important governmental interest furthered in a substantial manner by § 1409(a)(4) is the determination to ensure that the child and the citizen parent have some demonstrated opportunity or potential to develop not just a relationship that is recognized, as a formal matter, by the law, but one that consists of the real, everyday ties that provide a connection between child and citizen parent and, in turn, the United States. In the case of a citizen mother and a child born overseas, the opportunity for a meaningful relationship between citizen parent and child inheres in the very event of birth, an event so often critical to our constitutional and statutory understandings of citizenship. The mother knows that the child is in being and is hers and has an initial point of contact with him. There is at least an opportunity for mother and child to develop a real, meaningful relationship.

The same opportunity does not result from the event of birth, as a matter of biological inevitability, in the case of the unwed father. Given the 9–month interval between conception and birth, it is not always certain that a father will know that a child was conceived, nor is it always clear that even the mother will be sure of the father's identity. This fact takes on particular significance in the case of a child born overseas and out of wedlock. One concern in this context has always been with young people, men for the most part, who are on duty with the Armed Forces in foreign countries.

* * *

When we turn to the conditions which prevail today, we find that the passage of time has produced additional and even more substantial grounds to justify the statutory distinction. The ease of travel and the willingness of Americans to visit foreign countries have resulted in numbers of trips abroad that must be of real concern when we contemplate the prospect of accepting petitioners' argument, which would mandate, contrary to Congress' wishes, citizenship by male parentage subject to no condition save the father's previous length of residence in this country. In 1999 alone, Americans made almost 25 million trips abroad, excluding trips to Canada and Mexico. Visits to Canada and Mexico add to this figure almost 34 million additional visits. And the average American overseas traveler spent 15.1 nights out of the United States in 1999.

Principles of equal protection do not require Congress to ignore this reality. To the contrary, these facts demonstrate the critical importance of the Government's interest in ensuring some opportunity for a tie between citizen father and foreign born child which is a reasonable substitute for the opportunity manifest between mother and child at the time of birth. Indeed, especially in light of the number of Americans who take short sojourns abroad, the prospect that a father might not even know of the conception is a realistic possibility. Even if a father knows of the fact of conception, moreover, it does not follow that he will be present at the birth of the child. Thus, unlike the case of the mother, there is no assurance that the father and his biological child will ever meet. Without an initial point of contact with the child by a father who knows the child is his own, there is no opportunity for father and child to begin a relationship. Section 1409 takes the unremarkable step of ensuring that such an opportunity, inherent in the event of birth as to the mother-child relationship, exists between father and child before citizenship is conferred upon the latter.

The importance of the governmental interest at issue here is too profound to be satisfied merely by conducting a DNA test. The fact of paternity can be established even without the father's knowledge, not to say his presence. Paternity can be established by taking DNA samples even from a few strands of hair, years after the birth. Yet scientific proof of biological paternity does nothing, by itself, to ensure contact between father and child during the child's minority.

Congress is well within its authority in refusing, absent proof of at least the opportunity for the development of a relationship between citizen parent and child, to commit this country to embracing a child as a citizen entitled as of birth to the full protection of the United States, to the absolute right to enter its borders, and to full participation in the political process. If citizenship is to be conferred by the unwitting means petitioners urge, so that its acquisition abroad bears little relation to the realities of the child's own ties and allegiances, it is for Congress, not this Court, to make that determination.

*  *  *

Having concluded that facilitation of a relationship between parent and child is an important governmental interest, the question remains whether the means Congress chose to further its objective—the imposition of certain additional requirements upon an unwed father—substantially relate to that end. Under this test, the means Congress adopted must be sustained.

First, it should be unsurprising that Congress decided to require that an opportunity for a parent-child relationship occur during the formative years of the child's minority. In furtherance of the desire to ensure some tie between this country and one who seeks citizenship, various other statutory provisions concerning citizenship and naturalization require some act linking the child to the United States to occur before the child reaches 18 years of age.

*  *  *

In this difficult context of conferring citizenship on vast numbers of persons, the means adopted by Congress are in substantial furtherance of important governmental objectives. The fit between the means and the important end is "exceedingly persuasive." We have explained that an "exceedingly persuasive justification" is established "by showing at least that the classification serves 'important governmental objectives and that the discriminatory means employed' are 'substantially related to the achievement of those objectives.' " Section 1409 meets this standard.

## C

In analyzing § 1409(a)(4), we are mindful that the obligation it imposes with respect to the acquisition of citizenship by the child of a citizen father is minimal. This circumstance shows that Congress has not erected inordinate and unnecessary hurdles to the conferral of citizenship on the children of citizen fathers in furthering its important objectives. Only the least onerous of the three options provided for in § 1409(a)(4) must be satisfied. If the child has been legitimated under the law of the relevant jurisdiction, that will be the end of the matter. In the alternative, a father who has not legitimated his child by formal means need only make a written acknowledgement of paternity under oath in order to transmit citizenship to his child, hardly a substantial burden. Or, the father could choose to obtain a court order of paternity. The statute can be satisfied on the day of birth, or the next day, or for the next 18 years. In this case, the unfortunate, even tragic, circumstance is that Boulais did not pursue, or perhaps did not know of, these simple steps and alternatives. Any omission, however, does not nullify the statutory scheme.

Section 1409(a), moreover, is not the sole means by which the child of a citizen father can attain citizenship. An individual who fails to comply with '1409(a), but who has substantial ties to the United States, can seek citizenship in his or her own right, rather than via reliance on ties to a citizen parent. This option now may be foreclosed to Nguyen, but any bar is due to the serious nature of his criminal offenses not to an equal protection denial or to any supposed rigidity or harshness in the citizenship laws.

* * *

To fail to acknowledge even our most basic biological differences—such as the fact that a mother must be present at birth but the father need not be—risks making the guarantee of equal protection superficial, and so disserving it. Mechanistic classification of all our differences as stereotypes would operate to obscure those misconceptions and prejudices that are real. The distinction embodied in the statutory scheme here at issue is not marked by misconception and prejudice, nor does it show disrespect for either class. The difference between men and women in relation to the birth process is a real one, and the principle of equal protection does not forbid Congress to address the problem at hand in a manner specific to each gender.

The judgment of the Court of Appeals is Affirmed.

JUSTICE O'CONNOR, with whom JUSTICE SOUTER, JUSTICE GINSBURG, and JUSTICE BREYER join, dissenting.

In a long line of cases spanning nearly three decades, this Court has applied heightened scrutiny to legislative classifications based on sex. The Court today confronts another statute that classifies individuals on the basis of their sex. While the Court invokes heightened scrutiny, the manner in which it explains and applies this standard is a stranger to our precedents. Because the Immigration and Naturalization Service (INS) has not shown an exceedingly persuasive justification for the sex-based classification embodied in *8 U.S.C. § 1409*(a)(4)—*i.e.,* because it has failed to establish at least that the classification substantially relates to the achievement of important governmental objectives—I would reverse the judgment of the Court of Appeals.

Sex-based statutes, even when accurately reflecting the way most men or women behave, deny individuals opportunity. Such generalizations must be viewed not in isolation, but in the context of our Nation's " 'long and unfortunate history of sex discrimination.' " Sex-based generalizations both reflect and reinforce "fixed notions concerning the roles and abilities of males and females."

For these reasons, a party who seeks to defend a statute that classifies individuals on the basis of sex "must carry the burden of showing an 'exceedingly persuasive justification' for the classification." The defender of the classification meets this burden "only by showing at least that the classification serves 'important governmental objectives and that the discriminatory means employed' are 'substantially related to the achievement of those objectives.' "

Our cases provide significant guidance concerning the meaning of this standard and how a reviewing court is to apply it. This Court's instruction concerning the application of heightened scrutiny to sex-based classifications stands in stark contrast to our elucidation of the rudiments of rational basis review. To begin with, under heightened scrutiny, "the burden of justification is demanding and it rests entirely on [the party defending the classification]." *Virginia, supra, at 533* [United States v. Virginia, 518 U.S. 515 (1996)]. Under rational basis scrutiny, by contrast, the defender of the classification "has no obligation to produce evidence to sustain the rationality of a statutory classification."

\* \* \*

The most important difference between heightened scrutiny and rational basis review, of course, is the required fit between the means employed and the ends served. Under heightened scrutiny, the discriminatory means must be "substantially related" to an actual and important governmental interest. Under rational basis scrutiny, the means need only be "rationally related" to a conceivable and legitimate state end.

The fact that other means are better suited to the achievement of governmental ends therefore is of no moment under rational basis review.

\* \* \*

But because we require a much tighter fit between means and ends under heightened scrutiny, the availability of sex-neutral alternatives to a sex-based classification is often highly probative of the validity of the classification.

The gravest defect in the Court's reliance on this interest, however, is the insufficiency of the fit between § 1409(a)(4)'s discriminatory means and the asserted end. Section 1409(c) imposes no particular burden of proof on mothers wishing to convey citizenship to their children. By contrast, § 1409(a)(1), which petitioners do not challenge before this Court, requires that "a blood relationship between the person and the father [be] established by clear and convincing evidence." Atop § 1409(a)(1), § 1409(a)(4) requires legitimation, an acknowledgment of paternity in writing under oath, or an adjudication of paternity before the child reaches the age of 18. It is difficult to see what § 1409(a)(4) accomplishes in furtherance of "assuring that a biological parent-child relationship exists," *ante,* at 7, that § 1409(a)(1) does not achieve on its own. The virtual certainty of a biological link that modern DNA testing affords reinforces the sufficiency of § 1409(a)(1).

It is also difficult to see how § 1409(a)(4)'s limitation of the time allowed for obtaining proof of paternity substantially furthers the assurance of a blood relationship. Modern DNA testing, in addition to providing accuracy unmatched by other methods of establishing a biological link, essentially negates the evidentiary significance of the passage of time. Moreover, the application of § 1409(a)(1)'s "clear and convincing evidence" requirement can account for any effect that the passage of time has on the quality of the evidence.

\* \* \*

Indeed, the idea that a mother's presence at birth supplies adequate assurance of an opportunity to develop a relationship while a father's presence at birth does not would appear to rest only on an overbroad sex-based generalization. A mother may not have an opportunity for a relationship if the child is removed from his or her mother on account of alleged abuse or neglect, or if the child and mother are separated by tragedy, such as disaster or war, of the sort apparently present in this case. There is no reason, other than stereotype, to say that fathers who are present at birth lack an opportunity for a relationship on similar terms. The "physical differences between men and women," *Virginia, 518 U.S. at 533,* therefore do not justify § 1409(a)(4)'s discrimination.

# D. MARIANNE BLAIR & MERLE H. WEINER, STATE PRACTICES TOWARD NONMARITAL CHILDREN AND FATHERS

Family Law in the World Community 986–87 (2003).

In the United States, the Supreme Court has held that states can impose certain procedural requirements on nonmarital children before these nonmarital children can inherit intestate from their fathers. *See* Lalli V. Lalli, 439 U.S. 259 (1978). Consequently, there have sometimes been time limits for establishing paternity during the father's lifetime, or heightened pleading or evidentiary burdens. Recently, the U.S. Supreme Court upheld a distinction between nonmarital children living abroad who seek to acquire American nationality depending upon whether the child's mother or father is an American citizen... acquisition of American citizenship for a nonmarital child born abroad to an American father requires that a number of steps be taken. These steps include that a blood relationship between the child and father be established by clear and convincing evidence, that the father agree in writing to provide financial support for the child until the child reaches the age of eighteen years, and that before the child reached eighteen either a court establishes paternity, the father legitimates the child, or the father acknowledges paternity in writing under oath.

## Notes

1.   Is this case about immigration and citizenship, or about gender discrimination and equal protection? Compare and contrast the arguments set out in the majority opinion and the dissent. Which do you find more persuasive?

2.   Would it have made any difference if the Constitutional argument had focused on discrimination against non-marital children, as opposed to gender discrimination? As Professors Blair and Weiner summarize the decision in *Nguyen*:

> Using an intermediate level of scrutiny to evaluate the law's gender-based classifications, the Court stated that the law served the important governmental objectives of ensuring a biological parent-child relationship exists, and providing an opportunity for a parent-child relationship to develop. "To fail to acknowledge even our most basic biological differences—such as the fact that a mother must be present at birth but the father need not be—risks making the guarantee of equal protection superficial, and so disserving it," *Id*. at 2066. The Court also noted that Congress was afforded wide deference in the exercise of its immigration and naturalization power. *Id*. at 2065. Four justices vigorously dissented. Although the litigation focused on the alleged gender discrimi-

nation, the result probably would have been the same if the case had focused on discrimination between nonmarital and marital children. The standard applied to evaluate a gender discrimination claim is at least as strong as the standard applied to evaluate a discrimination claim by nonmarital children.

## CONVENTION ON THE RIGHTS OF THE CHILD
United Nations, 1989.
G.A. Document A/RES/44/25.

*Article 1*

For the purposes of the present Convention, a child means every human being below the age of eighteen years unless, under the law applicable to the child, majority is attained earlier.

*Article 2*

1.   States Parties shall respect and ensure the rights set forth in the present Convention to each child within their jurisdiction without discrimination of any kind, irrespective of the child's or his or her parent's or legal guardian's race, colour, sex, language, religion, political or other opinion, national, ethnic or social origin, property, disability, birth or other status.

2.   States Parties shall take all appropriate measures to ensure that the child is protected against all forms of discrimination or punishment on the basis of the status, activities, expressed opinions, or beliefs of the child's parents, legal guardians, or family members.

\* \* \*

*Article 7*

1.   The child shall be registered immediately after birth and shall have the right from birth to a name, the right to acquire a nationality and, as far as possible, the right to know and be cared for by his or her parents.

2.   States Parties shall ensure the implementation of these rights in accordance with their national law and their obligations under the relevant international instruments in this field, in particular where the child would otherwise be stateless.

## BARBARA STARK, BABY GIRLS FROM CHINA IN NEW YORK: A THRICE–TOLD TALE
2003 Utah L. Rev. 1231, 1293–95.

Historically, the illegitimate child was *filius nullius*, the child of no one, a nonperson. The child obviously had a mother, but an unmarried mother had no more legal status than her child. As feminist historian Gerda Lerner has explained, the law of legitimacy is grounded in patriarchy, in the idea of children as the property of the father.

This has been firmly repudiated in contemporary law. Under the Children's Convention, as well as under the family law of the United States and China, the adopted child is entitled to the same rights and legal status as a legitimate biological child. The rejection of illegitimacy as a status is grounded both in the recognition of women's equality and in the larger human rights project of which women's equality is a part. This project, in turn, is part of a larger normative shift from patriarchal authoritarianism to rights-centered egalitarianism. This shift is evident not only in the law, but in the bourgeoning numbers of out-of-wedlock births in the United States and western Europe. While laws renouncing illegitimacy are widespread, in practice the stigma remains strong in some parts of the world. International adoption enables babies born into a society where such a stigma still exists to grow up in a society where the stigma is less.

## HUGUES FULCHIRON, EGALITÉ, VÉRITÉ, STABIL-ITÉ: THE NEW FRENCH FILIATION LAW AFTER THE ORDONNANCE OF 4 JULY 2005

International Survey of Family Law 1, 203 (Andrew Bainham ed. 2006).

Thirty years after the great law of 3 January 1972, the ordonnance of 4 July 2005 has revolutionised French filiation law. Symbolically, the very categories of legitimate and natural filiation disappear. The same rules henceforth govern filiation in and out of wedlock. Advance notice had been given of the reform of family names and parental authority. In addition, in its main content, it commanded wide agreement. Nonetheless, directly and indirectly, it overturns French family law.

### *Notes*

1. Are there any reasons for discouraging, if not prohibiting, foreign adoptions of children born out of wedlock? *See* Part C of this Chapter, *Adoption*.

2. Why does Professor Fulchiron say that eradication of the distinction between 'legitimate' and 'natural' filiation "directly and indirectly ... overturns French family law"?

## JUNE CARBONE, LAW, POLITICS, RELIGION, AND THE CREATION OF NORMS FOR MARKET TRANSACTIONS: A REVIEW OF THE BIRTH OF SURROGACY IN ISRAEL BY D. KELLY WEISBERG

39 Fam. L.Q. 793, 800–801 (2005).

Israeli society is family-oriented, the government is explicitly pronatalist, and the Israeli medical profession has been in the forefront of reproductive technology for decades. Weisberg observes that Israelis feel particularly strong about the need to produce genetic offspring because of the legacy of the Holocaust (there were twenty million Jews worldwide in 1939, 13.5 million in 2004) and Israel's position as a Jewish enclave of five million surrounded by an Arab population thirty times larger with double the birthrate. The government provides universal health care and covers fertility treatments, including artificial insemination, in vitro fertilization, and ovum donation. Indeed, all Israeli women, irrespective of religion or marital status, have free unlimited access to in vitro fertilization up to the birth of two live children. In a society in which virtually all women marry (only 2% of Israeli women have not married by the age of forty) and the divorce rate is low (one in six Israeli marriages end in divorce compared to one of two in the U.S.), the pressures to reproduce are enormous. Carmel Shalev writes that: "The option of childlessness and its acceptance does not exist. Even alternative solutions such as intercountry adoption recede in the face of an unspoken imperative to realize genetic parenthood at whatever cost."

The importance of genetic offspring fueled creation of a sophisticated fertility industry. Israeli doctors pioneered innovations in fertilization techniques, and Israel has the highest concentration of IVF clinics on a per capita basis in the world. For women born without adequate uteruses, who suffered from repeated miscarriages, or who have had cancer or cancer treatments that interfere with their ability to carry a child, surrogacy offers the only way to produce genetic offspring. Once in vitro fertilization, with techniques pioneered by Israeli doctors, made it possible to ensure that the child would be genetically related to the intended parents, Israeli couples began to seek out surrogates abroad, lobby for subsidized Israeli doctors to perform the in vitro procedures in Israel, and ultimately challenge the validity of the government ban.

\* \* \*

After the initial births, the government declared a moratorium while it reviewed surrogacy procedures. A number of regulations adopted were similar to the Aloni Commission proposals intended to protect the surrogate. The new regulations standardized many of the contractual terms. They provided for the availability of psychological counseling for a period extending six months after the birth at the expense of the commissioning couple. They limited the permissible age and number of previous pregnancies by the surrogate and provided that she may perform no more than two surrogate births, both of which must be for the same family. They required the parties to agree in advance as to the nature and extent of contact, and the Approvals Committee took a more active role in screening applicants. Finally, the regulations provided for closer review of the compensation and for third-party transmission of payments to limit the opportunities for extortion, exploitation, nonpayment, and disputes.

Israel also adopted reforms intended to strengthen children's interests. The law, for example, limits surrogacy to two-parent couples, though it does not require marriage. Guidelines also require that intended fathers be no older than fifty-nine and intended mothers no older than forty-eight. And children born through surrogacy have an absolute right to learn their origins when they reach the age of majority.

\* \* \*

Weisberg concludes the book by emphasizing that surrogacy is now taking place in a global context. She reports the case of a British surrogate "inseminated in a Greek laboratory with sperm donated anonymously by an American at a Danish laboratory and mixed with the eggs of another British woman. The commissioning parents were an Italian man and his Portuguese wife who lived in France." And when the commissioning couple refused to accept the twin girls because they were the wrong gender, the surrogate arranged to have the babies adopted by a lesbian couple in California. Should the lesbian couple leave California, however, there is no guarantee their parentage will be recognized elsewhere.

Given the development of reproductive technology and the ease of international travel, the comprehensive regulation Weisberg seeks would have to be global. But the process of developing norms and practices that she describes so well in this book are local, the product, as she emphasizes, of religious, cultural, and national values and experiences. The book performs a valuable service in providing so comprehensive an account of law reform. It necessarily ends, however, with the evolution of understandings, even in the face of settled law, as an ongoing process.

## *Note*

How can the rights and interests of all the parties involved in globalized surrogacy be protected? If it is not possible to protect all of the parties' rights, whose are the most important? Who needs protection most?

# C. ADOPTION

International adoption brings children, often from less developed countries, into the homes of relatively affluent parents in the West. International adoptions have boomed in the United States since 1990, peaking at over 20,000 in 2004, and declining since then. This section addresses some of the legal issues raised by these new internationalized families. First, there may be technical problems arising from the lack of harmonization between different domestic laws. Second, international adoption may give rise to baby-selling or corruption in the children's countries of origin. Third, international adoptions may lead to 'wrongful' adoption claims, especially where serious medical conditions or histories of abuse are kept from prospective parents. This section concludes with an overview of the Hague Convention on Intercountry Adoption, which addresses some of these issues.

## MARRIAGE OF LUNINA AND POZDNYAKOV

Iowa Supreme Court, 1998.
584 N.W.2d 564.

\* \* \*

We have previously recognized that an adoption decree of a court of another nation is entitled to recognition if the court has jurisdiction to render it, at least to the extent of this state. *Corbett v. Stergios*, 257 Iowa 1387, 1391, 137 N.W.2d 266, 268 (1965). Given Ilya's failure to raise any objection below, this court must presume the certificate of adoption is valid and that Ilya adopted Olga in Azerbaijan in 1994.

### III. Iowa Code Section 600.15(2)

Ilya alternatively argues that even if an adoption occurred in Azerbaijan, Iowa Code section 600.15(2) required that further adoption proceedings occur in Iowa in order for the adoption to be valid. Iowa Code section 600.15(2) provides:

If an adoption has occurred in the minor person's country of origin, a further adoption must occur in the state where the adopting parents reside in accordance with the adoption laws of the state.

The district court rejected this argument and found a further adoption under section 600.15(2) is only required in situations in which U.S. residents adopt a foreign child in the child's country or origin. The district court concluded the statute did not apply in a case like this where a resident of Azerbaijan had adopted a child in Azerbaijan and then subsequently moved to Iowa.

## ADOPTION OF DAFINA T.G.

Surrogate's Court, New York, 1994.
161 Misc.2d 106, 613 N.Y.S.2d 329.

* * *

The court is cognizant of the fact that many proceedings for re-adoption pursuant to DRL 115–a(8) are complicated by the lack of due authentication of the foreign adoption documents. In this case, the court's file contains the original adoption documents from the Romanian court wherein the adoption of this child was finalized in 1991. The documents, however, are not properly authenticated although the court is satisfied as to their genuineness.

Accordingly, in re-adoption proceedings wherein due authentication of foreign adoption documents is lacking, the court will permit the proceeding to proceed to finalization in the absence of such authentication where the court is satisfied as to the genuineness of the documents submitted and hence the proof of the finalization of the adoption outside the United States as required by DRL 115–a(8). Where original foreign adoption documents are not available or where the court is not satisfied as to their adequacy, the court will nevertheless consider permitting the matter to proceed to finalization as permitted by DRL 115–a(6) where the child has resided with the adoptive couple for at least one year and where a home study conducted after the expiration of the one year period recommends approval of the petition.

## BARBARA STARK, ADOPTION

International Family Law: An Introduction 53–56 (2005).

Adoption is the process through which a legal relationship is established between a child and a person or couple who are not her biological parents. The primary purpose of adoption is to assure an otherwise parentless child a stable, secure and loving home. In addition, adoption enables those who want a child, or more children, to create or enlarge their families.

In intercountry adoption, this may be achieved through a simple adoption, in which the relationship with the child's biological parents is not completely severed, or a full adoption, in which it is. Termination of the parent/child relationship may be involuntary, initiated by the State in cases of neglect or abuse. In the alternative, the biological parents may terminate the relationship voluntarily, through abandonment of the child, or by surrendering the child to an agency or to the adoptive parents. In many States, a surrender is not valid unless it occurs after the birth. That is, a biological mother cannot be held to a pre-birth agreement to give the child up for adoption. This reflects the belief that a mother cannot agree to give up the baby in the abstract; only after the birth can she fully understand what she is giving up. Often there is an additional period in which she can revoke her decision.

This kind of protection may be extended to both parents. In the Czech Republic, for example, under the Family Law Reform of 1998, the parents may submit a written declaration to a court or appropriate agency in which they agree to their infant's adoption. This consent is not valid, however, unless it is given after the infant is six weeks old. In general, if the biological father is married to the child's mother, he also has rights to the child. If he is not married to the child's mother, he usually has fewer rights and may have none. If he has parental rights but does not want to exercise them, it is usually a simple matter for him to relinquish them. In many States, for example, he need only sign a statement to that effect.

Once the child's relationship with the biological parents is legally terminated, the child is eligible for adoption. Standards for those who are eligible to adopt are established by the national law of the country in which the adoption will take place. This may be the child's country of origin, the adoptive parents' country of residence, or both. These standards for adoptive parents vary widely, but may include: minimum (or maximum) age, proof of the ability to financially care for the child, and the absence of other children in the family.

Screening is often delegated to public or private agencies, which may impose additional requirements. In China, for example, adoptive parents are likely to be asked why they are adopting a Chinese child, whether they have any children now (either adopted or birth), details regarding their family background, an explanation as to their childlessness, and for assurances that the adopted child will be well-treated. A home study, in which a social worker visits the parents in the home where they plan to raise the child, is frequently part of the screening process. In countries where there are more parents seeking babies than babies needing parents, screening can become quite restrictive.

Once the parents have been screened, the child may be placed with them and the adoption provisionally granted. There may be a mandatory waiting period, typically between six months and a year, before the order of adoption is finalized. This final order typically gives the parents and child all of the legal rights and obligations of a biological family.

Intercountry adoption raises many important legal issues, some of which may be very sensitive. National laws regarding the disclosure of the identity of the biological parents vary widely, for example, as discussed in Section 3 below. The requirement of voluntary relinquishment, similarly, may be presumed from the circumstances or may be satisfied only by a formal oath before a court. In addition to the distinction between 'full' and 'simple' adoptions, noted above, some States create other categories for adoptions. The Czech Republic, for example, allows two types of adoption, one revocable on 'important grounds,' the other irrevocable. The legal issues which must be addressed in intercountry adoption are complicated, finally, by the emigration and citizenship laws of the involved States. These may require that a child be adopted before leaving her State of origin, and be adopted again under the laws of the parents' State.

### Agency or Independent Adoption

Some States allow adoptions to be arranged independently, that is, without the supervision of a State-authorized agency. In an independent adoption, the prospective parents may deal directly with the biological parent, or they may hire an intermediary. Independent adoptions must comply with all applicable local or national laws governing adoption in general, such as prohibitions against baby-selling and requirements for voluntary consent. But they are free of the additional requirements that may be imposed by agencies, whether as part of an effort to reduce the pool of applicants or to further what the agency views as the best interests of the child. Instead of agency criteria, independent adoptions may be based on the specific preferences of the parties, such as a biological mother's preference for parents of a particular religious denomination.

A major risk in an independent adoption is that if the adoption is not finalized—for whatever reason—the prospective parents, as well as the biological parent, must begin the process all over again. The prospective parents may lose any money advanced—for counseling, legal fees or medical care—depending on the terms of the contract between the parties. Even if they are entitled to reimbursement, as a practical matter it may be impossible to recover funds already spent by an impoverished mother. The psychological costs of a failed adoption may be devastating, especially where the prospective parents have bonded with the child.

While these psychological costs are not entirely avoided in an agency adoption, they may be reduced. Once the prospective parents are approved to receive a baby, the agency will generally find them another baby if an initial placement is not finalized through no fault of the parents. This should be explicitly set out in the agreement with the agency, however. Agency obligations vary from State to State, so prospective parents, as well as surrendering parents, must be wary. Risk-averse prospective parents may decide to work through two agencies, one in the sending and one in the receiving State. A domestic agency with a history of successfully finalized adoptions from the sending country—and with ties to agencies there—is a relatively safe choice, but it is not always an option.

### Alternatives to Adoption

It should be noted that some States, particularly Muslim States in the Middle East, do not recognize 'adoption' as described here. In such States responsibility for a parentless child is established through a system of kafalah, or guardianship, in which relatives of the child assume responsibility for the care of the child, who remains identified with the biological family. Kafalah is not subject to the Hague Convention on Intercounty Adoption and it will not be addressed in this chapter.

### Notes

1. The U.S. signed the Intercountry Adoption Convention in 1994 and enacted implementing legislation in 2000. Intercountry Adoption Act of 2000, 42 U.S.C. § 14901 et seq. The Convention will become effective in the U.S. when the regulations are complete and the providers accredited. The Act provides for recognition of adoptions finalized in other Convention countries. § 14 931(b). Would this have affected the decisions in *Dafina T.G.* and *Lunina*? How?

2. From 1995 to 2005, American families adopted 18,298 Guatemalan babies. Mothers in Guatemala are routinely paid for putting their babies up for adoption, although baby-selling is illegal under the Hague Convention, to which Guatemala is a party. As one commentator observes, "Critics of the adoption system here—privately run and uniquely streamlined—say it has turned this country of 12 million people into a virtual baby farm that supplies infants as if they were a commodity. The United States is the No. 1 destination. Marc Lacey, "Guatemala System is Scrutinized as Americans Rush In to Adopt", N.Y. Times 1, 8, November 5, 2006. What will happen to the babies if Washington stops approving adoptions from countries that do not meet the standards of the Hague Convention? What are the alternatives? See, e.g., Laura Daly, Note, To Regulate or Not to Regulate: The Need for Compliance with International Norms by Guatemala and Cooperation by the United States, 45 Fam. Ct. Rev. 621 (2007).

# CONVENTION ON THE RIGHTS OF THE CHILD

United Nations, 1989.
G.A. Document A/RES/44/25.

## *Article 20*

1.   A child temporarily or permanently deprived of his or her family environment, or in whose own best interests cannot be allowed to remain in that environment, shall be entitled to special protection and assistance provided by the State.

2.   States Parties shall in accordance with their national laws ensure alternative care for such a child.

3.   Such care could include, inter alia, foster placement, kafalah of Islamic law, adoption or if necessary placement in suitable institutions for the care of children. When considering solutions, due regard shall be paid to the desirability of continuity in a child's upbringing and to the child's ethnic, religious, cultural and linguistic background.

## *Article 21*

States Parties that recognize and/or permit the system of adoption shall ensure that the best interests of the child shall be the paramount consideration and they shall:

(a) Ensure that the adoption of a child is authorized only by competent authorities who determine, in accordance with applicable law and procedures and on the basis of all pertinent and reliable information, that the adoption is permissible in view of the child's status concerning parents, relatives and legal guardians and that, if required, the persons concerned have given their informed consent to the adoption on the basis of such counselling as may be necessary;

(b) Recognize that inter-country adoption may be considered as an alternative means of child's care, if the child cannot be placed in a foster or an adoptive family or cannot in any suitable manner be cared for in the child's country of origin;

(c) Ensure that the child concerned by inter-country adoption enjoys safeguards and standards equivalent to those existing in the case of national adoption,

(d) Take all appropriate measures to ensure that, in inter-country adoption, the placement does not result in improper financial gain for those involved in it;

(e) Promote, where appropriate, the objectives of the present article by concluding bilateral or multilateral arrangements or agreements, and endeavour, within this framework, to ensure that the placement of the child in another country is carried out by competent authorities or organs.

# BARBARA STARK, ADOPTION

International Family Law: An Introduction 57–59 (2005).

The full text of the Hague Convention on Adoption can be found at http://www.hcch.net/e/conventions/text33e.html. Rather than setting forth detailed substantive law, the Convention takes into account the different approaches of State parties to issues such as independent adoptions, the use of private intermediaries and the disclosure of identifying information. These differences are resolved by allocating responsibility for different stages of the adoption process to the sending or receiving State. In addition, the Convention allows either State to veto the action of the other at various points during the process, or under the comprehensive veto power of Art. 17(c), which requires the Central Authorities of both States to affirmatively agree that the adoption should proceed.

Chapter I sets forth the scope of the Convention, which applies to adoptions involving residents of different Contracting States. Art. 2. Chapter I also clarifies the Convention's objectives, specifically, 'to ensure that intercountry adoptions take place in the best interests of the child and with respect for his or her fundamental rights as recognized in international law.' Art. 1(a).

Chapter II establishes the requirements for intercountry adoptions, including, importantly, a determination 'that an intercountry adoption is in the child's best interest ... [after] possibilities for placement of the child within the State of origin have been given due consideration.' (emphasis added.) This provision reflects the assumption that it is in the child's best interest to remain in her country of origin, if she can be properly cared for there. Unlike the Convention on the Rights of the Child (CRC, Art. 21), however, the Hague Convention assumes that it is better for a child to be adopted abroad than raised in an institution in her country of origin.

Chapter II further requires the freely given consent, after counseling if needed, of all persons 'whose consent is necessary,' including that of a mature child. It expressly prohibits 'payment or compensation of any kind' to induce such consents. These provisions prevent the kind of problems that followed the U.S. 'Operation Baby Lift' at the end of its war in Vietnam. Babies were 'rescued' from orphanages in the final days of the war and placed with families in the U.S. It was later discovered that many of these babies had been placed in orphanages by their families with the understanding that such placement would be temporary, and that the child would be returned to its family when it was safe. The premature 'rescue' of these children resulted in several lawsuits, and courts ordered some of these babies returned to their biological parents... Finally, Chapter II addresses the placement of the child in the receiving State (Art. 5), requiring that the competent authorities of that State 'have determined that the prospective adoptive parents are eligible and suited to adopt' and that the children will be 'authorized to enter and reside permanently in that State.' Art. 5.1(c).

Chapter III requires the Contracting State to designate a Central Authority which will carry out the State's duties under the Convention. This allows other States, as well as agencies and prospective adoptive parents, to know who they should be dealing with in what is often a complex bureaucracy. The Central Authority is also responsible for providing information regarding national adoption laws and otherwise cooperating with their counterparts in other Contracting States. This includes the duty to 'reply, in so far as is permitted by the law of their State, to justified requests from other Central Authorities or public authorities for information about a particular adoption situation.' Art. 9(e).

The Central Authority is ultimately responsible for ensuring that adoptions proceed in accordance with Chapter IV of the Convention. These duties may be delegated to other public authorities or 'duly accredited' bodies, such as private adoption agencies. Under Art. 22(2), a State may declare that these functions may also be performed by other 'qualified' bodies or persons, such as lawyers or social workers. A sending State may specify, however, that adoption of its children may only take place where such functions are performed by public or accredited bodies.

The Procedural Requirements set out in Chapter IV include the preparation of a report about the applicants 'including information about their identity, eligibility and suitability to adopt, background, family and medical history, social environment, reasons for adoption, ability to undertake an intercountry adoption, as well as the characteristics of the children for whom they would be qualified to care.' Art. 15. This report is to be prepared by the Central Authority of the receiving State. After determining that a child is adoptable, the Central Authority of the child's State of origin is required to 'transmit to the Central Authority of the receiving State its report on the child, ... taking care not to reveal the identity of the mother and the father if, in the State of origin, these identities may not be disclosed.' Art. 16(d)

Chapter V requires Contracting States to recognize and give full legal effect to adoptions made in accordance with the Convention. Art. 23. Such recognition may be refused 'only if the adoption is manifestly contrary to its public policy, taking into account the best interests of the child.' Art. 24. This contemplates simple as well as full adoptions. Under Art. 26, recognition explicitly includes recognition of the 'legal parent-child relationship between the child and his or her adoptive parents' and 'the termination of a pre-existing relationship between the child and his or her mother and father, if the adoption has this effect in the Contracting State where it was made.' Under Art. 26, the law of the State of adoption governs. Under Art. 27, however, if the sending State grants a simple adoption, the receiving State may convert such adoption to a full adoption *unless* the consents were specifically limited.

Limited deference to the domestic laws of the Contracting States is also shown in Art. 29, which prohibits contact between the perspective adoptive parents and the biological parents until the required consents have been given, *unless* such contact is 'pursuant to conditions' established by the State of origin. Thus, independent adoptions are allowed under the Convention if such adoptions are allowed in the child's State of origin. Art. 30.1, similarly, requires the State to 'preserve' identifying information and medical histories of the child's biological parents, but leaves the question of actual access to such information to State law:

> (1) The competent authorities of a Contracting State shall ensure that information held by them concerning the child's origin, in particular information concerning the identity of his or her parents, as well as the medical history, is preserved.

> (2) They shall ensure that the child or his or her represen-tative has access to such information, under appropriate guid-ance, in so far as is permitted by the law of that State.

Other provisions reflect greater consensus among Contracting States, and their shared intention to establish some common stan-dards. Article 32, for example, provides that: '(1) No one shall derive improper financial or other gain from an activity related to an intercountry adoption. (2) Only costs and expenses, including reasonable professional fees may be charged or paid.' Art. 40, similarly, prohibits States from taking reservations to the Conven-tion. Some of the Convention's requirements are vague and the Convention expressly contemplates variations in domestic law. The Convention nevertheless establishes clear bottom lines B with re-gard to the parents' and child's rights, reporting requirements, monitoring and administration B to which all Contracting Parties are bound.

# MARGARET F. BRINIG, CHOOSE THE LESSER EVIL: COMMENTS ON BESHAROV'S "CHILD ABUSE REALITIES"

8 Va. J. Soc. Pol'y & L. 205 (2000).

In Lord v. Living Bridges [1999 WL 562713 (E.D. Pa. 1999)], the Lords approached an American adoption agency, Living Bridges, looking to adopt Mexican children. The couple noted that because they had a history of health problems themselves they "needed children in good health," and specifically mentioned that they were not capable of caring for children with "special needs." The Lords were told about a "premier" Mexican orphanage with which Living Bridges dealt and were told that the three girls they could adopt were "sweet and loving," "bright" and "had not been abused." Unfortunately, most of these representations proved to be untrue. Most of the children in the orphanage had been abused, including the three girls placed in the Lord's custody. The orphanage had records showing that the girls were the victims of physical abuse and, in the case of one, physical torture. One of the girls had intellectual impairments, possible brain damage and psychological problems. Almost immediately after placement, one of the girls showed signs of serious mental illness requiring hospitalization. Another was diagnosed with serious emotional problems that required therapy, and two of the girls had acted out violently. These problems cost the Lords not only money, but also caused severe emotional distress, and, in Mr. Lord's case, substantial cardiac problems. The Lords sued the placing agency for wrongful adoption, fraudulent and negligent misrepresentation, negligent nondisclosure, and intentional and negligent infliction of emotional distress.

## *Note*

Americans adopted approximately 48,500 children from China between 1989 and 2005. Almost 8,000 children were adopted from China in 2005 alone. See Joe McDonald, AP, "China Now Nixes Adoption Applicants Who are Obese or Single," Deseret News (Salt Lake City), Dec. 20, 2006. But China imposed new restrictions on foreign adoptions on May 1, 2007. As of that date, applicants who are unmarried, or have been married less than two years, as well as applicants who are obese, over 50 or who take antidepressants, are barred.

You represent a slightly overweight couple who have been married for eighteen months. The woman is 52; her husband is 49. He has been on a mild anti-depressant for the past four years. They are aware of the new restrictions, which they consider offensive, and still want to adopt a baby from China. They would like to try, and to challenge the restrictions if they fail. How do you advise them?

## BARBARA STARK, LOST BOYS AND FORGOTTEN GIRLS: INTERCOUNTRY ADOPTION, HUMAN RIGHTS, AND AFRICAN CHILDREN

22 St. Louis U. Pub. L. Rev. 275 (2003).

The "right to culture" in international human rights law is considered a group right, typically claimed by an indigenous group or other ethnic minority within a larger society. While the parameters of the right to culture are not precise, it generally encompasses the right to "a way of life"—language, customs, music, celebrations, food, and rituals—customarily practiced by the group. In Sweden, for example, the right to culture of the indigenous Sami has been recognized and linked to their traditional reliance on reindeer. Thus, under Swedish law, the Sami are assured the land needed to sustain a herd and continue their traditional practices. Group rights are grounded in the recognition that the group's traditions offer the richest, most satisfying way of life for its members, as well as a sense of pride and identity which may be particularly important for those living within a majority culture that marginalizes them. The right to culture is also crucial to the group's survival as a group, enabling it to maintain a distinct cultural identity and to resist pressure to assimilate.

The CRC explicitly endorses these assumptions. It assumes that it is better for a child to remain in her country of origin, even in an institution, than be sent to a foreign country where she will presumably be an ethnic minority. This preference for institutionalization in the country of origin over intercountry adoption is echoed in the African Charter. As Abdullahi An Na'im has observed, "If [western critics] encourage young girls to repudiate the integrity and cohesion of their own minority culture, how can the theorists then help to sustain the identity and human dignity of those women?"

The Hague Convention on Adoption, however, takes a different view. Under the Hague Convention, placement with a family abroad is preferred over institutionalization. In Minister for Welfare and Population Development v. Fitzpatrick, the Constitutional Court of South Africa held that intercountry adoptions could not be barred under the South African Constitution. This decision has opened the door for intercountry adoption of AIDS orphans, healthy children who have lost their families to AIDS and would otherwise languish in underfunded orphanages. This reflects the painful reality that in some cases, remaining in Africa may not be in the best interest of the child. While this decision obviously has no extraterritorial impact, the South African Court is highly regarded and its decisions are studied not only throughout Africa, but throughout the world.

### 3. TRANSRACIAL ADOPTION

Some of the Girls, along with other African orphans, might be adopted by African–Americans. Because of the demographics of adoption in the U.S., however, the majority of these children are likely to be adopted by white couples or single white women.

Interracial adoption is permitted in every state in the U.S .. Indeed, any effort to prohibit it would be subject to constitutional challenge as a violation of the Fourteenth Amendment equal protection guarantees. But many agencies have been reluctant to place Black children with white parents. The Association of Black Social Workers strongly opposed such placements for 30 years, on the grounds that they are not in the best interest of Black children. As Twila Perry recently observed, "The researchers on transracial adoption are still virtually unanimous in their conclusion that it remains preferable for Black children to be placed with Black adoptive parents, if possible."

James S. Bowen argues, for example, that white parents are unlikely to provide Black children with "Black survival skills", including: several learned abilities: to ignore (racial) insults, to decipher the appropriateness of fighting back or submission, to emphasize Black strength, beauty and worth as a countermeasure to the denigration of Blackness in America ... to evaluate objectively and subjectively the level of nepotistic advantage or same-group favoritism which precludes opportunities and advancement in education, employment and business. As Professor Derrick Bell has argued, moreover, because of the long and bitter history of slavery and racism in this country, discrimination against Blacks has been "particularly vicious." Domestic transracial adoptions involving the adoption of Black children by white parents has been problematic. As Black adoptee Susan Harris says, "I loved my parents, and I know that they loved me. I would not have traded them in for anyone, although I would have traded the all-white environment for an integrated one. And I know plenty of African–American transracial adoptees who feel the same."

In 1994, however, Congress enacted the Howard M. Metzenbaum Multiethnic Placement Act of 1994 ("MPA"). As amended by the Interethnic Adoption Provisions of 1996, any agency that receives federal financial assistance is prohibited from "delaying or denying a child's foster care or adoptive placement on the basis of the child's or the prospective parents' race, color, or national origin." Thus, race would not bar the Girls' placement in the U.S., although racism remains a factor to be taken into account. While recognizing "race" as an indeterminate concept, Professor Woodhouse, reject[s] the notion that their indeterminacy forecloses discussion of race in child placement. My premise is that race and culture of origin, no matter how hard to define with satisfying logic, do matter to children and therefore should matter in adoption law. They may well be contingent and socially constructed, but children's awareness of race and group identity indicate that they are 'real' for the purposes that matter her—the fostering and protection of children's identity.

The Girls would lose their foster families, their culture, language, religion, traditions, and friends. For some of them, however, these would not be major losses. First, as described previously, their role in their foster families is often that of unpaid servants. Second, they may be "sold" for a bride-price. Third, if they are ever repatriated to the Sudan, as women they would become second class citizens, since subordination on the basis of sex is legal in the Sudan and well-entrenched in domestic law. Fourth, the camps are dangerous. Finally, those Girls who have been raped and are outcasts have no future in Africa.

## SUZANA KRALIJĆ, LEGAL REGULATION OF ADOPTION IN SLOVENIA—DO WE NEED CHANGE?

International Survey of Family Law 1, 403–404,
405–406 (Andrew Bainham ed. 2006).

### INTERNATIONAL ADOPTIONS IN SLOVENIA— DESCRIPTION OF THE STATUS QUO

As mentioned, in Slovenia there are a lot more potential adopters than children available. This situation existed before in former Yugoslavia but owing to poor regulation in the other Yugoslav republics, Slovenian couples mainly adopted children from Macedonia, Kosovo, and Bosnia and Herzegovina. From independence, these internal adoptions became international.

Even today, when in Slovenia there is an interest in the adoption of foreign children, the interest is directed towards children coming from the countries of former Yugoslavia, mainly Macedonia and Bosnia and Herzegovina. However, none of these countries has signed the Hague Convention on Inter–Country Adoption, neither has Slovenia signed any bilateral agreement with a foreign country, in spite of the attempts made over the years. Yet countries being economically sand socially weaker are reluctant to enter such agreements, since every country protects its own citizens. However, Slovenia and Macedonia signed a letter of intent in February 2005 by which they expressed their readiness to start negotiations on the conclusion of an agreement on international adoptions. The draft agreement was prepared on the Slovenian side and will determine the conditions and proceedings for introducing international adoptions and guarantee the adoption will be carried out in the best interest of the child and that the rights of the child will be respected in accordance with recognized international law. The agreement between Slovenia and Macedonia is the first agreement of the sort to determine the proceedings of adoption. The Ministry of Labor, Family and Social Affairs planned the signing of this agreement for Autumn 2005, and the first children from Macedonia will be adopted by Slovenian couples after the signing of the agreement on international adoptions at the beginning of 2006. In spite of the agreement, we do not expect a significant rise in the number of adoptions in Slovenia, since the preparation for international adoption will demand readiness for children from a different cultural, religious and national surrounding than that of the adopters.

At the CSW in Maribor, being the largest in Slovenia, there have already been two single adoptions (where one of the spouses adopted the child of her or her partner) where the children were foreign citizens, i.e. citizens of White Russia and Ukraine, living in Slovenia. In this case, the proceedings were carried out through the Ministry of Labor, Family, and Social Affairs.

The question of international adoptions became especially pertinent at the end of 2004, when some Asian countries were hit by the tsunami. Immediately 'market offers of orphan children' for adoption emerged. But, because countries avoid international adoptions in such cases, especially when the primary principle in adoption is the principle of the best interest of the child, in the affected countries a moratorium on international adoptions was put in place. It is the task of the state to find the closest relatives of the child. That could not have been dones since the first offers were made on the second day of the tsunami. Tracing relatives under those conditions can take years. But, because in cases of adoption, internal as well as international, times runs against the children, it is knows that adopters are much easier to find than young children. On the other hand, the possibility of finding the child's parents reduces from year to year. In addition these children, who usually live their childhood in different institutions or fall into the hands of people using them for prostitution, slave labor or as 'organ donors', have to be considered as well.

\* \* \*

### CONCLUSION

In Slovenia, in economic terms, demand still exceeds supply. This means that there are many more potential adopters waiting to adopt a child than there are potential children available. In spite of Slovenia being a signatory of the Hague Convention on Inter–Country Adoption, there are practically no international adoptions. In Slovenia, soon, the first bilateral agreement, i.e. with Macedonia, will be signed, opening the path for Slovenian adopters to adopt Macedonian children, but here the question arises whether the number of adoptions will really rise. In the case of international adoptions even more preparations relating to future adopters will be necessary because different cultural, religious and national circumstances will be brought together.

In the same way, it is necessary to mention that between internal and international adoptions there are essential differences of which potential adopters should be informed. Couples deciding for international adoption from abroad look for the child by themselves, while for internal adoptions the CSW looks for the child. In international adoption the adopters also make contact in the country from which they wish to adopt a child by themselves with the institution there and send it an application for adoption. International adoption will demand much more personal, as well as financial, investment from the would-be adopters.

However, internal adoptions also reveal certain problems. Frequently, the children remain in foster families or move from one family to another for too long a time, which results in negative consequences for the child's whole life. In cases where it is obvious that the child will not be able to return to the original family, proceedings for adoption have to be advanced.

### *Notes*

1.  Why should adoption agencies, and adoption lawyers, get paid while birth mothers get nothing? Should birth mothers be reimbursed for their expenses, including medical expenses? What about their time? Is reproduction 'work'?

2. Birth parents may be giving up more than they think. The father of the Malawian boy who Madonna tried to adopt, for example, said, "Had they told us that Madonna wanted to adopt my son and make him her own son, we would not have agreed to that . . . I cannot read or write so I relied on what the officials told me, that the papers said Madonna would look after the child the way the orphanage planned to educate him, and then he comes back to me." "Boy's Father Now Opposes Madonna Adoption," N.Y. Times Oct. 23, 2006. The matter was argued before the High Court, during which the Human Rights Consultative Committee, an alliance of 67 human rights groups, contended that Malawi laws forbid international adoption, "even by celebrities". *Id.*

3. Problems in the countries of origin affect prospective parents as well as the children they hope to adopt. In the Ukraine, for example when the director of the new Department for Adoptions resigned, the futures of 90,000 orphans were left up in the air. This included children who had visited their prospective parents in the U.S., and were hoping to become part of a permanent family. As one commentator notes,

> In the largely unregulated world of international adoptions, these programs often lead to happily-ever-after, but sometimes end painfully. Ukraine and Russia place formidable obstacles in the path of parents, among them inaccurate information about children's availability and health status. Multiple families can wind up competing for the same child. And children themselves know they are auditioning for what the industry calls their "forever families." Then there is an entrenched system of favors—requests for cash or gifts from facilitators, translators, judges and others who handle the mechanics of adoption overseas.

Jane Gross, "A Taste of Family Life in U.S., But Adoption Is in Limbo," N.Y. Times, Jan. 13, 2007 at A1, A12. How would you advise prospective parents, who had paid fees to American and Ukrainian agencies and developed a strong attachment to a child, if they asked you whether there was any alternative to returning 'their' child to the orphanage in the Ukraine at the end of her visit?

# Chapter 5

# PARENTAL RIGHTS AND RESPONSIBILITIES

## A.  CUSTODY AND VISITATION

Laws governing child custody around the world are almost universally based on a principle of protecting the child's welfare, often referred to as the "best interests of the child." This standard is also embraced in the United Nations Convention on the Rights of the Child, excerpted below. In different cultures and legal systems, however, the standard is understood to mean different things. See generally Philip Alston, ed., The Best Interests of the Child: Reconciling Culture and Human Rights (1994). For a general survey of different national laws, see Symposium on Comparative Custody Law, 39 Fam. L.Q. 247 (2005).

### HOSAIN v. MALIK
Maryland Court of Special Appeals, 1996.
108 Md.App. 284, 671 A.2d 988.

DAVIS, JUDGE.

* * *

FACTS

This is a long and bitter child custody dispute involving orders of courts in both Maryland and Pakistan. Not too long ago, these parties and their dispute were before this Court in *Malik v. Malik*, 99 Md.App. 521, 638 A.2d 1184 (1994), which we decided on March 30, 1994. Needless to say, with the battle still raging, the parties have returned once again to this Court. * * *

As a matter of background, we recite the facts of this case as stated in *Malik*:

The parties to this appeal are battling for custody of their daughter (the child), who was born in Karachi, Pakistan on September 11, 1983. . . . [T]he child's father . . . is a citizen of Pakistan. [T]he child's mother, also a citizen of Pakistan, has obtained a student visa that permits her to remain in this country on a temporary basis. The parties were married on June 20, 1982 and lived together until September of 1990, at which time the child was attending St. Joseph's Convent School in Karachi.

On September 15, 1990, [the mother] left the marital home and moved in with her parents. She took the child with her. [The father] sued for custody. When [the mother] learned of [the father's] lawsuit, she fled the country, taking the child with her. Soon thereafter, [the mother] moved into the home of a man with whom she has continued to live and by whom she conceived a son who was born in 1991. [The mother] was represented by counsel in the Pakistani custody proceeding. She refused, however, to appear in person. She also refused to obey the judge's order that the child be produced. It appears that the judge did consider a written statement submitted by [the mother], but awarded custody to [the father].

Having obtained legal custody of his daughter, [the father] set out to find her. [The mother] hid the child from [the father] for over two years. In 1992, [the father's] private detectives were finally able to locate the child and [the mother] in Baltimore County. Once she realized that she had been discovered and that [the father] was about to seek enforcement of the order granting him custody of his daughter, [the mother] filed a complaint in the Circuit Court for Baltimore County, requesting custody of the child and a restraining order against [the father]. At the conclusion of an emergency hearing, the trial judge decided that the Circuit Court for Baltimore County had jurisdiction to determine custody, that the Pakistani custody order was not entitled to comity, that temporary custody should be granted to [the mother], and that [the father] should be enjoined from going within three hundred feet of the child, [the mother] or their residence.

The parties point out to this Court that appellant fled to the U.S. from Pakistan with the child shortly *before*—not after—appellee filed a petition for custody in Pakistan. In this regard, we stand corrected. Additionally, appellant has since married the man by whom she had a son.

In *Malik*, the father presented the following question for our review: "Did the chancellor err in exercising jurisdiction when custody proceedings were pending in a foreign country?" * * *

[W]e held that "the circuit court should decline to exercise jurisdiction unless persuaded that the Pakistani court either (1) did not apply the best interest of the child standard when it awarded custody to [the father], or (2) arrived at its decision by applying a law (whether substantive, evidentiary, or procedural) so contrary to Maryland public policy as to undermine confidence in the outcome of the trial." Accordingly, we remanded the case to the circuit court for an evidentiary hearing on these issues. In so doing, we set forth the law for the circuit court to apply in determining whether the evidence that would be introduced demonstrated that the Pakistani court did not apply law in "substantial conformity with Maryland law." In addition, we held that the burden was on the mother to prove these matters by a preponderance of the evidence.

LEGAL ANALYSIS

\* \* \*

## III

Turning to the heart of this appeal, appellant argues that the circuit court erred in determining that appellant failed to prove that Pakistani law was not in substantial conformity with Maryland law. In this regard, appellant's argument is two-pronged: first, appellant maintains that the Pakistani court did not apply the "best interest of the child" standard to the case at hand, although the standard exists in Pakistan; and second, even if the Pakistani court did apply the best interest of the child standard, the rules of law and procedure that the Pakistani courts followed were contrary to Maryland's public policy. \* \* \*

\* \* \*

## A

The evidence was overwhelming that, as a general principle, Pakistan follows the best interest of the child test in making child custody decisions. Both experts testified that the Guardians & Wards Act of 1890 applies to child custody disputes. Section 7 of the Act authorizes a court to appoint a guardian for a child where "the Court is satisfied that it is for the welfare of a minor...." GUARDIANS AND WARDS ACT § 7 (1992). Section 17 of the Act, in pertinent part, states:

> (1) In appointing or declaring the guardian of the minor, the Court shall, subject to the provisions of this section, be guided by what, consistently with the law to which the minor is subject, appears in the circumstances to be for the welfare of the minor.

(2) In considering what will be for the welfare of the minor, the Court shall have regard to the age, sex and religion of the minor, the character and capacity of the proposed guardian and his nearness of kin to the minor, the wishes, if any, of a deceased parent, and any existing or previous relations of the proposed guardian with the minor or his property.

(3) If the minor is old enough to form an intelligent preference, the Court may consider that preference.

GUARDIANS AND WARDS ACT § 17 (1992).

As noted above, the experts made it clear during the remand hearing that Section 17 of the Act encompasses many different types of factors considered by courts in determining the "welfare of the minor." The expert testimony was clear that, depending on the specifics of a given case, Pakistani courts examine a number of different facts to determine the welfare of the child.

In their seminal handbook on Maryland family law, Judge Fader and Master Gilbert, citing an exhaustive collection of Maryland case law, outlined the various factors that courts may consider in determining the best interest of the child, including: fitness of parents, character and reputation of the parties, the child's preference, the age, health, and sex of the child, adultery of parents, and material opportunities affecting the future life of the child. JOHN F. FADER, II & RICHARD J. GILBERT, MARYLAND FAMILY LAW, § 7.3 (1990 & Supp.1993). In addition, determining the best interest of the child involves a multitude of often ambiguous and intangible factors. Necessarily, therefore, this analysis is conducted on a case-specific basis, as the child's best interest "varies from each individual case." In view of the expert testimony and the language of the Guardians and Ward Act itself, there was substantial evidence supporting the circuit court's determination that Pakistan follows the best interest of the child standard in child custody disputes.

\* \* \*

\* \* \* [A]ppellant is correct that it was not enough under our mandate for the circuit court to merely find that the best interest of the child standard is the law in Pakistan in child custody disputes. We are persuaded, however, that substantial evidence before the circuit court indicated that the Pakistani courts in fact applied the best interest of the child standard.

\* \* \*

## B

We now address whether substantial competent evidence existed from which the circuit court could have determined that the best interest of the child standard was in fact applied in Pakistan.

Preliminarily, we believe it beyond cavil that a Pakistani court could only determine the best interest of a Pakistani child by an analysis utilizing the customs, culture, religion, and mores of the community and country of which the child and—in this case—her parents were a part, i.e., Pakistan. Furthermore, the Pakistani court could only apply the best interest standard as of the point in time when the evidence is being presented, not in futuro, the Court having no way of predicting that the child would be spirited away to a foreign culture. * * * Thus, faced with the facts of a Pakistani child of two Pakistani parents who had been raised in the culture of her parents all of her life, not only did the Pakistani court properly utilize the only mores and customs by which the family had been inculcated, but it used the only principles and teachings available to it at the time. * * * Hence, bearing in mind that in the Pakistani culture, the well being of the child and the child's proper development is thought to be facilitated by adherence to Islamic teachings, one would expect that a Pakistani court would weigh heavily the removal of the child from that influence as detrimental. It certainly is not our task on this appeal to attempt to reorder the priorities of the Pakistani court in its analysis of undeniably legitimate factors bearing on whether the best interest of the child is served by granting custody to appellee.

Based on a plain reading of the Pakistani court orders, we hold that the trial judge was not clearly erroneous in finding that the Pakistani courts applied the best interest of the child standard to this case. On their face, the Pakistani court orders—especially the August 1, 1993 order granting permanent custody to appellee— unambiguously indicate that the welfare of the child standard was in fact applied. Before analyzing each Pakistani order, we are guided by the widely-recognized principle that judgments must be construed in the same manner as other written documents, and accordingly, where its meaning is clear and unambiguous, we do not look beyond the order, as there is no room for construction. * * *

* * *

[On appeal of the Pakistani trial court order,] the Court of Vth Senior Civil Judge/ASJ & R.C. issued a judgment dated August 1, 1993, disposing of appellee's application under section 25 of the Act for the return of the child to appellee's custody and granting permanent custody to appellee. Section 25 states that, where a child is removed from the custody of her guardian, the court may order that the child be delivered into the custody of the guardian, if the court finds that "it will be for the welfare of the ward."

After reciting the facts of both sides of the dispute, the court set out to determine specifically "[w]ith whom the welfare of the minor [l]ies." In so doing, the court set forth the testimony of appellee. Appellee testified that appellant is living a "sin life" with her lover in the U.S., and that his daughter is not being properly cared for by appellant. In addition, appellee testified that when his child lived in Pakistan he paid for her to attend the St. Joseph School where she received an Islamic education, but that the child is not now receiving an Islamic education in the U.S. Moreover, appellee testified that appellant is controlling the child through fear, and that appellant lacks moral character. Appellee also informed the court of appellant's failure to comply with a Pakistani court order. Appellee further stated that the man with whom appellant was living was a stranger to the child. In sum, appellee's testimony before the Pakistani court was that the welfare of the child will suffer in the hands of appellant and her lover.

The Pakistani court then noted that appellant did not challenge or rebut appellee's testimony, "though she was given full chance for the same purpose." In addition, the court observed that appellant's counsel "also failed to argue the matter." Based on this uncontradicted *evidence* on the record, i.e., appellee's testimony, the Pakistani court reasoned that custody should be awarded to appellee in the interest of "the welfare and well being" of the child. In so doing, the court relied upon and considered several factors to which appellee testified, e.g., that appellant forcibly removed the child from appellee's access, that appellant lived with another man in adultery, that appellant had a child with her paramour, that the child was living in a non-Islamic society, that appellee is a businessman living in an Islamic society, and that appellee is of good moral character.

We believe it is pellucid that these orders unambiguously indicate that the Pakistani courts did in fact apply the welfare of the child test in awarding custody to appellee. Moreover, these orders clearly contravene the minority's assertion that the Pakistani courts considered only that appellant was purportedly living a life of sin in the United States and that appellant kidnapped the child from Pakistan to the United States, and ignored other relevant best interest factors. Indeed, in its August 1, 1993 final custody order, the Pakistani court plainly based its conclusion on appellee's testimony. We see nothing improper with the Pakistani court's reliance on appellee's testimony. * * *

* * *

C

Next, appellant argues that, even if the Pakistani court did in fact apply the best interest of the child standard, the circuit court erred in failing to conclude under the second part of our mandate in

*Malik* that the child custody law and procedure that the Pakistani courts followed was contrary to Maryland's public policy. We disagree. Appellant sets forth several arguments in support of her contention that Pakistani law is contrary to Maryland law. We shall address each argument in turn.

i

We reject appellant's argument that the Pakistani court applied a rule of law so "contrary to Maryland's public policy as to undermine confidence in the outcome of the trial," when it allegedly based its child custody order only on evidence that appellee presented. Initially, we observe that we are not called upon here to pass judgment on a trial by fire, trial by ordeal, or a system rooted in superstition, or witchcraft. In fact, the Pakistani child custody system is rooted in the Guardian and Wards Act of 1890—an enactment based on British common law. As we noted in part A, the great weight of evidence shows: (1) the Pakistani court proceeded in a manner quite similar to the manner in which a Maryland court would have proceeded had a parent failed to appear; (2) appellant had notice and an opportunity to present her side of the case in Pakistan; and (3) appellant was represented by counsel and by her father in Pakistan. As a result, the circuit court did not err by failing to conclude that basing the child custody decision only on evidence that was before the Pakistani court was "repugnant to Maryland public policy."

ii

Appellant also claims that the law as applied in Pakistan is repugnant to Maryland public policy because the Pakistani order was based on the right of Hazanit. In *Malik*, we stated the following:

> On the record before us, we cannot determine whether Pakistani law lacks conformity with Maryland law. We can, however, resolve the narrow issue of whether the Pakistani order should be denied comity because there is a paternal preference in Pakistani law. If the only difference between the custody laws of Maryland and Pakistan is that Pakistani courts apply a paternal preference the way Maryland courts once applied the maternal preference, the Pakistani order is entitled to comity. A custody decree of a sister state whose custody law contains a preference for one parent over another would be entitled to comity, provided, of course, the sister state's custody law applies the best interest of the child standard.... A Maryland court should not, therefore, refuse to enforce a Pakistani custody order merely because a paternal preference is found in that country's law.

As we previously noted, the doctrine of Hazanit embodies complex Islamic rules of maternal and paternal preference, depending on the age and sex of the child. Appellant describes the doctrine as follows:

Under the Islamic law, the Doctrine of Hazanit governs child custody. Under the Doctrine of Hazanit, the mother is entitled to custody of her male child up to the age of seven (7) and of her female child up to the age of puberty. However, the mother's right to Hazanit is subject to the control of the father who is the child's natural guardian. Moreover, if the father is unfit for custody once the child reaches the requisite age, the child's paternal male relatives, and not the mother, are given custody. Further, the mother can lose custody before the child reaches the requisite age if she is an "apostate" (wicked or untrustworthy). The mother can also lose custody before the child reaches the requisite age if she can not [sic] promote the religious or secular interests of the child.

Appellant states that in this case, the Pakistani court ruled that she lost Hazanit because she removed the child to the U.S. where appellee was unable to exercise his right to control as the child's natural guardian. Appellant further notes that she was considered "apostate" for living in an adulterous household.

Certainly, the doctrine of Hazanit is not a preference rule applied in Pakistan the same "way Maryland courts once applied the maternal preference." This, however, does not mean that it is therefore "repugnant to Maryland public policy." Our review of the record indicates that there was substantial competent evidence upon which the circuit court could base its conclusion that "the law there in Pakistan is not so repugnant to the law of Maryland that we should fail to grant comity in the case." Given this evidence, we are also satisfied that the circuit court was legally correct in this regard.

The circuit court had before it the expert testimony of Justice Dogar that, under the Act, Hazanit is but one of the factors to be considered in the welfare of the child test. He stressed that a Pakistani court does not blindly apply the doctrine of Hazanit in making child custody determinations. According to Justice Dogar, "If the personal law [as expressed in the doctrine of Hazanit] was to be the only thing on the basis on which [the welfare of the child] was decided, there would have been no Guardians and Wards Act . . ." Given the circuit court's opinion of the credibility of this expert, from this testimony, we hold that the circuit court could reasonably have found that Hazanit was merely one factor. In addition, consideration of this factor does not make Pakistani law repugnant to Maryland public policy.

We recognize that Hazanit is different in many respects from the traditional maternal preference once followed in this State. We recognize, however, that Hazanit is nonetheless similar to the traditional maternal preference in that they both are based on very old notions and assumptions (which are widely considered outdated, discriminatory, and outright false in today's modern society) concerning which parent is best able to care for a young child and with which parent that child best belongs. Viewed in this regard, standing as a factor to be weighed in the best interest of the child examination, Hazanit is no more objectionable than any other type of preference. As we noted in *Malik*, the courts of this State will not refuse to enforce child custody awards of those states still recognizing the maternal preference as a factor.

Given that Hazanit is only more doctrinaire in degree from the maternal preference and because the circuit court could have reasonably found it to be only a factor, we hold that the circuit court did not err in concluding that the principles of Pakistani law which were applied were not repugnant to Maryland law. In fact, the Pakistani court arrived at the same rule of maternal preference now recognized in Maryland by virtue of its decision that appellant had forfeited her right of Hazanit, i.e., the preference no longer was applied in the custody determination. Thus, had the right of Hazanit been considered as a factor, we would be obliged to note that we are simply unprepared to hold that this longstanding doctrine of one of the world's oldest and largest religions practiced by hundreds of millions of people around the world and in this country, as applied as one factor in the best interest of the child test, is repugnant to Maryland public policy. Since the Pakistani court decided the right to Hazanit was forfeited, it was not factored in and thus the effect of the preference was the same as that now recognized under Maryland law.

iii

Next, appellant asserts that the Pakistani custody orders were founded on principles of law repugnant to Maryland public policy because the orders were allegedly based on the Pakistani presumption that an adulterous parent is unfit for custody. We disagree. The record, including the Pakistani orders and the testimony of the experts, contains substantial evidence that adultery was only one factor considered.

There is nothing "repugnant," or even foreign, in a court considering adultery as a factor in determining the best interest of the child. In *Davis v. Davis*, 280 Md. 119, 127, 372 A.2d 231 (1977), the Court of Appeals stated that it is proper in certain cases to consider adultery. In *Swain v. Swain*, 43 Md.App. 622, 629, 406 A.2d 680, *cert. denied*, 286 Md. 754 (1979), we stated the following:

[T]here are now no presumptions whatsoever with respect to the fitness of a parent who has committed, or is committing, adultery. Rather, adultery is relevant only insofar as it *actually* affects a child's welfare. We will not presume a harmful effect, and the *mere* fact of adultery cannot "tip the balance" against a parent in the fitness determination. Thus, a chancellor should weigh, not the adultery itself, but only any actual harmful effect that is supported by the evidence.

While appellant argues in terms of "presumption of unfitness," the testimony at the remand hearing was sufficient to support a conclusion that adultery was only a factor. Accordingly, the circuit court did not err by failing to conclude that this aspect of the Pakistani welfare of the child test was repugnant to Maryland public policy.

\* \* \*

## *Notes*

1. Two judges dissented in *Hosain*, concluding that the Pakistani court had not applied a "best interests of the child" standard. The dissent argued that the trial court did not consider factors such as the fitness of either parent, the wishes of the child, or "the well-being of the child or the standard of living or surroundings in which [the child] would be reared." The dissenters also noted that the Pakistani court did not investigate the mother's allegations of substance abuse and domestic violence. In contrast to the majority, which accepted the conclusion that her allegations were not considered because she failed to appear at the hearing in Pakistan, the dissenters were troubled by the mother's testimony that she could not return to Pakistan without risking severe punishment as an adulterer, and by her argument that under Pakistani law the result would not have been different even if she had participated in the hearing. In addition, the dissent emphasized that the mother brought the child to the United States before any custody order had been entered in Pakistan, and therefore that she did not act in violation of any court decree. *Hosain* is criticized in June Starr, "The Global Battlefield: Culture and International Child Custody Disputes at Century's End," 15 Ariz. J. Int'l & Comp. L. 791 (1998).

Other cases considering whether to extend comity to custody decrees based on religious law include Marriage of Malak, 182 Cal. App.3d 1018, 227 Cal.Rptr. 841, 847–48 (1986) (upholding custody decree based on Islamic law), and Ali v. Ali, 279 N.J.Super. 154, 652 A.2d 253, 259–60 (Ch. Div. 1994)(refusing to extend comity to decree based on irrebuttable presumption that father was entitled to custody.) See also Amin v. Bakhaty, 798 So.2d 75, 85 (La. 2001).

2. Article 16 of the U.N. Convention on the Elimination of all Forms of Discrimination Against Women (CEDAW), reprinted above in

Chapter 2, requires that states parties ensure that women and men have "[t]he same rights and responsibilities with regard to guardianship, wardship, trusteeship and adoption of children" and that "in all cases the best interests of the children shall be paramount." Is the Pakistani custody law described in *Hosain* consistent with this standard?

### Comment on Jurisdiction and Recognition of Custody Orders

International private law issues concerning children are addressed in the 1996 Hague Convention on Jurisdiction, Applicable Law, Recognition, Enforcement, and Cooperation in Respect of Parental Responsibility and Measures for the Protection of Children, reprinted at 35 I.L.M. 1391 (1996), which entered into effect in 2002. More information is available on the Hague conference web site at www.hcch.net; see also Linda Silberman, "The 1996 Hague Convention on the Protection of Children: Should the United States Join?," 34 Fam. L.Q. 239 (2000). Within the European Community, these questions fall within the scope of a regulation known as "Brussels II revised" or Council Regulation (EC) 2201/2003 Concerning Jurisdiction and the Recognition and Enforcement of Judgments in Matrimonial Matters and the Matters of Parental Responsibility (2003) OJ L 338/1.

In the United States, these issues are governed primarily by the Uniform Child Custody Jurisdiction and Enforcement Act (UCCJEA), adopted in most of the states, which places jurisdiction over child custody determinations in the "home state" of the child, defined as "the State in which a child lived with a parent or a person acting as a parent for at least six consecutive months immediately before the commencement of a child custody proceeding." Under § 105, reprinted below, the child's "home state" might be found to be a foreign country. In this situation, a state court would not have jurisdiction, except on a temporary basis in an emergency situation. See generally D. Marianne Blair, "International Application of the UCCJEA: Scrutinizing the Escape Clause," 38 Fam. L.Q. 547 (2004).

Under the UCCJEA, once a court in the child's home state takes jurisdiction, it retains "exclusive, continuing jurisdiction" as long as a parent, a person acting as a parent, or the child continue to reside in that state, and its custody orders must be enforced in other states without modification except in an emergency situation. A number of cases have deferred to the jurisdiction of foreign courts under the UCCJEA; see, e.g., Atchison v. Atchison, 256 Mich.App. 531, 664 N.W.2d 249 (2003) (holding that Canadian court had exclusive continuing jurisdiction), Marriage of Medill, 179 Or.App. 630, 40 P.3d 1087 (2002) (deferring to Germany as the child's home state). See generally Robert G. Spector, "International Child Custody Jurisdiction and the Uniform Child Custody Jurisdiction and Enforcement Act," 33 N.Y.U. J. Int'l L. & Pol. 251 (2000). The UCCJEA requires deference to a foreign custody decree only if it was entered in factual circumstances that conform to the jurisdictional standards of the Act. These standards include requirements of notice and a hearing. See, e.g., Maqsudi v. Maqsudi, 363 N.J.Super. 53, 830 A.2d 929 (Ch. Div. 2002).

# UNIFORM CHILD CUSTODY JURISDICTION AND ENFORCEMENT ACT (UCCJEA)

9 U.L.A. (Part 1A) 649 (1999).

\* \* \*

## Section 105.  *International Application of Act*

(a) A court of this State shall treat a foreign country as if it were a State of the United States for the purpose of applying Articles 1 and 2.

(b) Except as otherwise provided in subsection (c), a child custody determination made in a foreign country under factual circumstances in substantial conformity with the jurisdictional standards of this Act must be recognized and enforced under Article 3.

(c) A court of this State need not apply this Act if the child custody law of a foreign country violates fundamental principles of human rights.

\* \* \*

## Section 303.  *Duty to Enforce*

(a) A court of this State shall recognize and enforce a child-custody determination of a court of another State if the latter court exercised jurisdiction that was in substantial conformity with this [Act] or the determination was made under factual circumstances meeting the jurisdictional standards of this Act and the determination has not been modified in accordance with this Act.

(b) A court may utilize any remedy available under other law of this State to enforce a child-custody determination made by a court of another State. The procedure provided by this article does not affect the availability of other remedies to enforce a child-custody determination.

\* \* \*

### *Notes*

1.  Section 105(c) provides an exception to the duty to enforce a foreign custody order on public policy grounds. When would the child custody law of a foreign country "violate fundamental principles of

human rights"? See D. Marianne Blair, "International Application of the UCCJEA: Scrutinizing the Escape Clause," 38 Fam. L.Q. 547 (2004); Carol S. Bruch, "Religious Law, Secular Practices, and Children's Human Rights in Child Abduction Cases under the Hague Child Abduction Convention," 33 Int'l L. & Pol. 49 (2000).

2. *Problem.* Magda, an Egyptian citizen, is married to Bakhaty, who has dual citizenship in the U.S. and Egypt. During their marriage, Magda has lived with her family in Egypt, and Bakhaty has spent most of his time in New Jersey, where he is a successful anesthesiologist. Bakhaty visits Egypt several times a year for a week at a time. Magda and Bakhaty have a son, Ahmed, who has lived exclusively with his mother.

When Ahmed was six years old, Magda brought him to the U.S. for a visit with her family in Baton Rouge, Louisiana. Soon after she arrived, she called her husband and asked him to meet her in Louisiana. Instead of joining Magda, Bakhaty flew to Egypt and brought criminal charges against her for removing Ahmed from Egypt with out his permission and for fraud in her procurement of Ahmed's Egyptian passport. When she was notified of the charges, Magda filed suit in the family court in Louisiana, seeking a divorce, sole custody, and child support. The next day, Bakhaty obtained a certificate of divorce and filed for a judgment declaring that he was entitled to temporary guardianship and physical custody of Ahmed under Egyptian law. He has asked the family court to dismiss Magda's petition. How should the court resolve this dispute? (See Amin v. Bakhaty, 798 So.2d 75 (La. 2001).)

# CONVENTION ON THE RIGHTS OF THE CHILD
United Nations, 1989.
G.A. Document A/RES/44/25.

### Article 3

1. In all actions concerning children, whether undertaken by public or private social welfare institutions, courts of law, administrative authorities or legislative bodies, the best interests of the child shall be a primary consideration.

2. States Parties undertake to ensure the child such protection and care as is necessary for his or her well-being, taking into account the rights and duties of his or her parents, legal guardians, or other individuals legally responsible for him or her, and, to this end, shall take all appropriate legislative and administrative measures.

\* \* \*

### Article 9

1. States Parties shall ensure that a child shall not be separated from his or her parents against their will, except when

competent authorities subject to judicial review determine, in accordance with applicable law and procedures, that such separation is necessary for the best interests of the child. Such determination may be necessary in a particular case such as one involving abuse or neglect of the child by the parents, or one where the parents are living separately and a decision must be made as to the child's place of residence.

2.   In any proceedings pursuant to paragraph 1 of the present article, all interested parties shall be given an opportunity to participate in the proceedings and make their views known.

3.   States Parties shall respect the right of the child who is separated from one or both parents to maintain personal relations and direct contact with both parents on a regular basis, except if it is contrary to the child's best interests.

4.   Where such separation results from any action initiated by a State Party, such as the detention, imprisonment, exile, deportation or death (including death arising from any cause while the person is in the custody of the State) of one or both parents or of the child, that State Party shall, upon request, provide the parents, the child or, if appropriate, another member of the family with the essential information concerning the whereabouts of the absent member(s) of the family unless the provision of the information would be detrimental to the well-being of the child. States Parties shall further ensure that the submission of such a request shall of itself entail no adverse consequences for the person(s) concerned.

\* \* \*

*Article 12*

1.   States Parties shall assure to the child who is capable of forming his or her own views the right to express those views freely in all matters affecting the child, the views of the child being given due weight in accordance with the age and maturity of the child.

2.   For this purpose, the child shall in particular be provided the opportunity to be heard in any judicial and administrative proceedings affecting the child, either directly, or through a representative or an appropriate body, in a manner consistent with the procedural rules of national law.

# B.   INTERNATIONAL CHILD ABDUCTION

One of the most widely ratified conventions produced by the Hague Conference on Private International Law is the 1980 Convention on the Civil Aspects of International Child Abduction, which has been ratified or acceded to by more than 75 nations, including more than 20 countries that are not members of the

Hague Conference. Information including a list of contracting states for the Child Abduction Convention is available on the Hague Conference web site at www.hcch.net.

# GIL v. RODRIGUEZ

U.S. District Court, Middle District of Florida, 2002.
184 F.Supp.2d 1221.

Presnell, District Judge.

THIS CAUSE came before the Court on Roger Francisco Barrios Gil's ("Petitioner") Petition for the Return of Child. Petitioner alleged that the child's mother, Diana del Valle Matheus Rodriguez ("Respondent"), wrongfully removed their daughter Diana Anaid Barrios Matheus ("Diana") from Venezuela. On January 16, 2002, the Court held an evidentiary hearing on this matter.

## I. Background

Diana was born on May 10, 1994. Petitioner and Respondent never married, but both parents have been actively involved in Diana's upbringing. For the first six years of Diana's life, Petitioner, Respondent and Diana lived together intermittently. During this time, Petitioner was actively involved in every facet of Diana's life. He picked her up from school on a daily basis and participated in school activities. He accompanied her to doctor's appointments. He exclusively financed her educational, medical and living expenses.

In July, 2000, Petitioner, Respondent and Diana moved into an apartment in Valencia, Carabobo State, Venezuela. Uncontroverted evidence, including testimony from Aurora Sierra de Munoz, the landlord of this apartment, established that for ten months, Petitioner, Respondent and Diana resided together as a family in this apartment.

On April 27, 2001, Respondent took Diana to school. Respondent alerted Petitioner that because she planned to take Diana to her mother's house, Petitioner did not need to pick Diana up from school. Shortly thereafter, Petitioner noticed that many of Diana and Respondent's possessions were missing from the family home. Petitioner called Respondent, but her cell phone had been disconnected. He visited Respondent's mother's house, but nobody was home. On May 3, 2001, Petitioner visited local airports and learned that Respondent and Diana had flown to Miami, Florida. Petitioner knew that Respondent had family members in Florida, and attempted to contact them about Diana's whereabouts. Although he was able to speak to one of Respondent's relatives, they did not reveal Diana's location.

On June 24 or 25, 2001, Respondent called Petitioner and informed him that she and Diana were in Florida, and that he should come to visit. When Petitioner arrived at a designated meeting place on June 28, 2001, Florida law enforcement officers served him with a Temporary Injunction for Protection against Domestic Violence filed by Respondent. Petitioner and Respondent appeared before a Circuit Court Judge on July 9, 2001. The Circuit Court dismissed the case against Petitioner for want of jurisdiction. Petitioner returned to Venezuela without seeing Diana.

Upon his return, Petitioner hired a private investigator, who eventually determined that Diana and Respondent were residing in Kissimmee, Florida. Petitioner finally learned of Diana's whereabouts on December 22, 2001. Meanwhile, Petitioner initiated proceedings in Venezuela to define his custodial rights. A Venezuelan Superior Court dismissed his petition, stating that he did not possess custody rights over Diana. A Venezuelan Court of Appeals reversed this decision and remanded the case to Superior Court.

## II. Law

Congress enacted the International Child Abduction Remedies Act ("ICARA") to implement the Hague Convention on the Civil Aspects of International Child Abduction ("Hague Convention"), a treaty to which the United States and Venezuela are signatories. 42 U.S.C. § 11601(b)(1) (West 2001). The objectives of the Hague Convention are: 1) to secure the prompt return of children wrongfully removed or retained in any Contracting State; and 2) to ensure that rights of custody and of access under the law of one Contracting State are effectively respected in other Contracting States. *Hague Convention on the Civil Aspects of Child Abduction*, Oct. 25, 1980, Art. 1, §§ a-b. Furthermore, the Hague Convention seeks to restore the pre-abduction status-quo and to deter parents from crossing borders in search of more sympathetic courts.

The Hague Convention and ICARA apply where a child has been removed from her habitual residence in breach of the petitioner's custody rights. *Hague Convention*, Art. 3. A petitioner establishes a prima facie case of wrongful removal by demonstrating by a preponderance of the evidence that: 1) the habitual residence of the child immediately before the date of the alleged wrongful removal was in the foreign country; 2) the removal breached the petitioner's custody rights under the foreign country's law; and 3) the petitioner exercised custody of the child at the time of her alleged removal. 42 U.S.C. at § 11603(e)(1)(A). A petitioner's custody rights may arise by operation of law, judicial or administrative decree, or by private agreement. *Hague Convention*, Art. 3. Children who are wrongfully removed under the provisions of the Hague Convention shall be promptly returned unless one of the exceptions provided in the treaty applies. *See* 42 U.S.C. at § 11601(a)(4).

A respondent may avoid returning the child to petitioner if respondent can demonstrate by clear and convincing evidence that: 1) return would "expose the child to physical or psychological harm or otherwise place the child in an intolerable situation" or; 2) if the child objects to return and is of sufficient age and maturity to do so; or 3) if return would not be permitted by fundamental American principles concerning the protection of human rights and freedoms. *Id*. at § 11603(e)(2). Furthermore, to avoid return, a respondent may demonstrate by a preponderance of the evidence that: 1) more than one year has elapsed since the child's removal and the child is settled in her new environment or; 2) the petitioner does not really have custody rights; or 3) petitioner has consented or acquiesced to the removal. *Id*.

This Court has proper jurisdiction over ICARA proceedings. *Id*. at § 11603(a). This jurisdiction exists, however, only to determine the merits of the abduction claim and not to consider the underlying custody dispute. *Hague Convention*, Art. 19.

### III.  DISCUSSION

Petitioner and Respondent stipulated that Diana habitually resided in Venezuela prior to her removal in May, 2001. Furthermore, Respondent invoked none of the exceptions to the Hague Convention or ICARA. Therefore, in order to prevail, Petitioner must demonstrate by a preponderance of the evidence that: 1) Respondent's removal of Diana breached Petitioner's custody rights under Venezuelan law; and 2) Petitioner was exercising custody over Diana at the time of her removal. Petitioner has met this burden.

### A.  Venezuelan Custodial Rights

By unilaterally removing Diana from Venezuela in May, 2001, Respondent breached Petitioner's custody rights under Venezuelan law.[3] The Venezuelan Constitution states that the father and mother of a child have a shared and irrevocable duty to raise, educate, support and assist their children. *Republic of Venezuela Const.*, Art. 76. Venezuelan law describes these responsibilities and obligations as *Patria Potestas* (parental authority). See *Organic Law for the Protection of Juveniles and Adolescents* (hereinafter "Organic Law"), § 1, Art. 347. "*Patria Potestas* encompasses the guardian-

---

**3.** The Court took judicial notice of sections of the Organic Law for the Protection of Juveniles and Adolescents, as well as sections of the Venezuelan Constitution. Furthermore, the Court heard expert testimony on custodial issues from Professor Leonardo D'Onofrio of the University of Carabobo, a former Venezuelan federal judge.

ship and representation of the offspring who are the subject of said *Patria Potestas*, as well as the management of the offspring's property." *Id.* at § 1, Art. 348. Guardianship, in turn, refers to "custody, material assistance, vigilance and moral as well as educational guidance.... Exercising parental authority requires direct contact with the offspring, and therefore the ability to decide their place of residence or domicile." *Id.* at § 2, Art. 358.

Undoubtedly, Petitioner fully exercised *Patria Potestas* over Diana. Uncontroverted testimony established that he actively and directly participated in every meaningful aspect of Diana's life except for her removal from Venezuela. On a daily basis, Petitioner picked up Diana from a school that he paid for her to attend. Furthermore, he signed the lease of the apartment where he, Diana and Respondent lived for the ten months prior to Diana's removal. Certainly, Petitioner possessed the ability to decide Diana's domicile during this time, thus establishing his parental authority and custodial rights under Venezuelan law.

### B. *Custodial Rights at Time of Removal*

When Respondent unilaterally removed Diana from Venezuela, Petitioner was exercising his custodial rights. Respondent relied almost exclusively upon Article 360 of the Organic Law in arguing that Petitioner possessed no custody rights at the time of Diana's removal.[5] Essentially, Respondent maintains that because Diana had not yet turned seven at the time of her removal, Respondent possessed exclusive custodial rights.

Respondent's reliance on Article 360 is misplaced. On May 3, 2001, Respondent agrees that she, Petitioner and Diana all lived in the same apartment, and had done so for ten months. Respondent never maintained that she and Petitioner held separate residences when she took Diana to Florida. In fact, when Respondent applied to the Florida Circuit Court for a domestic violence injunction against Petitioner, she signed a petition under penalty of perjury stating that she, Petitioner and Diana lived in one home, "as if a

---

**5.** Article 360 of the Organic Law states:

> In the cases of suit for final decree of divorce, physical separation, annulment of the marriage, or if the father and mother were to hold separate residences, they shall decide, by mutual agreement, which of them shall exercise guardianship over the children over seven years of age. The children that are seven years of age or less shall reside with the mother, except in the case in which she is not the legal holder of parental authority or in which, due to reasons of health or safety, it is most appropriate for them to be separated from her temporarily or for an indefinite period of time. In the absence of agreement between the father and the mother over which of the two exercises guardianship over their offspring, the competent judge shall determine to which of the two it shall belong....

Organic Law, § 2, Art. 360.

family." Therefore, Article 360 of the Organic Law does not apply to this case.

Finally, Respondent claims that because no formal custody agreement was in place when she removed Diana, Petitioner exercised no custodial rights. This argument embodies a continued misunderstanding of Article 360 and ignores Article 3 of the Hague Convention, which clearly states that custody rights need not be established by formal agreement, but can arise by operation of law. If Respondent's view were upheld, any parent who was not a party to an official custodial agreement could abscond with their child, leaving the remaining parent without legal recourse. The Hague Convention acknowledges that a parent seldom prepares legal documents in anticipation of such a shocking action, and safeguards their custodial rights in the country where their child habitually resided. See Id., Proclamation, Art. 1.

### IV.  CONCLUSION

The circumstances of this case represent a textbook example of why the United States signed the Hague Convention and enacted ICARA. The proper forum for the clarification of Petitioner and Respondent's custody rights over Diana is in Venezuela. Petitioner has met his burden under ICARA by establishing that: 1) Diana habitually resided in Venezuela prior to her removal on May 3, 2001; 2) by removing Diana, Respondent breached Petitioner's custodial rights under Venezuelan law; and 3) Petitioner possessed custodial rights at the time of Diana's removal. Therefore, Diana must be returned to Venezuela.

While recognizing the obvious personal dispute between Petitioner and Respondent, the Court has also clearly observed the deep love and concern both parties have for their daughter. The parties must comply with this Order in a manner that best reflects these sentiments and makes Diana's emotional and physical well-being a paramount concern. Therefore,

It is ORDERED and ADJUDGED that:

   1.   Petitioner's Petition for Return of Child is GRANTED.

   2.   The parties and Diana shall appear before the Court at 3:30 p.m. on January 23, 2002, to discuss arrangements for returning Diana to Venezuela, in a manner that is in the best interests of the child. The Respondent is responsible for bringing Diana to Court.

   3.   If the parties cannot reach agreement on a plan for returning Diana to Venezuela, the Court will enter a subsequent Order commensurate with this ruling.

  4. All prior Orders issued by the Court regarding travel limitations and visitation remain in force and effect.

### *Notes*

  1. The Child Abduction Convention was premised on the belief that custody issues are best resolved by the authorities in the child's place of habitual residence, and mandates prompt return of a child wrongfully removed from or retained outside the child's country of habitual residence. See Elisa Pérez-Vera, Explanatory Report on the 1980 Child Abduction Convention, available on the Hague Conference web site at www.hcch.net. *Gil* was brought under the International Child Abduction Remedies Act (ICARA), 42 U.S.C. §§ 11601–11610, which implements the Child Abduction Convention. Parties seeking a return order under ICARA, can file in either state or federal court. A court hearing a case under the Convention is prohibited from making a custody determination, and once a wrongful removal or retention is established there are very limited grounds on which a court may deny a return order. General information on the application of the Child Abduction Convention and ICARA in the United States is available on the website of the Department of State at www.travel.state.gov. See also Paul R. Beaumont & Peter E. McEleavy, The Hague Convention on International Child Abduction (1999).

  2. Many cases under the Child Abduction Convention begin with the problem of determining whether the petitioner had "rights of custody" under the law of the child's habitual residence at the time of the wrongful removal or retention. In addition to *Gil*, see, e.g., Whallon v. Lynn, 230 F.3d 450 (1st Cir. 2000) (applying Mexican law) and Furnes v. Reeves, 362 F.3d 702 (11th Cir. 2004) (applying Norwegian law). Visitation or access rights are not a sufficient basis to invoke the return remedy of the Convention, and a number of cases have struggled to determine whether visitation rights plus a *ne exeat* clause, which prohibits removing a child from the jurisdiction without the consent of both parents or a court order, constitutes a "right of custody" within the Convention. Compare Croll v. Croll, 229 F.3d 133 (2d Cir. 2000) with Furnes v. Reeves, 362 F.3d 702 (11th Cir. 2004).

## CONVENTION ON THE RIGHTS OF THE CHILD
United Nations, 1989.
G.A. Document A/RES/44/25.

### *Article 11*

  1. States Parties shall take measures to combat the illicit transfer and non-return of children abroad.

  2. To this end, States Parties shall promote the conclusion of bilateral or multilateral agreements or accession to existing agreements.

# CONVENTION ON THE CIVIL ASPECTS OF INTERNATIONAL CHILD ABDUCTION

Hague Conference on Private International Law, 1980.
T.I.A.S. No. 11,670, 1343 U.N.T.S. 89; 19 I.L.M. 1501.

## *Article 1*

The objects of the present Convention are—

a.  to secure the prompt return of children wrongfully removed to or retained in any Contracting State; and

b.  to ensure that rights of custody and of access under the law of one Contracting State are effectively respected in the other Contracting States.

## *Article 2*

Contracting States shall take all appropriate measures to secure within their territories the implementation of the objects of the Convention. For this purpose they shall use the most expeditious procedures available.

## *Article 3*

The removal or the retention of a child is to be considered wrongful where—

a.  it is in breach of rights of custody attributed to a person, an institution or any other body, either jointly or alone, under the law of the State in which the child was habitually resident immediately before the removal or retention; and

b.  at the time of removal or retention those rights were actually exercised, either jointly or alone, or would have been so exercised but for the removal or retention.

The rights of custody mentioned in sub-paragraph a above, may arise in particular by operation of law or by reason of a judicial or administrative decision, or by reason of an agreement having legal effect under the law of that State.

## *Article 4*

The Convention shall apply to any child who was habitually resident in a Contracting State immediately before any breach of custody or access rights. The Convention shall cease to apply when the child attains the age of 16 years.

## *Article 5*

For the purposes of this Convention—

    a.  'rights of custody' shall include rights relating to the care of the person of the child and, in particular, the right to determine the child's place of residence;

    b.  'rights of access' shall include the right to take a child for a limited period of time to a place other than the child's habitual residence.

## *Article 6*

A Contracting State shall designate a Central Authority to discharge the duties which are imposed by the Convention upon such authorities.

Federal States, States with more than one system of law or States having autonomous territorial organizations shall be free to appoint more than one Central Authority and to specify the territorial extent of their powers. Where a State has appointed more than one Central Authority, it shall designate the Central Authority to which applications may be addressed for transmission to the appropriate Central Authority within that State.

## *Article 7*

Central Authorities shall co-operate with each other and promote co-operation amongst the competent authorities in their respective States to secure the prompt return of children and to achieve the other objects of this Convention.

In particular, either directly or through any intermediary, they shall take all appropriate measures—

    a.  to discover the whereabouts of a child who has been wrongfully removed or retained;

    b.  to prevent further harm to the child or prejudice to interested parties by taking or causing to be taken provisional measures;

    c.  to secure the voluntary return of the child or to bring about an amicable resolution of the issues;

    d.  to exchange, where desirable, information relating to the social background of the child;

    e.  to provide information of a general character as to the law of their State in connection with the application of the Convention;

    f.  to initiate or facilitate the institution of judicial or administrative proceedings with a view to obtaining the return of the child and, in a proper case, to make arrangements for organizing or securing the effective exercise of rights of access;

g.  where the circumstances so require, to provide or facilitate the provision of legal aid and advice, including the participation of legal counsel and advisers;

h.  to provide such administrative arrangements as may be necessary and appropriate to secure the safe return of the child;

i.  to keep each other informed with respect to the operation of this Convention and, as far as possible, to eliminate any obstacles to its application.

\* \* \*

## *Article 12*

Where a child has been wrongfully removed or retained in terms of Article 3 and, at the date of the commencement of the proceedings before the judicial or administrative authority of the Contracting State where the child is, a period of less than one year has elapsed from the date of the wrongful removal or retention, the authority concerned shall order the return of the child forthwith. The judicial or administrative authority, even where the proceedings have been commenced after the expiration of the period of one year referred to in the preceding paragraph, shall also order the return of the child, unless it is demonstrated that the child is now settled in its new environment.

\* \* \*

## *Article 13*

Notwithstanding the provisions of the preceding Article, the judicial or administrative authority of the requested State is not bound to order the return of the child if the person, institution or other body which opposes its return establishes that—

a.  the person, institution or other body having the care of the person of the child was not actually exercising the custody rights at the time of removal or retention, or had consented to or subsequently acquiesced in the removal or retention; or

b.  there is a grave risk that his or her return would expose the child to physical or psychological harm or otherwise place the child in an intolerable situation.

The judicial or administrative authority may also refuse to order the return of the child if it finds that the child objects to being returned and has attained an age and degree of maturity at which it is appropriate to take account of its views.

In considering the circumstances referred to in this Article, the judicial and administrative authorities shall take into account the information relating to the social background of the child provided by the Central Authority or other competent authority of the child's habitual residence.

\* \* \*

## Article 16

After receiving notice of a wrongful removal or retention of a child in the sense of Article 3, the judicial or administrative authorities of the Contracting State to which the child has been removed or in which it has been retained shall not decide on the merits of rights of custody until it has been determined that the child is not to be returned under this Convention or unless an application under this Convention is not lodged within a reasonable time following receipt of the notice.

\* \* \*

## Article 19

A decision under this Convention concerning the return of the child shall not be taken to be a determination on the merits of any custody issue.

## Article 20

The return of the child under the provisions of Article 12 may be refused if this would not be permitted by the fundamental principles of the requested State relating to the protection of human rights and fundamental freedoms.

## Article 21

An application to make arrangements for organizing or securing the effective exercise of rights of access may be presented to the Central Authorities of the Contracting States in the same way as an application for the return of a child.

The Central Authorities are bound by the obligations of co-operation which are set forth in Article 7 to promote the peaceful enjoyment of access rights and the fulfilment of any conditions to which the exercise of those rights may be subject. The Central Authorities shall take steps to remove, as far as possible, all obstacles to the exercise of such rights.

The Central Authorities, either directly or through intermediaries, may initiate or assist in the institution of proceedings with a view to organizing or protecting these rights and securing respect for the conditions to which the exercise of these rights may be subject.

## *Notes*

1.  The 1980 Hague Convention on the Civil Aspects of International Child Abduction (Child Abduction Convention) marked a change from previous Hague conventions concerning children and families, because it was developed as a mechanism to promote international judicial cooperation rather than a tool for harmonizing laws on jurisdiction or recognition and enforcement of judgments. This cooperation is achieved through the designation of a Central Authority in each contracting state; for the United States, the Central Authority is the Office of Children's Issues in the Department of State.

Once a member state of the Hague Conference ratifies the Child Abduction Convention, it comes into effect between that state and those other member states that have also ratified the Convention. States that were not members of the Hague Conference at the time the convention was adopted in 1980 may accede to it, but must request that their accession be accepted by each of the contracting states. The Hague Conference web site includes a detailed table showing accessions and acceptances of these accessions. As the Child Abduction Convention is increasingly widely adopted, some contracting states may lack resources or capacity to carry out their obligations under the Convention, and this factors into the determination of other states whether to accept an accession. See William Duncan, "Action in Support of the Hague Child Abduction Convention: A View from the Permanent Bureau," 33 N.Y.U. J. Int'l L. & Pol. 103, 119–20 (2000); see also Carol S. Bruch, "Religious Law, Secular Practices, and Children's Human Rights in Child Abduction Cases under the Hague Child Abduction Convention," 33 Int'l L. & Politics 49, 49–51 (2000).

2.  For cases involving abductions from countries with which the United States does not have reciprocal relations under the Child Abduction Convention there is no federal court remedy. See, e.g., Taveras v. Taveras, 397 F.Supp.2d 908 (S.D. Ohio 2005). For cases involving abductions from the United States to non-Hague countries, the State Department can provide some types of assistance generally described on the website for the Office of Children's Issues at http://travel.state.gov. See also the International Parental Kidnapping Act (IPKA), 18 U.S.C. § 1204, which provides for federal criminal prosecution of anyone who "removes a child from the United States or retains a child (who has been in the United States) outside the United States with intent to obstruct the lawful exercise of parental rights." See generally Patricia E. Apy, "Managing Child Custody Cases Involving Non–Hague Contracting States," 14 J. Amer. Acad. Matrim. Lawyers 77 (1997).

# McMANUS v. McMANUS

U.S. District Court, Massachusetts, 2005.
354 F.Supp.2d 62.

MEMORANDUM AND ORDER

O'TOOLE, DISTRICT JUDGE.

The petitioner brought this action seeking the return of her four minor children to Northern Ireland pursuant to the 1980 Hague Convention on the Civil Aspects of International Child Abduction ("Convention"), Oct. 25, 1980, T.I.A.S. No. 11,670, 1343 U.N.T.S. 89, and its implementing statute, the International Child Abduction Remedies Act ("ICARA"), 42 U.S.C. §§ 11601–11610. Upon consideration of the evidence adduced at a two-day trial without a jury and the parties' submissions, I conclude that the petition ought to be denied and the return of the children to Northern Ireland refused. In support of that conclusion, I make the following findings of fact and rulings of law:

## I. Findings of fact

The petitioner, Dympna McManus, a citizen of Northern Ireland, and the respondent, Peter McManus, a citizen of the United States, were married in Massachusetts in 1988 and again in a religious ceremony in Northern Ireland in 1989. They have had four children: Daniel and Sean are fourteen-year-old twins, Stephanie is thirteen, and Peter is eleven.[1] The children were all born in the United States and are U.S. citizens.

The family lived together in Massachusetts until May 2001, at which time they relocated to Northern Ireland where Dympna's extended family lived. When they relocated, they sold their house and cars in Massachusetts and shipped their furniture and personal belongings to Northern Ireland. After arriving in Northern Ireland, they rented a house, purchased a car, and applied for government-provided health insurance. Peter did not have a job in Northern Ireland. The children attended school there and participated in numerous school and social activities.

Peter and Dympna's marriage was troubled for some years prior to the move to Northern Ireland. It was marked by poor communication, altercations, and estrangement. After the move, their relationship did not improve, and in December 2001, Peter returned alone to Massachusetts. Dympna and the four children

---

**1.** The parties' son Peter is often referred to by family members, particularly by his mother, as Peter Óg (Irish for "young Peter") to distinguish him from his father. For clarity, I will follow that convention here. "Peter" refers to the father, "Peter Óg" to the son.

remained in Northern Ireland. Peter visited the children a few times during 2002, and each time he returned alone to Massachusetts. He commenced divorce proceedings in the Massachusetts probate and family court in early 2003.

In July 2003, the children, with Dympna's consent, traveled to Massachusetts for what was to be a three-week visit with their father. They traveled with round-trip plane tickets and were scheduled to return to Northern Ireland on July 24, 2003. While visiting Peter, the children disclosed the unpleasant details of their living conditions in Northern Ireland. For example, the children had grown unruly and disobedient in Dympna's care, and she drank alcohol regularly to excess, which interfered with her ability to care for and control the children. The children testified that on several occasions Dympna struck them or threw objects at them. On at least two occasions, Dympna summoned her brother, Liam, and a neighbor, Graham, to help discipline the children. Liam and Graham struck at least two of the children. As it was described at trial, the household had become chaotic, and the children were quite unhappy.

After hearing of these conditions, Peter decided to keep the children in Massachusetts. He left two messages on Dympna's answering machine telling her that the children would not return to Northern Ireland as had been previously scheduled. Peter and Dympna did not speak about Peter's decision to keep the children. Dympna consulted a solicitor in Northern Ireland for advice about how to secure the return of the children, but aside from filing an application under the Convention with the proper authorities in Northern Ireland, she did not seek any relief from the courts of Northern Ireland or the United States. In December 2003, Peter obtained a divorce judgment from the Massachusetts probate and family court, including a grant of temporary custody of the children. Dympna filed the present petition under the Convention in April 2004.

*II.  Rulings of law*

*A.  Legal framework*

The Convention was adopted "to protect children internationally from the harmful effects of their wrongful removal or retention and to establish procedures to ensure their prompt return to the State of their habitual residence." The Convention's remedial scheme is designed "to restore the pre-removal status quo and discourage a parent from crossing international borders in search of a more sympathetic forum." *Whallon v. Lynn*, 230 F.3d 450, 455 (1st Cir.2000). It "seeks to deter those who would undertake such abductions by eliminating their primary motivation for doing so.

Since the goal of the abductor generally is to obtain a right of custody from the authorities of the country to which the child has been taken, the signatories to the Convention have agreed to deprive his actions of any practical or juridical consequences." *Mozes v. Mozes*, 239 F.3d 1067, 1070 (9th Cir.2001) (citations and internal quotations omitted). To achieve its goals, the Convention requires that "children who have been wrongfully removed from their country of habitual residence must be returned, unless the abductor can prove one of the defenses allowed by the Convention." *Danaipour v. McLarey*, 286 F.3d 1, 13 (1st Cir.2002).

Under ICARA, a petitioner seeking the return of a child must establish by a preponderance of the evidence that the child has been wrongfully removed or retained within the meaning of the convention. Under Article 3 of the Convention,

> The removal or retention of a child is to be considered wrongful where—
>
> (a) it is in breach of rights of custody attributed to a person, an institution or any other body, either jointly or alone, under the law of the State in which the child was habitually resident immediately before the removal or retention; and
>
> (b) at the time of removal or retention those rights were actually exercised, either jointly or alone, or would have been so exercised but for the removal or retention.

If the petitioner demonstrates that a child has been wrongfully retained, then the court must order the prompt return to the child's state of habitual residence, unless the respondent demonstrates that one of the exceptions expressed in Article 13 or Article 20 applies. 42 U.S.C. § 11601(a)(4); *Whallon*, 230 F.3d at 454.

### B. *Wrongful retention*

To prove that Peter's retention of the children in Massachusetts in July 2003 was wrongful, Dympna must prove that at the time of the retention Northern Ireland was the children's place of habitual residence and that she had been and was exercising custody rights in Northern Ireland. Neither the Convention nor ICARA defines the term "habitual residence." It has been left to the courts to develop a working definition. The Third Circuit has defined it this way:

> [W]e believe that a child's habitual residence is the place where he or she has been physically present for an amount of time sufficient for acclimatization and which has a 'degree of settled purpose' from the child's perspective. We further believe that a determination of whether any particular place satisfies this standard must focus on the child and consists of an analysis of

the child's circumstances in that place and the parents' present, shared intentions regarding their child's presence there.

*Feder v. Evans–Feder*, 63 F.3d 217, 224 (3d Cir.1995). To establish an habitual residence, it is not necessary to have an intention to stay in the place indefinitely. *Id*. at 223.

The Ninth Circuit, in a case where a child had a clearly established habitual residence in the native country of one parent and then took up residence in the native country of the other parent, found:

> When a child has no clearly established habitual residence elsewhere, it may become habitually resident even in a place where it was intended to live only for a limited time. The same is true if the child's prior habitual residence has been effectively abandoned by the shared intent of the parents. Where there is no such intent, however, a prior habitual residence should be deemed supplanted only where 'the objective facts point unequivocally' to this conclusion.

*Mozes*, 239 F.3d at 1082 (footnote and citation omitted).

Applying those principles here, I conclude that Northern Ireland was the children's place of habitual residence in July 2003 when Peter retained them in Massachusetts. It is clear that prior to May 2001 (when the family moved to Northern Ireland) their habitual residence was in Massachusetts; in fact, it was the only place where they had lived. Nevertheless, the evidence at trial demonstrated that when they moved to Northern Ireland in May 2001 the parents had decided to leave Massachusetts for at least the near foreseeable future and to make their home for an indefinite time in Northern Ireland. While the parents had not reached an agreement on how long they would stay in Northern Ireland, they nevertheless had no plans to return to the United States.

During the two years that they lived in Northern Ireland, the children became settled and acclimated to their new location. They enrolled in and attended schools, joined organized sports teams, participated in church activities, and engaged in other activities as residents of the country would.

Peter does not dispute the extent to which the children had become settled and acclimated in Northern Ireland and were participating in academic, civic, and family life there. Further, he does not suggest that he or Dympna had any plans to move the children away from Northern Ireland at the time they visited him in July 2003. On the contrary, he acknowledges that the children had round-trip plane tickets and were scheduled to return to Northern Ireland after a three-week stay in Massachusetts. It was only after they arrived in Massachusetts and he learned of the circumstances in Northern Ireland that Peter decided to retain the children here.

On the basis of this evidence, I find by a preponderance of the evidence that at the time the children visited their father in July 2003, Northern Ireland was their place of habitual residence as that concept is employed in the Convention.

The second proposition that Dympna must establish in order to show that the retention of the children in the United States was wrongful is that she was at the time exercising custody rights granted her under the laws of Northern Ireland. This proposition is not contested by Peter, for good reason. The undisputed evidence establishes that Dympna had physical custody of the children in Northern Ireland and was solely responsible for their care (except for financial assistance from Peter) for approximately eighteen months after Peter left Northern Ireland and returned to Massachusetts.

Accordingly, because Northern Ireland was the children's place of habitual residence and Dympna had and was exercising custody rights prior to their trip to Massachusetts in July 2003, the conclusion follows that Peter's retention of the children in Massachusetts was wrongful within the meaning of the Convention.

## C. *Exceptions*

Peter asserts that, notwithstanding his wrongful retention, there are two exceptions to the Convention's rule of summary return that apply and should persuade me to deny the petition for the return of the children to Northern Ireland. Invoking Article 13(b) of the Convention, he argues that "there is a grave risk that" return of the children would expose them "to physical or psychological harm or otherwise place [them] in an intolerable situation." He also invokes a second Article 13 exception that provides, "The judicial or administrative authority may also refuse to order the return of the child if it finds that the child objects to being returned and has attained an age and degree of maturity at which it is appropriate to take account of its views."

"The Convention establishes a strong presumption favoring return of a wrongfully removed child," and "[e]xceptions to the general rule of expedient return ... are to be construed narrowly." *Danaipour*, 286 F.3d at 13–14 (citations omitted). The party opposing return of a child has the burden of proving the Article 13(b) "grave risk" exception by clear and convincing evidence; the applicability of other Article 13 exceptions, including the "objection" exception, need only be proved by a preponderance of the evidence. 42 U.S.C. § 11603(e)(2). The Court has discretion to order the return of a wrongfully retained child even if the conditions for an exception are met. *Danaipour*, 286 F.3d at 14.

### 1.  Grave risk of harm

To sustain the burden under the Article 13(b) exception, Peter must show that, if the children are returned, the risk of physical and psychological harm is "grave," which is said to be "a great deal more than minimal," *Walsh v. Walsh*, 221 F.3d 204, 218 (1st Cir.2000), and "more than serious," *Danaipour*, 286 F.3d at 14. The First Circuit has explained:

> The text of the article requires only that the harm be 'physical or psychological,' but context makes it clear that the harm must be a great deal more than minimal. Not any harm will do nor may the level of risk of harm be low. The risk must be 'grave,' and when determining whether a grave risk of harm exists, courts must be attentive to the purposes of the Convention. For example, the harm must be 'something greater than would normally be expected on taking a child away from one parent and passing him to another'; otherwise, the goals of the Convention could be easily circumvented.

*Walsh*, 221 F.3d at 218 (citations omitted).

The First Circuit has also cautioned that "[t]he Article 13(b) defense may not be used 'as a vehicle to litigate (or relitigate) the child's best interests.' " *Danaipour*, 286 F.3d at 14 (citation omitted). Thus, in determining whether the petition for return ought to be granted, the task is not simply to determine where the child would be happiest or who would be the better parent. *Walsh*, 221 F.3d at 218; see also *Friedrich v. Friedrich*, 78 F.3d 1060, 1068 (6th Cir.1996). The Convention is designed to ensure that those and other issues underlying the custody dispute are presumptively to be adjudicated in the place of the child's habitual residence.

Further, a grave risk of harm is not "established by the mere fact that removal would unsettle the children who have now settled in the United States. That is an inevitable consequence of removal." *Walsh*, 221 F.3d at 220 n. 14. "A removing parent must not be allowed to abduct a child and then-when brought to court-complain that the child has grown used to the surroundings to which they were abducted. Under the logic of the Convention, it is the *abduction* that causes the pangs of subsequent return." *Friedrich*, 78 F.3d at 1068 (footnote omitted).

Applying those principles and considering all the circumstances of this case, I am not persuaded to the degree required that the children will be exposed to a grave risk of physical or psychological harm, or a situation that is otherwise "intolerable," if returned to Northern Ireland.

Prior to trial, I appointed a guardian ad litem, Dr. Sharon Gordetsky, a clinical psychologist with a specialty in children and families, to assess the risk of physical or psychological harm if the children were to be returned to Northern Ireland, and also to assess their degree of maturity and to determine the wishes of the children with respect to their being returned to Northern Ireland. Dr. Gordetsky prepared a comprehensive report and testified at trial.

The children had described to Dr. Gordetsky (as they had previously to a social worker in the probate court) that Dympna drank to excess on a regular basis, and that her drinking contributed to the bleak environment at the home in Northern Ireland. The children gave similar testimony in the trial. Dympna sometimes physically disciplined the children, and she solicited the assistance of her brother and a neighbor to physically discipline the children. There were two incidents described in the testimony that involved physical or violent discipline. In one incident, Dympna's brother Liam was said to have broken through a locked bathroom door and forcibly removed Daniel, striking him as he did so. In the other, the friend, Graham, was said to have slapped Sean on the head with the palm of his hand. There was no testimony about specific instances of physical violence directed at either Stephanie or Peter Óg. There was also general testimony about Dympna's striking the children and throwing household objects, but no specific instances were described. It is clear from the evidence that the children had grown troubled and fearful from the chaotic conditions and physical discipline to which they were subjected.

Dr. Gordetsky ultimately concluded in her written report that the children "were frequently exposed to situations that put them at serious risk for current and future psychological harm. Further, the children presented credible narratives that from a child's mental health perspective would constitute an intolerable situation." In reaching those conclusions, Dr. Gordetsky noted that the children had endured physical altercations with their mother, her brother, and her friend and that the home had deteriorated to a state of physical and emotional dysfunction and chaos. The relationship between Dympna and the children had become quite strained and has deteriorated further since they have been in the United States. Dr. Gordetsky testified that if returned to Northern Ireland the children would likely experience depression, anger, anxiety, shame, and betrayal.

I find that the children have been subjected to physical discipline and psychological distress while in their mother's care in Northern Ireland. I also find that, regardless of whether they stay in Massachusetts or return to Northern Ireland, they will likely continue to suffer some degree of psychological harm as a result of their parents' marital and parenting problems. I do not doubt Dr. Gordetsky's prognosis of continuing disruption and some level of consequent psychological harm if they were to be returned to Northern Ireland, especially in light of their own objections. The harm they have suffered and likely will suffer is not to be minimized and can certainly be characterized as "serious." However, in this circuit, at least, a "serious" risk of harm, short of a "grave" risk, does not rise to the level of prospective harm that the Article 13(b) exception recognizes as a reason for not returning a wrongfully removed or retained child.

Cases that have approved invocation of the Article 13(b) exception have focused on evidence of a sustained pattern of physical abuse and/or a propensity for violent abuse. *See, e.g., Walsh*, 221 F.3d at 219–220 (finding grave risk of harm where petitioner had severely beaten his wife over a number of years, including while she was pregnant, many of the beatings took place in front of her small children, and petitioner had a history of other violent activity and of chronic disobedience of court orders); *see also Danaipour v. McLarey*, 386 F.3d 289 (1st Cir.2004) (affirming district court finding of grave risk of psychological harm where petitioner had sexually abused one of the two children whose return was sought). Evidence of real but sporadic or isolated incidents of physical abuse, or of some limited incidents aimed at persons other than the child at issue, have not been found sufficient to support application of the "grave risk" exception. *See Whallon*, 230 F.3d at 460 (finding that allegations of physical and verbal abuse did not rise to the level needed to satisfy the Article 13(b) exception and stating that "[t]o conclude otherwise would risk substituting a best interest of the child analysis for the analysis the Convention requires"). Guided by these principles, I conclude that the respondent has not established the existence of a "grave risk" by clear and convincing evidence.

### 2. *The children object*

Peter also argues that I should take account of the children's own maturely formed objections to being returned to Northern Ireland and decline to order their return. In their trial testimony, each child expressed an objection to being returned to Northern Ireland. During their testimony, I observed the children to be intelligent, mature, and articulate. They displayed an appropriate understanding of and appreciation for the issues presented in this matter and effectively communicated their experiences and feelings concerning those issues. Among other reasons, the children testified that they do not respect their mother, she drinks too much, she fights with and hits them, and she had her brother and neighbor come to the house to discipline them. In contrast, the children testified that they preferred to remain in Massachusetts with their father because they have more respect for him, he does not drink, and he does not hit them. Generally, since July 2003, the children have become settled again at school and at home in Massachusetts, and they wish to remain in that environment. Their testimony appeared to represent their genuine thoughts and feelings; neither I nor Dr. Gordetsky (according to her) found indications that their testimony had been coached or otherwise unduly influenced by their father.

Dr. Gordetsky described in her report and testified at trial that she found each child to be cognitively and emotionally mature. She separately addressed for each child both the child's level of maturity and the substance of the child's objection to returning to Northern Ireland. She indicated that each child was capable of independent thought and was able to appropriately and effectively communicate his or her emotions and desires. Further, she found that each child demonstrated an appropriate appreciation for the implications of his or her expressed desire to remain in the United States, including a certain amount of ambivalence about the decision and its implications. She regarded the ambivalence as a sign of maturity, indicating an ability to weigh both sides of a question and an appreciation that decisions are not always "black-and-white."

With respect to Daniel and Sean, both 14, the judgment whether, under Article 13, to respect their objections is relatively easy. The Convention only applies to children who are under 16 years old, Convention, art. 4, and the authoritative commentary to the Convention suggests that children who are nearing 16 years should ordinarily have their own wishes respected. Elisa Pérez-Vera, *Explanatory Report on the 1980 Child Abduction Convention*, ¶ 30, at 433, in 3 Hague Conference on Private Int'l Law, Acts and Documents of the Fourteenth Session (1980), ("[T]he fact must be acknowledged that it would be very difficult to accept that a child of, for example, fifteen years of age, should be returned against its will."). The application of the exception is not automatic either for 15–year-olds or, as here, 14–year-olds, but it can be applied with more confidence the older the child. I have no trouble concluding, based on the evidence and my direct observations, that Daniel and Sean have attained an age and maturity such that their views ought to be taken into account. In my judgment, their objections to being returned to Ireland is thoughtfully and not reflexively reached and ought to be honored.

The decision regarding the objections of the younger two children, Stephanie and Peter Óg, is not as easy. Nevertheless, I place considerable reliance on Dr. Gordetsky's professional clinical assessment of them. Although recognizing that Stephanie and Peter Óg were not as mature as their older brothers, she nonetheless concluded that they were able to understand and appreciate the circumstances of the controversy concerning where they should reside and were similarly able to form and express a thoughtful opinion deserving of respect.

Additionally, Dr. Gordetsky noted that the four children were very close, in part having been pushed to band together by conditions in the home in Northern Ireland. With respect to Stephanie and Peter Óg, Dr. Gordetsky expressed the opinion that they would suffer some level of psychological harm if returned to Northern Ireland under any circumstances, and this would undoubtedly be exacerbated if they were ordered returned without Daniel and Sean. Thus, while the case for respecting the objections voiced by Stephanie and Peter Óg is not quite as strong as it is for Daniel and Sean, the additional factor of the psychological harm that the younger two would likely suffer if the children were separated gives support for the conclusion that they also should have their objections to return honored.

In the end, there are three possible choices: (1) return all the children to Northern Ireland, notwithstanding the validity of Daniel's and Sean's Article 13 objections; (2) honor Daniel's and Sean's objections and decline to order their return, but split the family and return the younger two whose objections may be somewhat less compelling; or (3) return none of the children, giving effect to Daniel's and Sean's objections and honoring Stephanie's and Peter Óg's objections as well on the basis of the combined assessment of the soundness of the objections and the prospect of harm from their return without their older siblings. The last of these seems the most satisfactory as the best accommodation of the various factors to be taken account of under the Convention.

It may be objected that this is simply a "best interests of the child" analysis masquerading as a "mature child's objection" analysis. The answer to that objection is that while the former is forbidden in proceedings under the Convention, the latter is invited. The Convention clearly contemplates that the objections of a mature child should be taken account of and can be relied on to override the return that would otherwise be mandated. Obviously, there may be some overlap between the two inquiries. One can easily appreciate that giving effect to the mature objection may in any given case also be thought to be in the child's best interest. But that coincidence surely should not defeat application of the Article 13 "objection" exception. It would be absurd to conclude that the child's mature objection should be honored *unless* it is in the child's best interest.

Congress has added to the Convention's endorsement of the exception the codicil that the factual predicate for finding that a mature objection has been made need only be established by the customary civil action standard of a preponderance of the evidence. In contrast to the other exception argued for in this case, the prospect of a "grave risk" of physical or psychological harm to the child if returned, establishing the "objection" exception to return is not subject to a stringent burden of proof, and thus a court may more readily find a valid objection than it could find the existence of a grave risk. This difference in stringency of examination is expressly mandated by ICARA. From this I conclude that the "objection" exception to a summary order of return is meant, both by the drafters and signers of the Convention and by Congress, to be used. Here, I find the conditions for its use satisfied.

### III.   Conclusion

Though Peter's retention of the children was wrongful under the Convention, I exercise the discretion granted by Article 13 of the Convention to refuse Dympna's petition for the return of the children to Northern Ireland.

It is SO ORDERED.

### Notes

1.   "Habitual residence" is an important concept in a number of the Hague conventions concerning children and family relations. The term is not defined in the Convention, and the drafters intended that it should be determined as a question of fact without all of the legal technicalities that surround the notions of domicile or nationality. *McManus* is straight forward in its analysis of this point, but some cases raise complex questions, particularly when the parents have different intentions as to the child's residence. See, e.g., Mozes v. Mozes, 239 F.3d 1067 (9th Cir. 2001).

2.   The Child Abduction Convention includes several affirmative defenses, set out in Articles 12, 13, and 20, that may be raised by a party who objects to return of a child. In the United States, ICARA requires proof by clear and convincing evidence of the "grave risk of harm" defense under Art. 13 (b), discussed in *McManus*, and the human rights defense under Art. 20. What kind of situation would suggest an argument under Article 20? See generally Merle H. Weiner, "Using Article 20," 38 Fam. L.Q. 583 (2004).

At the time the Child Abduction Convention was adopted, it was generally assumed in the United States that child abductions were usually carried out male non-custodial parents. Experience with the Convention, however, suggests that the majority of abductors are mothers, and these mothers often allege that they have been victims of domestic violence. See Merle H. Weiner, "International Child Abduction and the Escape from Domestic Violence," 69 Fordham L. Rev. 593 (2000). Because the Art. 13(b) defense focuses on the grave risk of harm to the child, it does not address the problem of spousal or partner violence. Domestic violence cases in which return orders were eventually denied under Art. 13(b) include Van De Sande v. Van De Sande, 431 F.3d 567 (7th Cir. 2005); Blondin v. Dubois, 238 F.3d 153 (2d Cir. 2001); and Walsh v. Walsh, 221 F.3d 204 (1st Cir. 2000). On the use of "undertakings" to attempt to ensure the safety of mothers and children when return is ordered, see Roxanne Hoegger, "What if She Leaves? Domestic Violence Cases Under the Hague Convention and the Insufficiency of the Undertakings Remedy," 18 Berkeley Women's L.J. 181 (2003). See also the excerpt reprinted below in Chapter 6 from Carol S. Bruch, "The Unmet Needs of Domestic Violence Victims and their Children in Hague Child Abduction Convention Cases," 38 Fam. L.Q. 529 (2004).

3. Article 12 of the Convention on the Rights of the Child provides that "States parties shall assure to the child who is capable of forming his own view s the right to express those views freely in all matters affecting the child, the views of the child being given due weight in accordance with the age and maturity of the child." Does the Child Abduction Convention adequately protect this right? See Rona Schuz, "The Hague Child Abduction Convention and Children's Rights," 12 Transnat'l L. & Contemp. Probs 393, 417–35 (2002).

4. *Problems.* (a) After a romance developed between Wim, who lived in Belgium, and Christina, who lived in New York, Christina learned that she was pregnant with Wim's child. Because there was free medical care available in Belgium, Wim persuaded Christina to have the baby there. Christina traveled to Belgium on a tourist visa, bringing only two suitcases, and lived there for six months until the child was born. By then, the parties' relationship had deteriorated, and Christina obtained a U.S. passport for the infant and returned with him to New York. Wim made several trips to New York over the next three months, but the parties' attempts to reconcile were not successful. Wim has filed a petition to return the baby to Belgium under the Hague Convention. What issues must the court resolve, and how should they be decided? (See Delvoye v. Lee, 329 F.3d 330 (3d Cir. 2003).)

(b) After planning their move for several years, Robert and Julie sold their house and moved from Minnesota to Israel in July 1999 with their two sons, who were 6 and 9 years old. The children enrolled in school, made friends, and began to learn Hebrew, but Julie was unhappy and wanted to return to the U.S. with the children. To prevent this, Robert procured an ex parte restraining order from the rabbinical court in Israel. He did agree that Julie could take the children back to Minnesota the next summer, however. Julie consulted a lawyer, who told her that she would probably lose custody of her children in the Israeli rabbinical court. Julie flew to Minnesota with the boys in June 2000, and filed for a legal separation and for custody in the state courts. She has refused to return to Israel with the children. In November 2000, Robert filed a petition under the Hague

Convention in federal district court. What arguments can Julie make in response to Robert's petition? (See Silverman v. Silverman, 338 F.3d 886 (8th Cir. 2003).)

# C.  CHILD SUPPORT

The modern trend toward increased enforcement of parental financial obligations is notable in both domestic and international law. Rates of divorce and nonmarital childbirth have increased substantially around the globe over the past generation; as these changes have taken place, the law of child support has taken on new importance.

## OFFICE OF CHILD SUPPORT v. SHOLAN

Vermont Supreme Court, 2001.
172 Vt. 619, 782 A.2d 1199.

In this international child support case, appellant and father Randall Sholan challenges the Caledonia Family Court's jurisdiction to enforce a child support order entered against him in the Federal Republic of Germany. We hold that the family court has jurisdiction to enforce the order, and affirm.

On November 8, 1995, in the Federal Republic of Germany, father signed a document acknowledging his paternity of Bianca Schwebler, daughter of Elisabeth Schwebler, and also acknowledging his obligation to support Bianca. The Schweblers are residents of Germany. On April 4, 1999, mother filed a complaint against father in Caledonia Family Court, seeking registration and enforcement of the foreign document as a child support order. The Vermont Office of Child Support joined in the action. Father responded with a motion to dismiss, claiming the family court lacked subject matter jurisdiction over the issue. The motion was denied, and after the June 15, 2000 enforcement hearing the magistrate entered an order enforcing the foreign child support order. Father appealed this order to the family court, which sustained the magistrate's decision. This appeal followed.

Father claims that the Federal Republic of Germany has not been declared by the United States Secretary of State to be a "foreign reciprocating country" pursuant to 42 U.S.C. § 659a(a)(1), and Vermont has not entered into a reciprocal arrangement with it for the establishment and enforcement of support obligations, pursuant to 42 U.S.C. § 659a(d). He further claims that these are the only remedies available for the enforcement of foreign child support orders, based on the constitutional principles of the exclusive power of the federal government to enter into relationships with foreign nations, the prohibition on states entering into treaties or alliances with foreign nations, and the exclusive right of the federal government to regulate commerce with foreign nations. Therefore, he argues, Vermont courts lack subject matter jurisdiction to enforce the foreign child support order. We note that, as the issue presented is a question of law, we review the family court's decision de novo.

Passed by Congress in 1996, 42 U.S.C. § 659a provides that the United States Secretary of State is authorized to declare any foreign country a "foreign reciprocating country" if "the foreign country has established, or undertakes to establish, procedures for the establishment and enforcement of duties of support owed to obligees who are residents of the United States." 42 U.S.C. § 659a(a)(1). Subsection (d) provides that "[s]tates may enter into reciprocal arrangements for the establishment and enforcement of support obligations with foreign countries that are not the subject of a declaration pursuant to subsection (a) of this section, to the extent consistent with Federal law." *Id.* § 659a(d). The statute was passed in recognition of the difficulties present in pursuing support orders across national boundaries, with the purpose of "allow[ing] and encourag[ing] the Secretary of State to pursue reciprocal support agreements with other nations." 1996 U.S.C.C.A.N. 2495.

It is uncontested by the parties that no formal declaration by the Secretary of State has been made under the authority of 42 U.S.C. § 659a recognizing the Federal Republic of Germany as a foreign reciprocating country. Nor is it contested that Vermont has not entered into a reciprocal arrangement, pursuant to 42 U.S.C. § 659a, with that country. This does not, however, preclude Vermont from giving effect to foreign child support orders under the doctrine of comity. *See State ex rel. Desselberg v. Peele*, 136 N.C.App. 206, 523 S.E.2d 125, 128–29 (1999) (recognizing state courts may recognize and enforce orders from foreign countries under principle of "comity of nations"); see also Restatement (Third) of Foreign Relations Law of the United States § 486(1) (1987) ("A court in the United States will recognize and enforce an order of a foreign court for support, valid and effective under the law of the state where it issued. . . .").

"State laws which 'interfere with, or are contrary to the laws of Congress' are invalidated by the Supremacy Clause of the United States Constitution." *Trustees of the Diocese of Vermont v. State*, 145 Vt. 510, 514, 496 A.2d 151, 153 (1985) (citing *Gibbons v. Ogden*, 22 U.S. (9 Wheat.) 1, 211, 6 L.Ed. 23 (1824); U.S. Const. art. VI). "When Congress chooses to legislate, pursuant to its constitutional powers, courts must find that local laws have been preempted by federal regulation if they stand as an obstacle to the accomplishment and execution of the full purposes and objectives of Congress." *Id.* (citing *Hines v. Davidowitz*, 312 U.S. 52, 67, 61 S.Ct. 399, 85 L.Ed. 581 (1941) (internal quotations omitted)). However, because domestic relations are "preeminently matters of state law," the United States Supreme Court has "consistently recognized that Congress, when it passes general legislation, rarely intends to displace state authority in this area." *Mansell v. Mansell*, 490 U.S. 581, 587, 109 S.Ct. 2023, 104 L.Ed.2d 675 (1989). Federal preemption of state family law mechanisms occurs where "Congress has positively required by direct enactment that state law be pre-empted." *Hisquierdo v. Hisquierdo*, 439 U.S. 572, 581, 99 S.Ct. 802, 59 L.Ed.2d 1 (1979) (internal quotation omitted). For preemption to exist, "[a] mere conflict in words is not sufficient. State family and family-property law must do major damage to clear and substantial federal interests before the Supremacy Clause will demand that state law be overridden." *Id.* (internal quotations omitted).

In the present case, there is neither an express preemption clause nor a conflict of words preventing Vermont from applying principles of comity to recognize and give effect to the foreign child support order at issue. The language of § 659a does not reflect in any way an intent by Congress to preempt state-level efforts at enforcement of foreign support orders. Cf. *Shute v. Shute*, 158 Vt. 242, 246, 607 A.2d 890, 893 (1992) (recognizing language of Parental Kidnapping Prevention Act, 28 U.S.C. § 1738A, indicated Congress's intent to preempt field of custody jurisdiction). Section 659a does not provide the sole mechanism by which foreign support orders may be enforced in state courts. The purpose of the statute, as reflected in its express language and the legislative history behind its passage, is to provide the United States Secretary of State with the power to enter into reciprocal agreements with foreign nations so as to promote the recognition and enforcement of foreign support orders, and not to prevent states from giving effect to foreign support orders. Nor does the statute require states to enter into reciprocal enforcement arrangements with the foreign nations from which the orders originated before seeking to enforce those orders. We also note that father has not argued that any clear and substantial federal interests will suffer major damage by the family court's recognition and enforcement of this child support order.

As § 659a does not preempt state law jurisdiction over this foreign support order, we next examine whether the family court properly applied the principles of comity in recognizing and enforcing the foreign support order. As a general matter, under principles of comity, final judgments of courts of foreign nations which concern recovery of sums of money, the status of a person, or determine interests in property, are conclusive between the parties to the action and are entitled to recognition in United States courts. Restatement (Third) of Foreign Relations Law of the United

States § 481 (1987). The Restatement further refines the principle of comity, providing that "[a] foreign judgment is generally entitled to recognition by courts in the United States to the same extent as a judgment of a court of one State in the courts of another State." Reciprocity between the foreign state which issued the order and the domestic state which seeks to recognize and enforce it is unnecessary for the order to be recognized or enforced in the domestic state. For a court to recognize and give effect to a foreign order, the judgment must have been rendered under a judicial system which provides impartial tribunals and procedures compatible with due process of law, and the issuing court must have had jurisdiction over the defendant sufficient to support rendering such a decision in the state in which the order is sought to be enforced. *Id.* § 482(1). If these prerequisites have been met, the state court may still decline to recognize the foreign order, if the issuing court lacked subject matter jurisdiction over the action; the defendant was not accorded adequate notice of the proceeding; the judgment was obtained by fraud; the original action or judgment is in conflict with state or federal public policy; the judgment conflicts with another judgment entitled to recognition; or the foreign proceeding was contrary to an agreement by the parties to submit the controversy to another forum for resolution. *Id.* § 482(2).

In assessing whether the foreign order met these requirements, the family court had before it evidence that the Federal Republic of Germany has enacted laws and procedures similar to Vermont laws concerning child support, and are compatible with due process; that defendant was under the jurisdiction of the body which issued the order, and that body also had jurisdiction over the action; that the cause of action was consistent with Vermont public policy, "ensuring that parents make their best efforts to provide monetary support for their minor children"; and that there was no indication or contention by either party that the judgment against defendant was obtained by fraud or was in conflict with another judgment. Based on the evidence presented concerning these factors, the court properly found that the fairness requirements of the Restatement § 482 had been met, and correctly concluded that it was required to recognize and enforce the support order at issue.

Affirmed.

### Notes

1. Since passage of 42 U.S.C. § 659(a) in 1996, the United States has reached agreements with various Canadian provinces and a number of other foreign countries concerning child support enforcement. A list of these "foreign reciprocating countries" is available on the website of the Department of State at www.travel.state.gov.

The Uniform Interstate Family Support Act (UIFSA), which has been adopted in some form in all of the United States, is available as a tool for enforcement of some foreign child support orders. UIFSA § 102(21) achieves this by defining "State" to include those foreign jurisdictions with child support laws and procedures that are substantially similar to the procedures under UIFSA, as well as those that have been declared to be foreign reciprocating jurisdictions under federal law and those that have established a reciprocal child support arrangement with a particular state. See, e.g., Willmer v. Willmer, 144 Cal.App.4th 951, 51 Cal.Rptr.3d 10 (2006).

2. Harmonization of laws concerning child support enforcement has been a difficult project, marked by a series of Hague conventions addressing recognition of judgments and choice of law problems as well as a variety of regional agreements on enforcement of family maintenance obligations. A large group of nations, not including the United States, participates in the 1956 New York Convention on the Recovery Abroad of Maintenance, 268 U.N.T.S. 32–47 (1957). See generally Ann Laquer Estin, "Families and Children in International Law: An Introduction," 12 Transnat'l L & Contemp. Probs. 271; 277–79 (2002); Gary Caswell, "International Child Support: 1999," 32 Fam L.Q. 525 (1998).

A new Hague Convention on International Recovery of Child Support and Other Forms of Family Maintenance is scheduled for completion during 2007; information on the Maintenance Convention is available on the Hague Conference website at www.hcch.net. See William Duncan, "The Development of the New Hague Convention on the International Recovery of Child Support and Other Forms of Family Maintenance," 38 Fam. L.Q. 663 (2004).

# CONVENTION ON THE RIGHTS OF THE CHILD

United Nations G.A. Document A/RES/44/25 of December 5, 1989. 28 I.L.M. 1448.

## *Article 27*

1. States Parties recognize the right of every child to a standard of living adequate for the child's physical, mental, spiritual, moral and social development.

2. The parent(s) or others responsible for the child have the primary responsibility to secure, within their abilities and financial capacities, the conditions of living necessary for the child's development.

3. States Parties, in accordance with national conditions and within their means, shall take appropriate measures to assist parents and others responsible for the child to implement this right and shall in case of need provide material assistance and support programmes, particularly with regard to nutrition, clothing and housing.

4.  States Parties shall take all appropriate measures to secure the recovery of maintenance for the child from the parents or other persons having financial responsibility for the child, both within the State Party and from abroad. In particular, where the person having financial responsibility for the child lives in a State different from that of the child, States Parties shall promote the accession to international agreements or the conclusion of such agreements, as well as the making of other appropriate arrangements.

### Notes

1.  To what extent does the law in the United States fulfill the obligations suggested by Article 27 of the Convention on the Rights of the Child?

2.  For comparative perspectives on child support, see Mavis Maclean and Andrea Warman, "A Comparative Approach to Child Support Systems: Legal Rules and Social Policies," in Child Support: The Next Frontier (J. Thomas Oldham and Marygold S. Melli, eds. 2000) and John Eekelaar, "Child Support as Distributive and Commutative Justice: The United Kingdom Experience," in Child Support: The Next Frontier, supra. See also J. Thomas Oldham, "Lessons from the New English and Australian Child Support Systems," 29 Vand. J. Transnat'l L. 691 (1996).

# Chapter 6

# FAMILY VIOLENCE

'Family violence' includes all forms of violence within families, whether between spouses, or partners between parents and children, or between siblings. It appears in a range of legal contexts, including custody, visitation, divorce, abduction and asylum.

Global issues arise in this context, in part, because of cultural conflicts about what constitutes 'violence' and the circumstances, if any, under which it is allowed. What may be regarded as criminal in one state may be viewed in another as appropriate punishment or discipline to which one person, typically the husband or father, may properly subject another.

This chapter addresses two major forms of family violence: spousal abuse and child maltreatment. While commentators often use the term 'domestic violence' to refer to violence between partners, including but not limited to married partners, we use the term 'spousal abuse', including abuse in spouse-like relationships, to distinguish between adult/adult and adult/child abuse. The focus is on those legal contexts in which the abused or maltreated person seeks protection from the state, rather than cases in which one party seeks compensation from the other.

## A. SPOUSAL ABUSE

### BARBARA STARK, DOMESTIC VIOLENCE AND INTERNATIONAL LAW: GOOD–BYE EARL
47 Loy. L. Rev. 255 (2001).

Domestic violence is a global problem and international lawyers deal with it in three specific contexts. My purpose here is simply to introduce those contexts to the non-international lawyer or law student and, as a corollary, to introduce the relevant domestic violence law to international lawyers.

First, several "private" international treaties have been ratified and come into force, such as the Hague Convention on the Civil Aspects of International Child Abduction ("Hague Convention on Abduction"). These treaties resolve conflicts of law issues by coordinating the national laws of states parties. While these treaties do not explicitly refer to domestic violence, it is often a relevant issue in the underlying domestic law, which must be taken into account under the treaty. Second, as part of public international law, domestic violence has recently been recognized as a violation of women's human rights. Finally, domestic violence has been the subject of several important initiatives, as well as sustained efforts at education and intervention, by a number of international organizations ("IO"s) and nongovernmental organizations ("NGO"s). Thus, domestic violence is a recurring theme in the study of international law, vividly illustrating the many ways in which international law interacts with and shapes domestic norms.

*The Hague Convention on Abduction*

Article 13b of the Hague Convention is triggered in domestic violence cases. It provides:

> Notwithstanding the provisions of the preceding Article, the judicial or administrative authority of the requested State is not bound to order the return of the child if the person, institution or other body which opposes its return establishes that there is a grave risk that his or her return would expose the child to physical or psychological harm or otherwise place the child in an intolerable situation.

Under the Act, there are only three affirmative defenses available to defeat a demand that the child be returned under the Convention. These are set out at: (1) [There exists a] court order granting the defendant legal custody or visitation rights and that order was obtained pursuant to the Uniform Child Custody Jurisdiction Act and was in effect at the time of the offense; (2) The defendant was fleeing an incidence or pattern of domestic violence; (3) The defendant had physical custody of the child pursuant to a court order granting legal custody or visitation rights and failed to return the child as a result of circumstances beyond the defendant's control, and the defendant notified [the other parent].

While the Supreme Court of Canada has held that "the physical or psychological harm contemplated by the first clause of Article 13 is harm to a degree that also amounts to an intolerable situation," the United States Court of Appeals for the First Circuit has rejected such a narrow reading. Rather, in Walsh v. Walsh, the court held that the district court erroneously required a showing of an "immediate, serious threat" to the children under Article 13b. The court found that respondent mother had proven by clear and convincing evidence that the children faced a grave risk of exposure to physical or psychological harm should they be returned to Ireland.

The court explicitly noted "credible social science literature" showing that serial spousal abusers are also likely to be child abusers. The court further noted that "both state and federal law have recognized that children are at increased risk of physical and psychological injury themselves when they are in contact with a spousal abuser." Thus, the court concluded that the requisite "threshold showing of grave risk of exposure to physical or psychological harm" had been made.

### The Hague Convention on Adoption

Domestic violence is an issue under the Hague Convention on Adoption in at least two distinct contexts. First, the Convention requires that the birth parents voluntarily relinquish the child. Thus, it must be asked whether the mother's relinquishment is effectively coerced by domestic violence or the threat of domestic violence. Second, the Convention requires a determination as to the suitability of the adoptive parents. Thus, it must be asked whether the adoptive parents have been screened for domestic violence. As the death of Lisa Steinberg made so brutally clear, a child being adopted into an abusive relationship is at risk not only of witnessing abuse but of being abused herself.

### As a Violation of Women's Human Rights

Historically, domestic violence was not viewed as a violation of women's human rights because it is not perpetuated by the state. Rather, it was considered "private," "natural," or "cultural." International consciousness has been raised in the last decade, however. The three World Conferences on Women that the UN organized in connection with the UN Decade for Women between 1975 and 1985 (Mexico City 1975, Copenhagen 1980, Nairobi 1985) provided an opportunity to bring the issue of violence against women to international attention.

This raised consciousness is grounded in the work of women's groups on several fronts. Some groups lobbied for recognition of rape as a war crime before the ad hoc criminal tribunals in Rwanda and the former Yugoslavia. Others urged the international community to mobilize against female genital surgeries. Still others explicitly focused on domestic violence. On virtually every issue, women's groups worked on the regional and national as well as the international level.

Their work culminated in the 1993 Declaration on the Elimination of Violence Against Women, which recognizes that violence against women "both violates and impairs or nullifies the enjoyment by women of human rights and fundamental freedoms." It also resulted in the appointment of the Special Rapporteur on Violence Against Women, Radhika Coomaraswamy.

The Special Rapporteur, through a series of fact-finding missions and over two dozen reports prepared by her office on the topic of violence against women, brought international consciousness to a new level. Now, a state's acquiescence, or failure to take effective measures to combat domestic violence, is recognized as a violation of women's human rights. While the Declaration was aspirational, its prohibition of violence against women can now be characterized as emerging customary international law.

With the unanimous adoption of the Declaration on the Elimination of Violence Against Women in 1993, 180 states recognized domestic violence as a violation of women's international human rights. The issue of state responsibility is explicitly addressed in Article 4: "States should condemn violence against women and ... pursue by all appropriate means and without delay a policy of eliminating violence against women." Such measures should include: ratifying the Women's Convention (or withdrawing reservations), preventing, investigating and punishing violence against women, whether on the part of the state or private persons, and modifying social and cultural conduct based on stereotyped roles. Finally, the state should document its efforts in self-monitoring reports submitted to existing treaty bodies.

Although the Declaration was aspirational, its unanimous adoption in conjunction with the proliferation of domestic legislation, executive action, and national judicial decisions which followed, along with the repeated references to state responsibility for domestic violence in reports of the Human Rights Commission, the Special Rapporteur on Domestic Violence, and other international instruments as well as regional human rights instruments, supports the proposition that states may indeed be held responsible for domestic violence.

Once state responsibility is established, the substance of international norms against domestic violence may be understood as a clarification and elaboration of existing human rights norms. The Declaration explicitly recognizes that violence against women violates their "human rights and fundamental freedoms." "Violence against women" has been defined by the Committee on Human Rights as "any act of gender-based violence that results in, or is likely to result in, physical, sexual or psychological harm or suffer-

ing to women, including threats, domestic violence, crimes committed in the name of honor...." Paragraph 15(d) reiterates state
obligations, including the state's obligations to pass domestic legislation prohibiting violence against women.

As the Special Rapporteur explains in her Report of 21 January
1999, the "fundamental human rights to be free from torture,
gender discrimination and the inherent right to life are directly
applicable to ... violence against women." These rights, i.e., to be
free from torture, gender discrimination and the right to life, are
well established in CIL. Indeed, their lineage is cited in the Declaration itself. Thus, in a general sense, the rights set out in the
Declaration are already CIL. The Declaration, accordingly, represents the codification and clarification of general rights already
recognized in CIL in the specific context of domestic violence. The
concrete substance of the right, of course, is a function of the
concrete context in which it is recognized.

*The Convention on the Elimination of All Forms of Discrimination
Against Women (the Women's Convention")*

The Women's Convention does not explicitly prohibit violence
against women. As Joan Fitzpatrick notes, however, the Committee
on the Elimination of Discrimination Against Women ("CEDAW")
has attempted to retroactively fill in the gaps through "creative
interpretation" of the Women's Convention. In General Recommendation No. 19, for example, CEDAW explained that "gender-based
violence is a form of discrimination" and thus included in the
Women's Convention's bar against gender discrimination in general. In addition, the Women's Convention requires all parties to
"take all appropriate measures to eliminate discrimination against
women by any person, organization or enterprise." CEDAW read
this as making states responsible for private acts "if they fail to 'act
with due diligence to prevent violations of rights, or to investigate
and punish acts of violence, and to provide compensation.' "

United States is not a party to the Women's Convention, but it
is a signatory. Thus, the United States has the obligation at the
very least to refrain from any action that would contravene the
Convention.

*The Convention Against Torture ("CAT")*

The CAT has been ratified by the United States and the
necessary implementing legislation, the Foreign Affairs Reform and
Restructuring Act of 1998, has been enacted. "Torture" is defined
in Article 1 as the "intentional infliction of severe pain and of
suffering" with a view to achieving a wide range of purposes, by, or

with the acquiescence of, a person acting in an official capacity. As Rhonda Copelon and others have argued, and as the Special Rapporteur has confirmed, domestic violence may be torture. As such, it is subject to the penalties set out in the United States implementing legislation.

In addition, Article 3 of the CAT expressly provides for the withholding of removal of any individual seeking asylum in the United States who would "more likely than not" face a risk of torture should she be returned to her native country. Thus, the CAT offers what one commentator characterizes as a "viable alternative legal remedy" for immigrant women fleeing domestic violence.

*Inter-American Convention on Violence Against Women*

The Inter–American Convention on the Prevention, Punishment, and Eradication of Violence Against Women ("Convention of Belém Do Pará") was open for ratification in 1995. This Convention explicitly bars violence against women, but the United States is not yet a party. Article 10 defines violence against women as "any act of conduct, based on gender, which causes death or physical, sexual or psychological harm or suffering to women, whether in the public or private sphere." Article 6 affirms a woman's right to be free from all forms of discrimination, including "stereotyped patterns of behavior and social practices based on concepts of inferiority or subordination."

Article 8 requires the state to support educational and training programs, to change attitudes that contribute to violence against women, to provide specialized services for women who are the victims of violence, to develop guidelines for the media to promote more positive images of women, to support research on the causes, consequences, and frequency of violence against women, and to foster "international cooperation for the exchange of ideas and experiences and the execution of programs aimed at protecting women." Article 11 authorizes the Inter–American Court of Human Rights to give advisory opinions on its interpretation at the request of the state signatories and the CIM, and Article 12 permits individuals as well as NGOs to file petitions with the Inter–American Commission on Human Rights regarding violations of Article 7, which requires the state to "pursue policies to prevent, punish, and eradicate ... violence." Chapter IV of the Inter–American Convention sets out additional enforcement mechanisms, including self-monitoring.

## CAROL S. BRUCH, THE UNMET NEEDS OF DOMESTIC VIOLENCE VICTIMS AND THEIR CHILDREN IN HAGUE CHILD ABDUCTION CONVENTION CASES

38 Fam. L.Q. 529 (2004).

The 1980 Hague Child Abduction Convention, as currently applied, imposes unnecessary hardships on domestic violence victims and their children. These difficult cases require better solutions, and this article suggests how they can be accomplished. Courts need only return to the original structure and purposes of the Convention and inform themselves about the realities of abusive relationships.

The Abduction Convention was written to remove the advantages of self-help in child custody cases. Its primary goal was to defeat an abductor's hoped-for advantages, whether practical or legal. Its solution for most cases was to restore the status quo ante as expeditiously as possible by returning the child to its habitual residence. The courts of that place, it was believed, would be in the best position to deal with the merits of any custody dispute.

This aspect of the Convention has been well understood and, if anything, perhaps too well implemented. Without doubt, it works well in a great number of cases. It was never intended, however, to apply to all cases.

\* \* \*

Several fact patterns were left outside the remedy, and the Convention's Rapporteur, Professor Perez–Vera, explained why:

> Two objects of the Convention—[to deter abductions and] to secure the immediate reintegration of the child into the habitual environment—both correspond to a specific idea of what constitutes the 'best interests of the child.' However, even when viewing [the Convention] from this perspective, it has to be admitted that the removal of the child can sometimes be justified by objective reasons which have to do either with its person, or with the environment with which it is most closely connected. Therefore the Convention recognizes the need for certain exceptions to the general obligations assumed by States to secure the prompt return of children who have been unlawfully removed or retained. For the most part, these exceptions are only concrete illustrations of the overly vague principle whereby the interests of the child are stated to be the guiding criterion in this area.

In other words, although the basic scheme of the Convention leaves the hearing on an individual child's best interests to the courts of the habitual residence, its exceptions are intended as a deviation from this norm. Each defense to return, as Professor Perez–Vera indicates, addresses a concrete factual situation in which an individual child's best interests are, indeed, meant to control the outcome of the Hague proceeding.

\* \* \*

Widespread inattention to this history has caused much of the difficulty we now see in domestic violence cases. Those who had opposed any exceptions continued to caution judges about the dangers of loopholes that might eviscerate the Convention. Simultaneously, some courts expanded the Convention's definition of custody rights. The consequence is that many petitioners now obtain return orders although it is very unlikely that their children's best interests could be served by an award of custody to them—a situation the drafters sought to avoid. This unfortunate development stems in part from judicial opinions that have emphasized the perceived virtues of returning children as a matter of discretion even if valid defenses exist. In the context of abuse, a judge in one legal system may assert, for example, that it would be offensive to another legal system to suggest that it might not be able to protect a domestic violence victim or a child who has suffered abuse. No proof of the judicial system's adequacy is required; indeed—to the contrary—the victim is asked to carry the burden of establishing its inadequacies.

Nothing in the Convention requires such assumptions, and they have been challenged at last. American and Australian courts alike concluded in 2001 that judges who presume the habitual residence can protect the victims of violence abdicate their judicial responsibilities. As a federal judge in Michigan put it, a court's power to order a return as a matter of discretion after a defense has been established "does not equate to license; even where the Court has discretion, it must not exercise that discretion before it considers the relevant facts." This reasoning also appeared in a decision of the High Court of Australia as it set aside two return orders from the Full Court of the Australian Family Court.

\* \* \*

### *Note*

For fuller discussions of the Intercountry Adoption Convention and the Child Abduction Convention, see Chapters 4C and 5B of these materials.

# EMMANUEL QUANSAK, PROGRESS AND RETROGRESSION ON DOMESTIC VIOLENCE LEGISLATION IN GHANA

International Survey of Family Law 1, 241–242 (Andrew Bainham ed. 2006).

Perhaps the most sustained criticism of the [proposed Domestic Violence] Bill has been is abrogation of the immunity of a husband from criminal prosecution for raping his wife. The Ghanaian common law follows the English common law principle that by marriage a wife consents to intercourse with her husband and this confers on the husband a privilege which the wife cannot withdraw whenever she pleases. It follows from this principle that a husband cannot be guilty as a principal in the first degree of rape on his wife. However, after from 350 years of operation of the common law immunity, the English House of Lords unanimously held in R v. R that ... in modern times the supposed marital exemption in rape forms no part of the law of England. There is no indication as yet that the Ghanaian courts will follow the English example by jettisoning this archaic principle.

In the context of customary law, it has been stated that:

'[T]he conceptual idea that a wife in a customary marriage can be raped by her husband does not even exist because all sex within a customary marriage is considered "consensual", whether or not the woman consents. This is true because ... marriage results in a women's physical person and her sexuality becoming part of her husband's property. [I]t is a general rule all over Africa that a man can never be said to rape his own wife. As such, forced sex within marriage does not constitute an offense either under customary law or statutory law.'

It is in the context of these principles that the Bill has been strongly criticized. Another citric, Mr. F. Koonsom of the Ahmadiya Muslim Missions, contends that the definition of sexual abuse as contained in clause 3(1)(ii) of the Bill will enlighten and exhort women to refuse their husbands sex. This, in his view, will exacerbate the incidence of divorce cases.

A corollary to the above criticism is that the prosecution, conviction and sentencing of husbands for marital rape would destroy the sanctity of marriage. The National Coalition on Domestic Violence Legislation has countered this criticism by stating that experiences in 26 countries that have laws to prosecute marital rape belie this criticism. Furthermore, it is the view of the Coalition that one of the basic tenets of Ghanaian culture is the respect for the dignity of the human being. The Bill advocates respect for the dignity of every person in the domestic setting and abhors abuse in every form. They point out, for example, that in Akan culture, a married woman has the right to sexual satisfaction and can complain where her husband does not provide this. They contend that this example demonstrates that sexual abuse is definitely not accepted in this culture because the presence of sexual satisfaction precludes sexual abuse.

# BARBARA STARK, DOMESTIC VIOLENCE

International Family Law: An Introduction, 227–228 (2005).

At the same time, there is ongoing resistance to [international law] developments and there are new backlashes against them. Some States, such as Bangladesh and the Sudan, for example, have enacted religious laws or Shariah, interpretations of Islam that severely limit the rights of women. This is often presented as a defense of local norms, including the traditional prerogative of the patriarch within the home, and resistance to Western cultural imperialism.

Cultures may vary within a State as well. In the United States, for example, a comprehensive study was done to determine the effectiveness of mandatory arrest policies in connection with domestic violence. Under such policies, adopted on the municipal level, a city would require its police force to arrest the defendant whenever a domestic violence complaint was made. In the absence of such policies, in contrast, when the police appeared in response to a domestic violence complaint, the complainant would often recant and withdraw her complaint.

The study showed mixed results. In some cities, mandatory arrests was effective in reducing domestic violence (or at least, domestic violence complaints) over time. In others, however, mandatory arrest policies produced an apparent *increase* in domestic violence complaints. The researchers determined that the different results correlated to the racial makeup of the cities studied. In predominately black cities, mandatory arrests produced a backlash, while in predominately white cities, mandatory arrest policies were an effective deterrent. Where the arrest had negative consequences for the defendant (in addition to those directly attributable to the arrest itself), such as shame, loss of status in the community, or loss of a job, such policies were apt to be effective. Where the defendants did not have an image to protect in the community, and may even have regarded the complaint against them as a betrayal, there was more likely to be retaliatory violence once the defendant was released. Thus, the promulgation of laws and policies to address domestic violence, as set forth below, may show a good faith effort on the part of State officials to address the problem. Unless such measures are carefully tailored to the culture in which they are expected to operate, however, they may be futile or even counterproductive.

## *Notes*

1. As noted in the excerpts above, in Ghana the proposed Domestic Violence Bill has been criticized as contrary to the 'general rule all over Africa that a man can never be said to rape his own wife.' In the United States, mandatory arrest produced a backlash in some cities. How would you reply to critics of efforts to stem domestic violence in both countries?

2. Domestic violence is often a politically sensitive issue. Campaigns against domestic violence by those outside the country, such as human rights activists, are often criticized as 'Western' or 'imperialist.' The same arguments may be repeated within a country, with different factions replicating the larger debate. In Pakistan, since the enactment of the Hudood Ordinance thousands of women have been jailed for adultery. Women have been jailed under this law when they have been raped or when their former husbands refuse to recognize their divorces. President Pervez Musharraf introduced the Women's Protection Bill to improve his country's image in the West. But strong opposition, including some from his own coalition, has put the measure on hold. See Carlotta Gall & Salman Masood, "Pakistan Bid to End Abuse of Women Reporting Rape Hits Snag", N.Y. Times, September 14, 2006. See also Michelle A. McKinley, "Emancipatory Politics and Rebellious Practices: Incorporating Global Human Rights in Family Violence Laws in Peru." N.Y.U.J. Int'l L. & Pol. 75–139 (2006).

3. Why are the laws against domestic violence so often ineffective? What can be done to strengthen them? Is strengthening the laws the most promising approach? What else can be done?

## THE REFUGEE ACT OF 1980
### 8 U.S.C. § 1101(a)(42).

The term "refugee" means (A) any person who is outside any country of such person's nationality * * * and who is unable or unwilling to return to * * * that country because of persecution or a well-founded fear of persecution on account of race, religion, nationality, membership in a particular social group, or political opinion * * *.

## IN RE R–A–, RESPONDENT
### Decided by Attorney General (January 19, 2001).
### WL 1744475(BIA).

The question before us is whether the respondent qualifies as a "refugee" as a result of the heinous abuse she suffered and still fears from her husband in Guatemala. Specifically, we address whether the repeated spouse abuse inflicted on the respondent makes her eligible for asylum as an alien who has been persecuted on account of her membership in a particular social group or her political opinion.

\* \* \*

The respondent is a native and citizen of Guatemala. She married at age 16. Her husband was then 21 years old. He currently resides in Guatemala, as do their two children, immediately after their marriage, the respondent and her husband moved to Guatemala City. From the beginning of the marriage, her husband engaged in acts of physical and sexual abuse against the respondent. He was domineering and violent. The respondent testified that her husband "always mistreated me from the moment we were married, he was always . . . aggressive."

\* \* \*

As their marriage proceeded, the level and frequency of his rage increased concomitantly with the seeming senselessness and irrationality of his motives. He dislocated the respondent's jaw bone when her menstrual period was 15 days late. When she refused to abort her 3– to 4–month-old fetus, he kicked her violently in her spine. He would hit or kick the respondent "whenever he felt like it, wherever he happened to be: in the house, on the street, on the bus." The respondent stated that "[a]s time went on, he hit me for no reason at all."

The respondent's husband raped her repeatedly. He would beat her before and during the unwanted sex. . .

The respondent ran away to her brother's and parents' homes, but her husband always found her. Around December 1994, the respondent attempted to flee with her children outside the city, but her husband found her again. He appeared at her door, drunk, and as she turned to leave, he struck her in the back of her head causing her to lose consciousness. When she awoke, he kicked her and dragged her by her hair into another room and beat her to unconsciousness.

\* \* \*

The respondent's pleas to Guatemalan police did not gain her protection. On three occasions, the police issued summons for her husband to appear, but he ignored them, and the police did not take further action. Twice, the respondent called the police, but they never responded. When the respondent appeared before a judge, he told her that he would not interfere in domestic disputes. . . The respondent knew of no shelters or other organizations in Guatemala that could protect her. The abuse began "from the moment [they] were married," and continued until the respondent fled Guatemala in May 1995. One morning in May 1995, the respondent decided to leave permanently. With help, the respondent was able to flee Guatemala, and she arrived in Brownsville, Texas, 2 days later.

A witness, testifying for the respondent, stated that she learned through the respondent's sister that the respondent's husband was "going to hunt her down and kill her if she comes back to Guatemala."

We struggle to describe how deplorable we find the husband's conduct to have been.

* * *

The Immigration Judge found the respondent to be credible, and she concluded that the respondent suffered harm that rose to the level of past persecution. The Immigration Judge also held that the Guatemalan Government was either unwilling or unable to control the respondent's husband. The balance of her decision addressed the issue of whether the respondent's harm was on account of a protected ground.

The Immigration Judge first concluded that the respondent was persecuted because of her membership in the particular social group of "Guatemalan women who have been involved intimately with Guatemalan male companions, who believe that women are to live under male domination." She found that such a group was cognizable and cohesive, as members shared the common and immutable characteristics of gender and the experience of having been intimately involved with a male companion who practices male domination through violence. The Immigration Judge then held that members of such a group are targeted for persecution by the men who seek to dominate and control them.

The Immigration Judge further found that, through the respondent's resistance to his acts of violence, her husband imputed to the respondent the political opinion that women should not be dominated by men, and he was motivated to commit the abuse because of the political opinion he believed her to hold . . .

As noted above, we agree with the Immigration Judge that the severe injuries sustained by the respondent rise to the level of harm sufficient (and more than sufficient) to constitute "persecution." We also credit the respondent's testimony in general and specifically her account of being unsuccessful in obtaining meaningful assistance from the authorities in Guatemala. Accordingly, we find that she has adequately established on this record that she was unable to avail herself of the protection of the Government of Guatemala in connection with the abuse inflicted by her husband. The determinative issue, as correctly identified by the Immigration Judge, is whether the harm experienced by the respondent was, or in the future may be, inflicted "on account of" a statutorily protected ground . . .

Nowhere in the record does the respondent recount her husband saying anything relating to what he thought her political views to be, or that the violence towards her was attributable to her actual or imputed beliefs. Moreover, this is not a case where there is meaningful evidence that this respondent held or evinced a political opinion, unless one assumes that the common human desire not to be harmed or abused is in itself a "political opinion."

As we understand the respondent's rationale, it would seem that virtually any victim of repeated violence who offers some resistance could qualify for asylum, particularly where the government did not control the assailant. Under this approach, the perpetrator is presumed to impute to the victim a political opinion, in opposition to the perpetrator's authority, stemming simply from an act of resistance . . .

In this case, even if we were to accept as a particular social group "Guatemalan women who have been involved intimately with Guatemalan male companions, who believe that women are to live under male domination," the respondent has not established that her husband has targeted and harmed the respondent because he perceived her to be a member of this particular social group . . .

The Immigration Judge's nexus analysis fails to limit consistently the source of persecution to the respondent's husband. At one point, the Immigration Judge seems to identify all Guatemalan males who abuse their partners as the persecutors, but the record indicates that the respondent suffered and feared intimate violence only from her own husband.

Indeed, the record does not reflect that the respondent's husband bore any particular animosity toward women who were intimate with abusive partners, women who had previously suffered abuse, or women who happened to have been born in, or were actually living in, Guatemala. There is little doubt that the respondent's spouse believed that married women should be subservient to their own husbands. But beyond this, we have scant information on how he personally viewed other married women in Guatemala, let alone women in general.

The respondent in this case has been terribly abused and has a genuine and reasonable fear of returning to Guatemala. Whether the district director may, at his discretion, grant the respondent relief upon humanitarian grounds—relief beyond the jurisdiction of the Immigration Judge and this Board—is a matter the parties can explore outside the present proceedings. We further note that Congress has legislated various forms of relief for abused spouses and children. The issue of whether our asylum laws (or some other legislative provision) should be amended to include additional protection for abused women, such as this respondent, is a matter to be addressed by Congress. In our judgment, however, Congress did not intend the "social group" category to be an all-encompassing residual category for persons facing genuine social ills that governments do not remedy.

DISSENTING OPINION:

\* \* \*

This case presents two questions: (1) whether a woman trapped in a long-term relationship with an abusive spouse, in a country in which such abuse is tolerated by society and ignored by governmental officials, is a member of a particular social group entitled to the protection of asylum law; and, (2) whether the domestic abuse in the instant case was at least partially motivated by an actual or imputed political opinion.

This is not merely a case of domestic violence involving criminal conduct. The respondent's husband engaged in a prolonged and persistent pattern of abuse designed to dominate the respondent and to overcome any effort on her part to assert her independence or to resist his abuse. His mistreatment and persecution of her in private and in public was founded, as the majority states, on his view that it was his right to treat his wife as "his property to do as he pleased." He acted with the knowledge that no one would interfere. His horrific conduct, both initially and in response to her opposition to it, was not that of an individual acting at variance with societal norms, but one who recognized that he was acting in accordance with them.

The harm to the respondent occurred in the context of egregious governmental acquiescence. When the respondent sought the aid and assistance of government officials and institutions, she was told that they could do nothing for her . . .

The fundamental purpose of domestic violence is to punish, humiliate, and exercise power over the victim on account of her gender:

At its most complex, domestic violence exists as a powerful tool of oppression. Violence against women in general, and domestic violence in particular, serve as essential components in societies which oppress women, since violence against women not only derives from but also sustains the dominant gender stereotypes and is used to control women in the one space traditionally dominated by women, the home.

# DEBORAH ANKER, MEMBERSHIP IN A PARTICULAR SOCIAL GROUP: RECENT DEVELOPMENTS IN U.S. LAW

1514 PLI/Corp 119, 131.

Another area of gender asylum law that is undergoing a profound change is domestic violence-based claims. Women who face domestic violence fear a form of harm that is gender-based– that is, the harm they fear is because of their gender. For many years, advocates won cases on this basis, but one critical case where the Board held the other way was In Re R–A-where a Guatemalan woman who faced horrific abuse and oppression at the hands of her husband sought asylum. The IJ unfortunately adopted a poorly formulated PSG construction (poorly constructed for the reasons stated above): "Guatemalan women who have been involved intimately with Guatemalan male companions, who believe that women are to live under male domination." (Although he also suggested an alternative construction based on gender per se, which the Board did not address). The BIA denied R–A-'s claim and found that PSG was not "cognizable" and lacked the required "nexus" between membership in the group and the abuser's motivation to inflict harm

Attorney General Reno vacated the Board's R–A-decision, which Attorney General Ashcroft then recertified to himself. Following a major amicus effort, and significant advocacy, Mr. Ashcroft reconsidered any initial inclination to deny R–A-'s claim, and instead, like Reno before him, sent the case back to the Board, with instructions to decide the case after regulations were promulgated. The regulations, originally proposed in 2000, formally recognized gender as a potential "particular social group." Those regulations are still pending, as is R–A-'s case.

Importantly, the DHS submitted a brief to Mr. Ashcroft in R–A-, in which, in addition to recommending that R–A-be granted asylum, adopted a well-reasoned, "immutability' modeled analysis of MPSG, and essentially recognized that gender could define a PSG. With respect to domestic violence, gender and its general policy approach, the DHS adopted a position, embodied back in 1995 in then-INS Gender Asylum Guidelines, which state core principles and doctrine that have defined and guided the development of law in this area.

# ANN LAQUER ESTIN, FAMILIES AND CHILDREN IN INTERNATIONAL LAW: AN INTRODUCTION

12 Transnat'l L. & Contemp. Probs. 271 (2002).

Despite the new guidelines, women face significant obstacles when they seek asylum on the basis of domestic violence, cultural practices that are harmful to women, or governmental policies that discriminate against women. Women refugees must claim that these types of persecution are based on their membership in a "particular social group" or their "political opinion." Women refugees also confront the belief that domestic violence and cultural practices that are harmful to women do not constitute persecution because they result from "private" rather than governmental conduct. In response, advocates argue that the state shares responsibility for these harms when it proves to be unable or unwilling to protect women from these practices. Canadian immigration decisions have begun to approve refugee status for victims of private violence who establish a failure of protection by the state. In the United States, the Bureau of Immigration Appeals (BIA) has approved asylum in this context. One case involved a young woman facing genital cutting and a forced marriage, while another involved an applicant who had been severely beaten by her father for refusing to conform to his "fundamentalist Muslim beliefs." The BIA has only been willing to consider domestic violence as persecution within the meaning of the asylum statute, however, when the violence is expressed within a particular tribal or religious context. Serious spousal abuse, combined with a complete failure of protection by the public authorities, is still not deemed an adequate basis for refugee status in the United States.

## *Notes*

1. Domestic violence may drive women from their homes. Where the state does not protect them, it may drive them from their homelands. Do victims of domestic violence fit within the traditional definition of "refugee"? Why did R–A– lose? After this decision, what would you tell a client with a similar problem? See Angelica Chazaro & Jennifer Casey, "Getting Away with Murder: Guatemala's Failure to Protect Women and Rodi Alvarado's Quest for Safety," 17 Hastings Women's L.J. 141–185 (2006).

2. How is spousal abuse like other forms of persecution set out in The Refugee Act of 1980; i.e., persecution on "account of race, religion, nationality, membership in a particular social group, or political opinion"? How is it different? What are the legal alternatives to protect abused spouses in the US or in their home countries?

3. The Violence Against Women Act (VAWA), enacted in the U.S. in 1994, amended the Immigration and Nationality Act to allow victims of domestic violence to leave their abusive partners and sponsor their own applications for permanent residence. 8 U.S.C. § 1154(a)(1). Amendments also allowed 'cancellation of removal' for victims of domestic violence in cases of extreme hardship. 8 U.S.C. § 1229(b)(a).

# B. CHILD MALTREATMENT

This section focuses on child maltreatment within the family, as opposed to maltreatment facing children living apart from their families, including trafficked and enslaved children. International as well as domestic law assumes that children are more likely to be protected and cared for within families. As set out in the U.N. Report at the end of this section, however, it is increasingly recognized that children in families may also be at risk.

## THERESA HUGHES, THE NEGLECT OF CHILDREN AND CULTURE: RESPONDING TO CHILD MALTREATMENT WITH CULTURAL COMPETENCE AND A REVIEW OF CHILD ABUSE AND CULTURE: WORKING WITH DIVERSE FAMILIES

44 Fam. Ct. Rev. 501 (July 2006).

As I write from the most culturally diverse place on the planet, Queens, New York, it is plainly evident that cultural competence ought to be an undercurrent of professional society. Within only 109 square miles of the county, nearly 2.25 million people live, and 138 languages are spoken. Nationally, there are 31.1 million foreign-born people. Millions of Americans identify themselves as members of minority cultural and religious traditions. Yet, cultural competence is a skill that has for too long been overlooked in normative legal practice.

Although child maltreatment is a phenomenon familiar to all ethnic groups, ethnic minorities are appreciably overrepresented in the family court system. As different cultures come into contact with each other, conflicting cultural child-rearing practices create a situation ripe with the potential for disputes concerning what is child abuse or neglect. The apparent threat is the mishandling of the child maltreatment case due to bias toward particular cultural views, standards, and norms. In order to respond to child abuse and neglect effectively, increased attention must be given to the role of families' race and culture and appropriate threshold trainings must be routinely incorporated to establish a professional standard of cultural competence. The principal question this article speaks to is how these children are going to receive appropriate services, counseling, and representation given their varying cultural, ethnic, and racial backgrounds.

\* \* \*

### CHILD MALTREATMENT

The term "child maltreatment," also known as "child abuse and neglect," refers to violence or mistreatment that a child or adolescent experiences at the hands of someone who is caring for him or her. Federal legislation provides a foundation for states by identifying a minimum set of acts or behaviors that define child abuse or neglect. There are numerous forms of abuse, and definitions vary from one jurisdiction to another, as each state is responsible for providing its own definitions of child abuse and neglect. However, most states recognize four major types of maltreatment: neglect, physical abuse, sexual abuse, and emotional abuse.

Many states define abuse in terms of harm or threatened harm, while other standards include acts or omissions, recklessly failing or refusing to act, willfully causing or permitting, and failing to provide. These standards guide mandatory reporters in their decision on whether to make a report to child welfare. Case workers or investigators for child welfare agencies investigate reports by speaking with parents, others (e.g., medical personnel, teachers, etc.), and if possible, the child, to determine if abuse or neglect has occurred and if further risk is posed. The case workers will typically make one of two findings: "unfounded" (unsubstantiated) or "founded" (substantiated), meaning there was insufficient or sufficient evidence to conclude that a child was maltreated. However, there is a good deal of room for misinterpretation and subjectivity, based on personal bias and stereotypes. Evidence has shown that there is considerable variation between social workers as to what they consider "good parenting." The notions of "race" and "ethnicity" are laced throughout social work practice and policy, especially during the assessment process which can "reflect the power relationships between professionals and service users." Hence, therein rests the need for appropriate training on understanding and appreciating the significance of culture in child protection work.

### WHAT CAUSES CHILD MALTREATMENT

Many abusive parents report having been abused as children themselves. However, many have not. Some factors identified in abusive parents include: low self-esteem, low intelligence, hostility, isolation, depression, immaturity, dependency, drug or alcohol abuse, lack of parenting skills, inappropriate attitudes, physical illness, marital conflicts, financial stress, and so on. These factors may in fact lead to behavior on the part of the parent which causes what many subjectively categorize, define, and understand as child abuse or neglect. Immigrant families bring with them parenting practices and belief systems, including belief systems surrounding the use of corporal punishment, that may conflict with local U.S. laws and customs. How child maltreatment is statutorily defined affects most immigrant parents in a very different way than nonimmigrant parents. For example, in Vietnam, physical punishment is a traditional way of raising children, and is part of the culture that has existed for many years. But when immigrating to the United States, for many there is a clashing of maintaining traditional ways and cultures with assimilating when it comes to discipline. A Vietnamese child will be taught in an American school that her parents do not have a right to use excessive corporal punishment, and if such child is physically punished at home, she may relay this to a teacher or friend resulting in a child abuse report to child welfare, in turn causing stress between the child and parent, and confusion on the parents' part, not understanding why they have lost their authority to raise their own child.

### STATISTICS: RACIAL IMBALANCE

There are approximately 2.9 million child maltreatment reports made annually in the United States. Of those, almost 1 million are actual victims of child abuse or neglect. Estimates as of April 2005 hold that there are over 500,000 children living in the foster care system, ranging in age from newborn to over 19 years old. The median length of stay in foster care is 18 months, females are the slight majority, and the greater part live in nonrelative (a.k.a. "stranger") homes. Although heartbreaking, these numbers are not, at the present time, actually startling. What is indeed shocking is the disproportionate numbers related to the race/ethnicity of these children, with an elevated 59% being children of color. Among the more than 72 million children living in the United States, 41% are considered to be children of color: Black, Latino, Native American, Asian, or some race other than White. There is an unbalanced overrepresentation of children of color throughout the child welfare system, as children of color account for twice that of the general population. For every 1,000 Black children, 17 are in foster care, but for every 1,000 White children, 5 are in foster care; for every 1,000 Black children, 17 are substantiated as victims of child abuse or neglect, but for every 1,000 White children, 9 are substantiated as victims of abuse or neglect. Black, Hispanic, and Asian/Pacific Islander children have disproportionately higher investigations of child abuse and neglect than White children, regardless of the race of the investigator. Additionally, the racial and ethnic diversity of children in the United States continues to increase.

### RESPONDING TO CHILD MALTREATMENT WITH CULTURAL COMPETENCE

Child welfare agencies across the continent are mandated to investigate reported cases of suspected child abuse and neglect. The investigation consists of interviews of the subject children, siblings, parents, relatives, neighbors, teachers, medical personnel, police officers, and so on. When necessary, children may be removed (temporarily or permanently) from their homes, criminal prosecution may ensue, family court civil cases may be filed against the parents or persons legally responsible, and mental health and rehabilitative services may be ordered.

Child maltreatment research often does not take notice of ethnicity in its analyses and design. Indeed, prior to the 1990s, literature on cultural competence in the field of child protection was virtually nonexistent. However, there has been a more assertive movement within the last decade to raise awareness and provide training to better serve and represent ethnically diverse clients. Conferences, classes, and lectures have been held, and models and suggestions have been proposed to address the issues of sensitivity and competence. It may be fair to say that at this juncture, the term "cultural competence" is a reasonably commonly used phrase. But the need remains for professional training to develop abilities to cross cultural boundaries, especially for those dealing with child protection cases.

Why is training cultural competence so difficult? Cultures are highly subjective, always changing, with nebulous boundaries, and are highly heterogeneous. Generally, models seem to recommend that professionals should be aware of their own cultural biases and ideals, and be more sensitive to their clients' worldviews. However, it is unclear how to actually carry this out.

Despite pioneering efforts to teach cultural competence in the field of child welfare, stereotypic thinking nonetheless clouds professionals' evaluations, intervention efforts, and representation. Although relying on stereotypes can be convenient, storing a considerable amount of information in quickly accessible form, it is clearly potentially harmful and laced with bias. For example, in an assessment situation, certain stereotyping could lead a worker to assume that all families from certain ethnic backgrounds use harsh forms of punishment to discipline their children. Asking one to be culturally competent is asking that the professional shed the belief that others see the world as he does. It requires more than just acknowledging different perspectives and creating an illusion of understanding. No one is suggesting that child safety should be compromised in the name of cultural competence, but rather the distinction between harmful traditions and those traditions which positively enhance the child's cultural identity need to be drawn.

# MOHAMMED v. GONZALES

Ninth Circuit Court of Appeals, 2005.
400 F.3d 785.

\* \* \*

We reviewed BIA rulings on motions to reopen and reconsider for abuse of discretion and reverse only if the Board acted arbitrarily, irrationally, or contrary to law.

\* \* \*

As described above, Mohamed's case is characterized by a series of errors committed by the agency responsible for adjudicating her claim, and by her attorneys.

\* \* \*

We note that none of the "typographical," "scribner," or other errors that complicate our task appear to be the fault of Mohamed herself. As we have previously emphasized, "[t]he role of an attorney in the deportation process is especially important. For the alien unfamiliar with the laws of our country, an attorney serves a special role in helping the alien through a complex and completely foreign process." Furthermore, the obligation of counsel is greater where, as here, the client is a minor.

\* \* \*

To establish eligibility for asylum on the basis of past persecution, Mohamed "must show: (1) an incident ... that rise[s] to the level of persecution; (2) that [wa]s 'on account of' one of the statutorily-protected grounds; and (3) [wa]s committed by the government or forces the government is either 'unable or unwilling' to control." We address each element in turn.

First, we have no doubt that the range of procedures collectively knows as female genital mutilation rises to the level of persecution within the meaning of our asylum law. As the Seventh Circuit has written, the mutilation of women and girls is "a horrifically brutal procedure, often performed without anesthesia" that causes both short- and long-term physical and psychological consequences. The practice has been internationally recognized as a violation of the rights of women and girls. Within the Unites States, the practice of genital mutilation of female minors has been prohibited by federal law since 1996 ... In making such mutilation a criminal offense, Congress found that the procedure "often results in the occurrence of physical and psychological health effects that harm the women involved."

\* \* \*

Furthermore, the BIA has held that female genital mutilation constitutes "persecution within the meaning of section 101(a)(42)(A) of the [Immigration and Naturalization] Act ... In sum, the extremely painful, physically invasive, psychologically damaging and permanently disfiguring process of genital mutilation undoubtedly rises to the level or persecution.

\* \* \*

The second question is whether Mohamed's subjection to mutilation was "on account of" a protected ground. However, other circuits, as well as the BIA have recognized that female genital mutilation "constitute[es] persecution *on account of membership in a particular social group ...*"

\* \* \*

Once a petitioner demonstrates past persecution within the definition of the Act, she is entitled to a presumption of a well-founded fear of future persecution. The government must then rebut that presumption by demonstrating by a preponderance of evidence that circumstances have fundamentally changed or that relocation is possible, so that the petitioner no longer has a well-founded fear that she would be persecuted.

The government argues, quoting that Mohamed cannot be eligible for asylum because she has already suffered genital mutilation and therefore, "there is no chance that she would be personally tortured again by the procedure." ... In fact, there are several reasons why the agency and the court would be compelled to conclude that the government has failed to rebut the presumption of a well-founded fear of future persecution.

\* \* \*

The primary reason that such a conclusion is necessary is that persecution in the form of female genital mutilation is similar to forced sterilization and, like that other persecutory technique, must be considered a continuing harm that renders a petitioner eligible for asylum, without more.

\* \* \*

Like forced sterilization, genital mutilation permanently disfigures a woman, causes long term health problems, and deprives her of a normal and fulfilling sexual life. The World Health Organization reports that even the least drastic form of female genital mutilation can cause a wide range of complications such as infection, hemorrhaging from the clitoral artery during childbirth, formation of abscesses, development of cysts and tumors, repeated urinary tract infections, and pseudo infibulation. Many women subjected to genital mutilation suffer psychological trauma. In addition, it "can result in permanent loss of genital sensation and can adversely affect sexual and erotic functions."

\* \* \*

Because Mohamed has demonstrated that she was prejudiced by her attorney's ineffective assistance, the BIA abused its discretion in denying her motions to reopen and reconsider. We grant her petition for review and remand with instructions to grant the motion to reopen.

## BARBARA STARK, HUMAN RIGHTS OF THE FAMILY AND HUMAN RIGHTS OF INDIVIDUALS WITHIN THE FAMILY

International Family Law: An Introduction, 251 (2005).

International family law is at the center of a major faultline in international human rights law; that is, the ongoing debate between universalism and cultural relativism. Put simply, the argument of the universalists is that human rights are basically the same everywhere. While there may be some variation in the ways in which these rights are expressed or enjoyed, the prohibition against torture, for example, applies everywhere. Freedom of expression, similarly, cannot be interpreted to mean "freedom of expression as consistent with Islamic law" or "freedom of expression as understood in the U.S. Constitution." While freedom of religion may require the State to allow religious authorities some leeway (in sanctioning violations of religious law, for example) this cannot amount to abdication of the State in favor of those authorities.

Cultural relativists, on the other hand, insist that any conception of 'human rights' necessarily determined by the cultural context in which it is defined. It has been argued, for example, that a Muslim cannot truly practice his religion in a secular State. The right to practice one's religion, under this view, may well require a State which affirmatively supports that religion.

A well-known and contentious example may clarify the universalist/relativist debate. Human rights advocates have long demanded an end to female genital mutilation (FGM) or circumcision of girls as a rite of passage. It has been condemned as a violation of children's rights and as a form of torture. Cultural relativists, in contrast, first point out that FGM encompasses a range of practices, from removal of the external genitalia to more symbolic and less invasive procedures. They have argued that it is a rite of passage through which a girl becomes a member of her social group. In addition, they have pointed out that within some groups, a girl is considered unclean and thus ineligible for marriage unless she has undergone FGM. Finally, they point out that sanctions against the practice, including its criminalization in many Western States, merely drives it underground and deters women who have undergone the procedure from seeking medical attention. Rather, they argue for a coordinated approach, including grassroots education and respectful consultation with those who actually perform the surgeries.

## D. MARIANNE BLAIR & MERLE H. WEINER, THE UNITED STATES APPROACH TO FGS

Family Law in the World Community 434–35 (2003).

The Center for Disease Control estimates that in 1990, 168,000 people were subjected to or were at risk for FGM in the United States ... Should the United States' concern about FGM differ depending upon whether the procedure is practiced here or practiced abroad? If so, does it matter if it is practiced abroad in children of immigrants who travel from the Unites States to have FGM performed on their daughter? We have already mentioned that the United States ties its development aid, at least in theory, to efforts by governments to prevent FGM through education. *See* 22 U.S.C. § 262k–2(a) (2000). How does the United States address the practice at home? The material that follows considers the response to the practice in the United States through criminal, child protection, and immigration laws.

### A. CRIMINAL LAWS

Federal law states that "whoever knowingly circumcises, excises, or infibulates the whole or any part of the labia majora or labia minora or clitoris of another person who has not attained the age of 18years shall be fined under this title or imprisoned not more than 5 years, or both." *See* 188 U.S.C. § 166. There is a limited exception where necessary for the person's health and when performed by a doctor or other designated medical professional. In applying the health exception, "no account shall be taken of the effect on the person on whom the operation is to be performed of any belief on the part of that person, or any other person, that the operation is required as a matter of custom or ritual." Could a federal prosecutor use this law to prosecute parents who travel abroad with their daughter in order to obtain the procedure?

The law does not require international or even interstate travel for its violation. Can such a law be constitutional? Would the law survive a federalism challenge? Congress made six findings when it passed the law:

(1) the practice of female genital mutilation is carried out by members of certain cultural and religious groups within the

United States; (2) the practice of female genital mutilation often results in the occurrence of physical and psychological health effects that harm the women involved; (3) such mutilation infringes upon the guarantees of rights secured by Federal and State law, both statutory and constitutional; (4) the unique circumstances surrounding the practice of female genital mutilation place it beyond the ability of a single State of local jurisdiction to control; (5) the practice of female genital mutilation can be prohibited without abridging the exercise of any other law; and (6) Congress has the affirmative power under section 8 of article 1, the Necessary and Proper clause, section 5 of the Fourteenth Amendment, as well as under the Treaty Clause, to the Constitution to enact such legislation.

Would the law survive a First Amendment challenge by a parent or by a girl who wanted the procedure?

Fourteen states have also criminalized FGM. (California, Colorado, Delaware, Illinois, Maryland, Minnesota, Nevada, New York, North Dakota, Oregon, Rhode Island, Tennessee, West Virginia, and Wisconsin). The authors explain that the laws sometimes differ from the federal law by 1) prohibiting the practice also for women over 18 years old or 2) holding parents liable if they consent to the procedure. *Id.* "To date, there have been no criminal prosecutions at the federal or state level."*id.*

### Notes

1.  Does the parents' motivation matter? That is, does it matter whether the parents have female genital mutilation performed on their daughter to improve her chances of a good marriage? See generally, Kimberly Sowders Blizzard, Note, "A Parent's Predicament: Theories of Relief for Deportable Parents of Children Who Face Female Genital Mutilation," 91 Cornell L. Rev. 899–926 (2006).

2.  Does it matter whether a parent injures a child in a moment of anger or in the course of dispassionately administered 'discipline'? What if the parent threatens the child, but does not actually injure her? A Kenyan diplomat was accused of beating his 9–year-old son with a stick and chasing him with a knife in New York in 2006. The man was arrested but released when his status as a diplomat was discovered. The Administration for Children's Services took custody of his children temporarily, while officials explored their legal options. How should this have been resolved? See N.Y. Times, Metro Briefing, "Queens: Custody Battle Over Diplomat's Children", Nov. 14, 2006.

# UNIVERSAL DECLARATION OF HUMAN RIGHTS

United Nations, 1948.

G.A. Res. 217, U.N. GAOR, 3d Sess., pt. 1 at 71, U.N. Doc. A/810.

## *Article 26*

\* \* \*

3.   Parents have a prior right to choose the kind of education that shall be given to their children.

# INTERNATIONAL COVENANT ON ECONOMIC, SOCIAL AND CULTURAL RIGHTS

United Nations.

Jan. 3, 1976, 993 U.N.T.S. 3.

## *Article 10*

The States Parties to the present Covenant recognize that:

1.   The widest possible protection and assistance should be accorded to the family, which is the natural and fundamental group unit of society, particularly for its establishment and while it is responsible for the care and education of dependent children. Marriage must be entered into with the free consent of the intending spouses.

2.   Special protection should be accorded to mothers during a reasonable period before and after childbirth. During such period working mothers should be accorded paid leave or leave with adequate social security benefits.

3.   Special measures of protection and assistance should be taken on behalf of all children and young persons without any discrimination for reasons of parentage or other conditions. Children and young persons should be protected from economic and social exploitation. Their employment in work harmful to their morals or health or dangerous to life or likely to hamper their normal development should be punishable by law. States should also set age limits below which the paid employment of child labour should be prohibited and punishable by law.

\* \* \*

## *Article 11*

1.   The States Parties to the present Covenant recognize the right of everyone to an adequate standard of living for himself and his family, including adequate food, clothing and housing, and to the continuous improvement of living conditions. The States Par-

ties will take appropriate steps to ensure the realization of this right, recognizing to this effect the essential importance of international co-operation based on free consent.

2. The States Parties to the present Covenant, recognizing the fundamental right of everyone to be free from hunger, shall take, individually and through international co-operation, the measures, including specific programmes, which are needed:

(a) To improve methods of production, conservation and distribution of food by making full use of technical and scientific knowledge, by disseminating knowledge of the principles of nutrition and by developing or reforming agrarian systems in such a way as to achieve the most efficient development and utilization of natural resources;

(b) Taking into account the problems of both food-importing and food-exporting countries, to ensure an equitable distribution of world food supplies in relation to need.

\* \* \*

### Article 12

1. The States Parties to the present Covenant recognize the right of everyone to the enjoyment of the highest attainable standard of physical and mental health.

2. The steps to be taken by the States Parties to the present Covenant to achieve the full realization of this right shall include those necessary for:

(a) The provision for the reduction of the stillbirth-rate and of infant mortality and for the healthy development of the child;

(b) The improvement of all aspects of environmental and industrial hygiene;

(c) The prevention, treatment and control of epidemic, endemic, occupational and other diseases;

(d) The creation of conditions which would assure to all medical service and medical attention in the event of sickness.

\* \* \*

### Article 13

1. The States Parties to the present Covenant recognize the right of everyone to education. They agree that education shall be directed to the full development of the human personality and the sense of its dignity, and shall strengthen the respect for human rights and fundamental freedoms. They further agree that edu-

cation shall enable all persons to participate effectively in a free society, promote understanding, tolerance and friendship among all nations and all racial, ethnic or religious groups, and further the activities of the United Nations for the maintenance of peace.

2.   The States Parties to the present Covenant recognize that, with a view to achieving the full realization of this right:

(a) Primary education shall be compulsory and available free to all;

(b) Secondary education in its different forms, including technical and vocational secondary education, shall be made generally available and accessible to all by every appropriate means, and in particular by the progressive introduction of free education;

(c) Higher education shall be made equally accessible to all, on the basis of capacity, by every appropriate means, and in particular by the progressive introduction of free education;

(d) Fundamental education shall be encouraged or intensified as far as possible for those persons who have not received or completed the whole period of their primary education;

(e) The development of a system of schools at all levels shall be actively pursued, an adequate fellowship system shall be established, and the material conditions of teaching staff shall be continuously improved.

3.   The States Parties to the present Covenant undertake to have respect for the liberty of parents and, when applicable, legal guardians to choose for their children schools, other than those established by the public authorities, which conform to such minimum educational standards as may be laid down or approved by the State and to ensure the religious and moral education of their children in conformity with their own convictions.

4.   No part of this article shall be construed so as to interfere with the liberty of individuals and bodies to establish and direct educational institutions, subject always to the observance of the principles set forth in paragraph I of this article and to the requirement that the education given in such institutions shall conform to such minimum standards as may be laid down by the State.

\* \* \*

### Article 17

1.   No one shall be subjected to arbitrary or unlawful interference with his privacy, family, home or correspondence, nor to unlawful attacks on his honour and reputation.

2. Everyone has the right to the protection of the law against such interference or attacks.

\* \* \*

## *Article 23*

1. The family is the natural and fundamental group unit of society and is entitled to protection by society and the State.

2. The right of men and women of marriageable age to marry and to found a family shall be recognized.

3. No marriage shall be entered into without the free and full consent of the intending spouses.

4. States Parties to the present Covenant shall take appropriate steps to ensure equality of rights and responsibilities of spouses as to marriage, during marriage and at its dissolution. In the case of dissolution, provision shall be made for the necessary protection of any children.

# CONVENTION ON THE RIGHTS OF THE CHILD

United Nations, 1989.
G.A. Res. 44/25, U.N. Doc. A/44/49.

PREAMBLE

The States Parties to the present Convention,

\* \* \*

Recalling that, in the Universal Declaration of Human Rights, the United Nations has proclaimed that childhood is entitled to special care and assistance,

Convinced that the family, as the fundamental group of society and the natural environment for the growth and well-being of all its members and particularly children, should be afforded the necessary protection and assistance so that it can fully assume its responsibilities within the community,

Recognizing that the child, for the full and harmonious development of his or her personality, should grow up in a family environment, in an atmosphere of happiness, love and understanding,

Considering that the child should be fully prepared to live an individual life in society, and brought up in the spirit of the ideals proclaimed in the Charter of the United Nations, and in particular in the spirit of peace, dignity, tolerance, freedom, equality and solidarity,

\* \* \*

Recognizing that, in all countries in the world, there are children living in exceptionally difficult conditions, and that such children need special consideration,

Taking due account of the importance of the traditions and cultural values of each people for the protection and harmonious development of the child,

Recognizing the importance of international co-operation for improving the living conditions of children in every country, in particular in the developing countries,

Have agreed as follows:

### Article 11

1. States Parties shall take measures to combat the illicit transfer and non-return of children abroad.

2. To this end, States Parties shall promote the conclusion of bilateral or multilateral agreements or accession to existing agreements.

### Article 12

1. States Parties shall assure to the child who is capable of forming his or her own views the right to express those views freely in all matters affecting the child, the views of the child being given due weight in accordance with the age and maturity of the child.

\* \* \*

### Article 19

1. States Parties shall take all appropriate legislative, administrative, social and educational measures to protect the child from all forms of physical or mental violence, injury or abuse, neglect or negligent treatment, maltreatment or exploitation, including sexual abuse, while in the care of parent(s), legal guardian(s) or any other person who has the care of a child.

2. Such protective measures should, as appropriate, include effective procedures for the establishment of social programmes to provide necessary support for the child and for those who have the care of the child, as well as for other forms of prevention and for identification, reporting, referral, investigation, treatment and follow-up of instances of child maltreatment described heretofore, and, as appropriate, for judicial involvement.

\* \* \*

### Article 23

1. States Parties recognize that a mentally or physically disabled child should enjoy a full and decent life, in conditions which

ensure dignity, promote self-reliance and facilitate the child's active participation in the community.

* * *

*Article 27*

1. States Parties recognize the right of every child to a standard of living adequate for the child's physical, mental, spiritual, moral and social development.

## URSULA KILKELLY, ANNUAL REVIEW OF INTERNATIONAL FAMILY LAW

International Survey of Family Law 1, 5–6 (Andrew Bainhan ed. 2006).

* * *

(D) SECRETARY-GENERAL'S STUDY ON VIOLENCE AGAINST CHILDREN

A further area of attention in the United Nations in recent years has been the issue of violence against children. As reported in last year's Survey, in 2001 the General Assembly requested the Secretary–General to conduct an in-depth international study on violence against children, and in 2003, following the suggestion of the Commission on Human Rights in 2002, Mr. Paulo Sergio Pinheiro was appointed to direct the Study. There followed the publication of a concept paper for the study in July 2003 in which it was explained that the purpose of the Study was to provide an in-depth global picture of violence against children and to propose clear recommendations for the improvement of legislation, policy and programmes relating to the prevention of and responses to violence against children. Since that time, the study has been in consultation mode with governments, non-governmental organisations and the public being given the opportunity to participate. In March, 2004, the Study issued all governments with a questionnaire designated to gather material on the laws, policies and programmes in place to address violence against children. To date, almost 120 governments have responded. In addition, nine regional consultations were carried out by Mr. Pinheiro, his partners in the Study, UNICEF, WHO and the Office of the High Commissioner for Human Rights—and other non-governmental and state partners. Consultations in individual countries were then used to supplement the regional problems of violence against children. Also, in 2004–2005, public submissions on the issue of violence against children were invited, a number of expert thematic meetings were held and the Expert participated in a number of academic meetings, colloquiums, workshops and seminars related to the topic of violence against children. He has also considered the issues raised by the Committee on the Rights of the Child in its Concluding Observations. The participation of children and young people in the Study is also a priority and the Expert's website had a child-friendly section as well as a toolkit to facilitate this participation. For example, children and young people were involved in regional consultations and published statements at the end of the consultation.

In his report to the General Assembly in 2005, the Expert highlighted the key areas identified through the consultation processes regarding violence against children, which will be the focus of his work in the coming year. These included the continued legality and prevalence of corporal punishment against children in the home, schools, alternative care institutions and the juvenile justice system, the vulnerability of children in conflict with the law, as well as street children, to violence; and the persuasiveness of harmful traditional practices. He has also become very aware of the underlying conditions, such as community attitudes to violence; and the persuasiveness of harmful conditions, such as community attitudes to violence, discrimination, poverty, the unequal status of women and girls, lack of access to quality education and denial of human rights generally, which exacerbated children's vulnerability to violence. Lack of systematic and quality data and the importance of capacity building for those working with children have also become clear. His final report to the Secretary–General is expected to be presented in the spring of 2006.

## VIOLENCE AGAINST CHILDREN IN THE HOME AND FAMILY

United Nations, 2006.

http://www.unicef.ca/portal/Secure/Community/502/WCM/WHATWEDO/ChildProtection/assets/World%20Report%20on%20Violence%20Against%20Children%20-%20full%20report.pdf

But families can be dangerous places for children and in particular for babies and young children. The prevalence of violence against children by parents and other close family members—physical, sexual and psychological violence, as well as deliberate neglect—has only begun to be acknowledged and documented. Challenging violence against children is most difficult in the context of the family in all its forms. There is a reluctance to intervene in what is still perceived in most societies as a 'private' sphere.

\* \* \*

Younger children tend to be more vulnerable to violence in the home. In some industrialized States, where child deaths are most rigorously recorded and investigated, infants under one year of age face around three times the risk of homicide, almost invariably by parents, than children aged one to four, and twice the risk of those aged five to 14.

\* \* \*

Forced sex within families and early marriage is common in many States. So-called 'honour killings' of adolescent girls, regarded as having breached moral codes, occur in some countries. Despite legislation and advocacy efforts, female genital mutilation or cutting (FGM) remains widespread: in parts of North and Eastern Africa, over 90% of girls undergo this operation, usually at around the age of seven.

### *Notes*

1.  What are the competing state interests here? How are they reflected in the cited international human rights conventions? Does human rights law provide useful guidance for resolving these competing interests?

2.  How can domestic family law be used to protect children? Some states provide for the termination of parental rights, and the removal of the child from the family, in cases of serious abuse or neglect. In many states, however, this is not an option, either because of lack of resources of because it would be viewed as an impermissible intrusion. Does international human rights law suggest other possibilities, such as policy or educational initiatives, that might be helpful in this context?

# Index

References are to Pages

†